T0414029

Metaphysical Institutions

SUNY series in Islam

Seyyed Hossein Nasr, editor

Metaphysical Institutions

Islam and the Modern Project

CANER K. DAGLI

Published by State University of New York Press, Albany

For information, contact State University of New York Press, Albany, NY
www.sunypress.edu

Library of Congress Cataloging-in-Publication Data

Name: Dagli, Caner K., author.
Title: Metaphysical institutions : Islam and the modern project / Caner K. Dagli.
Description: Albany : State University of New York Press, [2024]. | Series: SUNY series in Islam | Includes bibliographical references and index.
Identifiers: LCCN 2023029851 | ISBN 9781438497006 (hardcover : alk. paper) | ISBN 9781438497020 (ebook)
Subjects: LCSH: Islamic countries—Civilization. | Islam—21st century. | Metaphysics. | Civilization, Modern.
Classification: LCC DS35.62 .D34 2024 | DDC 909/.09767—dc23/eng/20230731
LC record available at https://lccn.loc.gov/2023029851

10 9 8 7 6 5 4 3 2 1

To the Illuminated and the Lion,
the two biggest blessings of my life

Contents

Acknowledgments

In the Name of God, the Compassionate, the Merciful

Part of the research for this book was carried out while I was a Senior Research Fellow in the Humanities Research Fellowship program at the Research Institute at New York University Abu Dhabi (NYUAD) during the 2016–17 academic year.

My sincere appreciation to the two anonymous readers for SUNY whose helpful comments helped to improve the text.

I am truly grateful to my friends who gave me encouragement and feedback during the writing of this book. May God make any good that comes from this book be a blessing for you as well.

Introduction

What is real, possible, and good when it comes to human beings thinking together about the real, the possible, and the good? In this book, these ultimate questions will be explored on their own terms, and will be made particular through a question that is often limited to history, anthropology, and religious studies, namely, "What is Islam?" This latter topic continues to attract a great deal of scholarly attention oriented toward establishing a "useful concept" of Islam or a guideline by which to judge something "Islamic," but it has deep metaphysical implications far beyond this definitional question's relevance to any particular research program. At root, the work at hand is both a philosophical treatise about shared thinking that uses the encounter between the Modern Project and Islam as an illustrative example, and also an exploration of the conceptualization of Islam in light of the metaphysics of consciousness and meaning.

The most common and consequential concepts scholars use to explore and conceptualize Islam are religion, culture, civilization, and tradition, but what are *they*? Islam itself is said to be one or more of them. They are the most basic, underlying ideas used to classify things as Islamic or not, yet one finds little consensus across the relevant fields in the humanities and social sciences as to what belongs in what category. Is some practice *religious* or *cultural*? Is some idea Islamic *religion* or Islamic *civilization*? Is Islam as a whole better thought of as a *tradition* or a *religion*? Disagreements about such questions are the rule, and convergence the exception. Furthermore, one cannot get around such divergences by resorting to the specialized versions of the terms "culture," "religion," "civilization," and "tradition" in the academic disciplines that are devoted to them, because one finds that these ubiquitous and essential ideas have remained undefined and seemingly undefinable (or have too many definitions, which amounts to the same

1

problem) for well over half a century, with no clear path forward for how to improve the situation.

This definitional problem reveals deeper philosophical questions. When human beings in the modern world want to name their most ultimate sense of belonging, or their collective state of wisdom and maturity, it is these ideas they reach for, yet even in academic scholarship the concepts culture, religion, civilization, and tradition remain at the level of folk knowledge and are not well defined, partly because these kinds of realities are much more mysterious than commonly assumed, and partly because of a certain reticence to explore the deepest reasons *why* they are so hard to define.

Not only can "we" not conceptualize Islam, "we" have yet to properly conceptualize the "we" that is doing the conceptualizing or to come to grips with the very nature of that collective act of conceptualization. What we all need, therefore, is a consistent, coherent, and comprehensive way of theorizing the nature of human beings in their act of thinking together and living as a conscious "we."

This book develops a comprehensive theory of the *institution* (a surprisingly undertheorized concept itself) that incorporates the metaphysics of consciousness and demarcates both the necessary and empirically variable features of all institutions. It then expands this concept's scope to include a category called *metaphysical institutions*: realities that constitute the social dimension of human beings navigating ultimate questions of what is real, what is possible, and what is good. The result is a universal rubric—the first time that this has been attempted—that enables one to navigate the conceptual space of the religious, the cultural, the civilizational, and the traditional. A persistent theme of the book is that many of the ambiguities and difficulties in existing theorizations of these ideas arise first and foremost from the way that we answer that most ultimate of questions: *What is a human being?* More specifically, how is the social element of human consciousness conceived?

The new model is put to use to analyze how the Modern Project thinks about Islam, touching on the relationship of authority and autonomy, rationality and imitation, the universal and the particular, and other important questions. The overall approach of the book is to delineate the parameters and dimensions of the conceptual space in which such questions can be systematically and transparently explored, by tackling universal problems of what it means for human beings to know, reason, create, and choose together, and makes these themes concrete by exploring the case of navigating the "Islamic" in the humanities and social sciences. Its central method is logical and conceptual, taking important terms that have been poorly theorized, or whose theorizations are irretrievably contested, and placing them into a framework that will allow us to situate them against a larger horizon, rather than trying to stop using them (which is unlikely) or adding even more definitions to the pile (which is pointless), thus enabling greater understanding of social reality as well as greater sophistication and clarity for work in various fields.

At root this work is a philosophical treatise about ultimate questions, but one which simultaneously contributes to certain theoretical debates in various fields in the humanities and social sciences, as it engages existing viewpoints while offering its own solution to questions about the relationship of subjectivity and objectivity, essentialism and anti-essentialism, dynamism and change, and the interests of power versus the motives of purpose. In part it does this by drawing certain logical and metaphysical insights from within Islamic thought into a broader conversation, while also knocking down arbitrary walls between philosophy and the humanities and social sciences, especially as far as Islamic studies is concerned. Being "interdisciplinary," as that term is used today, already presupposes a certain division of intellectual disciplines in the modern world that is a reflection of a deep fragmentation of human thought resulting from a series of philosophical decisions that began in the early modern period in Europe and is now a defining feature of the Modern Project.[1] The interdisciplinarity of this book taps the spirit of Islamic intellectual culture at its height, where historians write about the spiritual life, philosophers write Quran commentaries, jurists write mystic treatises, theologians explore logic, mathematicians write poems, and poets teach law.[2] When one can, one should wander the landscape as if there were no borders, since those boundaries are only where we imagine them to be.

❧

Chapter 1, "What Kind of Thing Is Islam?," discusses the definitional hurdles related to the terms religion, culture, civilization, tradition, and institution, and brings out the underlying logical and metaphysical ambiguities that have plagued these concepts and the academic disciplines devoted to them for generations.

Chapter 2, "The Nature of Institutions and Shared Thinking," is a comprehensive presentation of the nature of institutions. Its three sections are meant to address the conceptual shortcomings described in chapter 1. Section 1 sets out the necessary or invariant features of all institutions;

section 2 lays out the nature of the empirical or contingent variation that can exist within those invariant parameters; and section 3 focuses on what institutions are not, namely, those realities that resemble some features of institutions but that must be distinguished from them.

Chapter 3, "The Metaphysics of Antidualism," is the first of three metaphysical chapters of part 2 of the book. The chapter's central theme is that antidualism as a general metaphysical stance—sometimes referred to as materialism, physicalism, naturalism, or scientism—makes the proper understanding of social reality impossible. This chapter begins to address the metaphysically laden concept of structure as well as the nature of basic validity claims related to rationality.

Chapter 4, "The Metaphysics of Meaning," turns to the nature of meaning and examines it in light of the model of institutions established in chapter 2, demonstrating that a conceptualization of human beings thinking together that attempts to remain within the strictures of antidualism can only be incoherent and self-undermining.

Chapter 5, "The Metaphysics of Paradox," discusses the nature of genuine paradox as it relates to consciousness and extends this to the nature of shared consciousness. The central theme of this chapter is that the difficulties of theorizing consciousness at the individual level do not disappear in the social domain, and that analytical clarity at the social level must take into account the difficulties of conceptualizing consciousness in the first place.

Chapter 6, "The Language Analogy," begins part 3 of the book, taking the general picture established by parts 1 and 2 and turning to the encounter between Islam and the Modern Project. It is an extended meditation on the nature of one language studying another, insofar as that encounter can be used as a template for understanding the relationship of metaphysical institutions with each other.

Chapter 7, "Project and Tradition," continues some of the themes of the language analogy from chapter 6 by incorporating the question of how metaphysics bears upon the encounter of the Modern Project with Islam, and specifically how the Modern Project's apex communities conceive of themselves as uniquely universal and how this self-image undermines its understanding of Islam and of itself.

Chapter 8, "One Islam, Many Islams, or No Islam?," brings the discussion to the academic humanities and social sciences. Against the backdrop of the conceptualization established in earlier chapters, it is a survey and evaluation of some of the most influential or representative attempts by modern scholars to conceptualize Islam.

The conclusion, "The Sighted Men and the Elephant," reflects upon how the ideas in this book can be used in the future, and how consideration of ultimate questions of the real, the possible, and the good must be a part of any useful discussion of human beings thinking together.

Readers can consult the end of each chapter to find a synopsis of the main points of that chapter.

Part I

Institutions

Chapter 1

What Kind of Thing Is Islam?

Religion. Civilization. Culture. Tradition. These are the things Islam is said to be. However else Islam is described and defined, one or more among this tetrad of terms is always going to show up and be primary. But which category is the most correct? Can Islam be more than one of them, or can it be all of them at once?

If one answers the question "What is Islam?" by beginning with "Islam is one of *these* (a religion, a civilization, a tradition, a culture)," then one had better know how to explain what those things are, yet it turns out that the best that scholars can say about civilization, culture, religion, and tradition is *we know it when we see it.* That means that when one defines Islam in terms of these categories, the resulting conceptualization adds no theoretical clarity because these categories are not well-defined themselves. They are not part of a reliable classification scheme that can illuminate one's thinking about Islam or clarify whether some practice, person, or belief is Islamic. And because these four ideas are primary in all other conceptualizations of Islam, it follows that all such efforts are deeply flawed or at least incomplete.

Scholars of religious studies have debated the meaning of "religion" for decades and have offered definition upon definition without nearing any consensus. Wilfred Cantwell Smith, writing in 1962, said, "There has been in recent decades a bewildering variety of definitions; and no one of them has commanded wide acceptance."[1] Over a half century later, in 2013 Brent Nongbri writes, "Scholars have had (and continue to have) an extremely difficult time agreeing on a definition of religion."[2] One of the main textbooks of contemporary religious studies notes:

Today, it is fair to say, no single theory exercises an influence comparable to that of the leading perspectives half a century ago. There are instead various competing patterns of interpretation that build upon the classic theories we have examined in this book even as they refine and apply them in different ways. We can perhaps best describe them as centers of theoretical interest—as programs that give to certain kinds of explanation a kind of first conceptual priority, or as paths of inquiry that from the start find explanations of certain types more compelling than others.[3]

Anthropologists since the nineteenth century have produced literally hundreds of definitions of "culture" with a similar absence of convergence on a conception that the field can accept. In their 1947 work *Culture: A Critical Review of Concepts and Definitions*, A. L. Kroeber and Clyde Kluckhohn categorized and analyzed 164 definitions of culture from the previous decades reaching back to the nineteenth century, remarking finally: "As yet we have no full theory of culture. We have a fairly well-delineated concept, and it is possible to enumerate conceptual elements embraced within that master concept. But a concept, even an important one, does not constitute a theory. . . . In anthropology at present we have plenty of definitions but too little theory."[4] Given the dizzying variety of conceptions described in their book, it is unclear how "concept" here means much more than that which important anthropologists happen to find themselves interested in and what they already assume to be culture. Half a century later one reads, "The ten-volume *Encyclopedia of Language and Linguistics* . . . summarized the problem as follows: 'Despite a century of efforts to define culture adequately, there was in the early 1990s no agreement among anthropologists regarding its nature.' "[5] The concept of "civilization" fares no better. Historians of various kinds have left us often magisterial taxonomies built upon sweeping chronicles of large swathes of geography and time, but in the end it seems there are as many different ways of cutting up the pie of history as there are scholars with informed opinions, and there exists no final arbiter to say where one civilization ends and another begins, or even an answer to the question as to what qualifies a civilization as such in the first place.[6]

At the start of his *History of Civilizations* (1963) Fernand Braudel wrote, "It would be pleasant to be able to define the word 'civilization' simply and precisely, as one defines a straight line, a triangle, or a chemical element. The vocabulary of the social sciences, unfortunately, scarcely permits decisive definitions. . . . In the social sciences, in fact, as in philosophy, there are wide and frequent variations in the meaning of the simplest words, according to the thought that uses and informs them."[7] In a journal devoted to civilization studies, a half century later, one scholar notes, "There are dozens, if not hundreds, of definitions of *civilization* around. I am told by the members of the International Society for the Comparative Study of *Civilizations* that they have made numerous previous attempts at their annual meetings to generate a consensus definition of *civilization*—without success."[8] Writing in 1996, Samuel Huntington, whose name is associated as much as any scholar with the notion of civilization, notes of a reference work from 1968: "Interestingly, the International Encyclopedia of the Social Sciences (New York: Macmillan and Free Press, ed. David L. Sills, 17 vols., 1968) contains no primary article on 'civilization' or 'civilizations.' The 'concept of civilization' (singular) is treated in a subsection of the article called 'Urban Revolution' while civilizations (plural) receive passing mention in an article called 'Culture.' "[9] He also quotes observations from other historians (e.g., Durkheim and Mauss, Braudel, Spengler, and Dawson) who use the concept of civilization but none of whom actually defined it formally either.

Huntington's own discussion of the nature of civilizations is a survey of what he takes to be the common scholarly understanding of civilization, which he characterizes as essentially "the broadest cultural entity,"[10] observing that "culture is the common theme in virtually every definition of civilization,"[11] and that "civilization is a culture writ large."[12] But elsewhere he elevates religion to a privileged place above culture and says, for example, "Of all the objective elements which define civilizations, however, the most important usually is religion,"[13] and he agrees with the statement of Christopher Dawson that "the great religions are the foundations on which the great civilizations rest."[14] So is a civilization essentially a cultural or religious entity? What are religion and culture in the first place, and how do they differ? Huntington's observations about civilizations do not amount to a formal definition beyond a vague sense that there exists some broadest identification with respect to notions such as culture and religion. In somewhat circular fashion, he says, "The civilization to which he belongs is the broadest level of *identification* with which he strongly *identifies*,"[15] a vagueness echoed in the assertion that "civilizations are the biggest 'we' within which we feel culturally at home as distinguished from all the other 'thems' out there."[16] Huntington's understanding of the nature of civilizations does not even cohere with his own claims about which civilizations happen to exist right now. He tells us that the West is a civilization, but it is an exception to his rule that civilizations be based on a religion. Buddhism is a major world religion, but it is not associated with a civilization, unlike the other four world religions of Islam, Christianity, Hinduism, and Confucianism. These are not trivial exceptions, and Huntington's many ad hoc adjustments to his notion of civilization belie any sense of a reliable definition or concept.

When it comes to the concept of "tradition" as an academic subject, there is no similar profusion of competing definitions as in the case of culture and religion, even though the words "tradition" and "traditional" are widely used in academic literature. Aside from a few important exceptions, the *concept* of tradition as a formal matter has suffered from either neglect or deliberate exclusion, unlike the other three terms of our tetrad.[17] It is far less frequently treated as a topic of academic scholarly interest worth theorizing, but often functions informally as a foil or as a symbolic antipode to the modern, the rational, and the properly historical.[18] Tradition is evoked as a lingering or outdated human tendency toward ossification and imitation, a relic of immaturity or dogmatism, a power impulse or ideology, but not usually treated as an analytic or theoretical idea.[19] Such attitudes are also commonly directed toward religion, but unlike religion, which is decidedly outside the self-image of the enterprise of modern scholarship, and which therefore can be comfortably theorized and defined with low stakes, many scholars will find themselves referring to their own "tradition of . . ." or "traditional . . ." despite their generally disapproving stance toward tradition when it comes to others. Modern intellectual life has a "tradition of" this or that but never a "religion of" those same things. Perhaps because tradition is still alive, half-hidden, in the self-image of modernity it is treated more as a subjective or psychological tendency than as a coherent reality standing on its own like the other three terms above.[20] Even thinkers who were willing to grapple with tradition—such as Karl Popper in the philosophy of science,[21] Jaroslav Pelikan in his history of the Christian tradition,[22] and Hans-Georg Gadamer in his approach to hermeneutics[23]—did not attempt a serious formal treatment of it, preferring to stick to concrete examples and historical cases and relying always on the idiomatic sense of the term.

Regarding the social sciences more generally, Edward Shils pointed out:

> Social scientists avoid the confrontation with tradition and with their omission of it from explanatory schemes by having recourse to "historical factors." In this way, they treat tradition as a residual category, as an intellectual disturbance which is to be brushed away.[24]

> On the whole . . . historians and anthropologists have not
> been reflective about tradition. The more they come into the
> present, the less they are inclined to observe the influence of
> tradition and the more they fall into the idiom of contemporary
> social science. Traditionality as a property of beliefs, actions, and
> institutions is dissolved into other things.[25]

But even among those few who are more systematic about theorizing tradition, there is very little by way of convergence on a reliable formal definition.[26] René Guénon, the founder of the traditional school, while providing many profound meditations on the nature of tradition, did not arrive at or even aim for a precise demarcation, while at the same time also formulating notions such as antitradition and countertradition based upon his understanding of tradition. In one example of terminological ambiguity, René Guénon critiqued the notion of "traditionalist," which he contrasted with a "truly traditional spirit,"[27] even though later members of the school such as S. H. Nasr embraced the label of traditionalist. The state of the use of the word "tradition" is somewhat different from the other three terms of our tetrad (as will be discussed in the concluding chapter), but generally the same set of problems apply to all four as a matter of definitions and scholarly use.

These open questions of definition leave contemporary scholars and philosophers in a curious situation. The result of generations of inability to demarcate their subject matter is that no scholar in the Euro-American academy and the broader modern intellectual culture can assert final authority over the correct use of the terms "culture," "civilization," "religion," and "tradition," or claim on the basis of consensus that someone else is using such terms *incorrectly*—to be clear, incorrectly as a certain kind of technical term, not as idiomatic English. How can there be an incorrect usage when the literature gives *hundreds* of allegedly correct meanings?[28] Neither anthropology, sociology, religious studies, nor history has a consensus or even majority definition for any of these concepts, and they have not for several decades. Nearly every theorist has an alternative suggestion about the right way to use them. The relevant literature on definitions is generations old and is making no progress.

Indeed, half a century of attempts is long enough for scholars to ask why this failure in the realm of definition persists. One reason might be that, in fact, one does not actually learn what a religion is, or what a culture is, or what a civilization is by mastering a concept or a definition.

Instead, one comes to understand how to use these concepts through exposure to the habits and priorities of a certain class of authorities and mentors (usually in the Euro-American academy). The official (or tentative) definitions of these concepts accomplish no theoretical or analytical work in any of the relevant fields—they solve no intellectual problems and only register opinions. There is no shortage of sentences labeled "definitions," but such formulations have no power to exclude or include on their own. That is to say, if some belief or action counts as "religion," then it already *did* count as such in the eyes of the scholar, and no definition will be able to change that status.[29] It may be that over time some belief or practice will shift from being "cultural" to "religious" or the reverse, but that change will never happen because any definition or theory demanded it. One defines religion, culture, civilization, and tradition in order to reflect usage and presuppositions, not to decide them.

When used appropriately, there is nothing intrinsically wrong with such definitions, and they can have a certain value, if only to communicate the definer's (or a field's) approach.[30] Indeed, a lack of definitional precision is not always a hindrance to understanding a great deal about an area of interest and to pursuing valuable research about it. The claim in this book is not that humanities and social science scholars are shooting in the dark when they use the concepts of religion, culture, tradition, civilization, and the like. Nor is it the case that unassailably precise definitions of a subject matter are a precondition for exploring it. When studying the realities denoted by religion, civilization, culture, and tradition, scholars are often making good faith efforts to be precise, and they can be highly erudite and empathetic about their subject matter, but the conceptual boundaries of what they have in mind can be *undertheorized* relative to the kind of analytical work these concepts are sometimes called upon to carry out—tasks such as delineating *other* concepts, like Islam. They function like floodlights, not spotlights. A chain is only as strong as its weakest link, and a definition is only as precise as its most ambiguous term.

Rather than being thought of as theoretically explanatory or analytical ideas, the Euro-American academic concepts of religion, civilization, culture, and tradition should be recognized for what they are: extremely rich folk concepts that register the received usage by relevant people about how to think about those areas of human experience that are pointed to by these concepts. Such ideas are understood through reliance upon the cultivated sensibilities of the people who use them, or in some cases simple everyday meaning. You just have to *know it when you see it*, because there is little analytical or theoretical consensus—no reliable systematic demarcations and guidelines—on what the categories of religion, civilization, culture, and tradition include and what they exclude, whether they are analyzed singly or taken together. The problems are amplified by the fact that these terms are almost always defined in terms of *each other*, as if taken together they will achieve a form of collective clarity that no one can achieve on its own (as we saw in Huntington's use of culture, civilization, and religion). That these most capacious and philosophically consequential terms lack any consistent definition—in fact, each one seems to have dozens or hundreds of definitions—is one of the most startling facts about modern intellectual life.

Coming back to the "What is Islam?" question: the situation of folk notions often being used as clarifying concepts leaves scholars of Islam in a curious predicament. Islam is defined as being a religion, civilization, tradition, or culture, but finding out what such things are requires absorbing the outlook and presuppositions of the *people* who are describing Islam as being religion, civilization, or culture, since there is no reliable procedure to follow that will tell you what counts as religion and what does not, what counts as civilization and what does not, what counts as a tradition and what does not, what counts as culture and what does not. One has to learn by reliance on authority. Only after having become thoroughly modern or "academic" in one's knowledge, habits, and preferences can one then understand how it is that Islam is a religion, or is a civilization, or is a tradition, or is a culture, or is a society, or is a system, et cetera. A years-long apprenticeship is, to put it mildly, a hefty price to pay just to get a definition of something so important. And, in fact, one never gets to a definition even after having gone to the trouble of becoming modern (or becoming competent in mimicking it). One masters its usage only through emulation and absorption, having developed the right kind of reflexes and intuitions. One observes one's mentors "knowing it when they see it" and, over a long period of time and in subtle and indefinable ways, one begins to also "know it when one sees it." Then, at some appropriate time, one offers one's own "definition" of religion, or civilization, or culture, which will no doubt be different in some way from those that went before and which will also fail to be widely accepted, if a century of scholarly history is any indicator.

This simply will not do. If the inclusion of Islam in some category like religion or civilization is to move beyond idiom and have analytical and theoretical power, then the nature of whatever category Islam is said to belong to must be adequately defined *first*. Otherwise, one should abandon the idea that one is clarifying what Islam is or answering any important theoretical questions about it by classifying Islam into one of these categories.

One can look at this question from the starting point of certain particular objects of study that may interest humanities and social science scholars. Consider the following assortment of items that are associated with Islam as a religion, culture, tradition, or civilization: Ibn Rushd's commentaries on Aristotle, ʿUmar Khayyām's poetry, land tax, miniature paintings of the Prophet, law, astrology, the rules of fasting, the prohibition against *ribā* (usury), atomic theory in *kalam*, the sari, the virtue of compassion, the *tafsīr* of al-Ṭabarī, the Taj Mahal, belief in bodily resurrection, art, coffee, the Constitution of Madinah, the visitation of saints' tombs, marriage, formal logic, *jizyah*, lullabies, qawwali, Persian carpets, *taʿarrof*, *waḥdat al-wujūd*, prayer beads, ethics, *uṣūl al-fiqh*, *al-ṭibb al-yūnānī*, the uncreatedness of the Quran, hip-hop music, *niqāb*, astronomy, streetlights, prophethood (*nubuwwah*). A list such as this could go on for thousands of pages, but it is a sufficient sample to think practically about the problem. If one attempts to classify the items above into just one of the categories of religion, culture, tradition, or civilization, the exercise will begin to feel arbitrary in many cases, and different scholars will classify different items according to their own presuppositions. If one were to limit oneself to just three categories for the sake of simplicity—religion, culture, and civilization—and one were to take a poll of scholars of Islam regarding these items, one would notice that some ideas and practices would show up only in one category, but some would appear in two, and some in three. It is clear that people mean substantially different things by religion, culture, and civilization, but it is also the case that in many instances it seems hard to draw a line between them and to know with clarity whether some particular reality is best classified as one or the other.

Put simply, between the categories of religion, culture, and civilization there is both overlap and difference. How does one identify and clarify those boundaries?

If one maps this situation as a Venn diagram (fig. 1.1) reflecting how scholars might categorize these realities, the result is three partially intersecting circles, with some items appearing at the conjunction of all three spheres (e.g., art), some at the conjunction of two out of three (e.g., law, carpet weaving, ethics), and some appearing only in one (e.g., belief in bodily resurrection, ship making, lullabies):

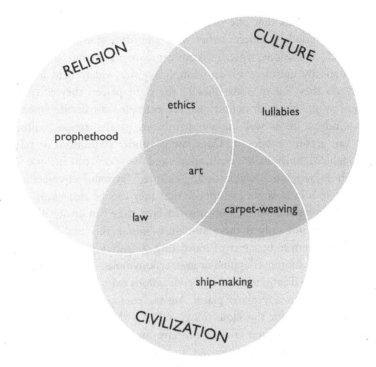

Figure 1.1. Venn diagram of civilization, religion, and culture.

Such a diagram constitutes a snapshot of what scholars *already* know about how they use these ideas and classify things into them. One could never use it as a tool to decide whether something belongs to religion or culture. It simply provides a visual metaphor for how already existing habits of thought relate to each other in a certain way.

The same ambiguity becomes apparent if one begins from already existing definitions of our tetrad and tries to use them as sorting procedures for classifying different particulars as listed above. Suppose one were to say: if some item from the list above fulfills conditions set out in a given definition of "civilization," then it belongs to the category of civilization; if it fulfills a certain definition of "culture" then It belongs to the category of culture; and if it fulfills conditions a certain definition of "religion," it belongs to the category of religion. No matter how carefully one tries to articulate these definitions (which are numerous and often mutually contradictory), one will never overcome the demarcation problem—the definitions will always either exclude particulars that one believes ought to be included in some category, or include particulars that one believes must be excluded. One always falls back on one's good judgment rather than any kind of formal concept. In real life such definitions typically require too many ad hoc modifications to be analytically useful at all, and simply register widely held folk usage. Not only do they fail to draw lines in the right places, they often fail to draw lines at all. No such definitions, for example, can decide where "art" will go—indeed, most well-known definitions of civilization, culture, or religion can accommodate art. Does law go under civilization or religion? All reasonable definitions of "civilization" and "religion" can include law. If terms such as "religion," "civilization," "culture," "system," et cetera are this ambiguous, it is impossible to suppose that they can be *theoretically* useful. They do not solve analytical problems. In fact, they can create new ones.

Moreover, not only is there ambiguity *within* the uses of terms, but there does not seem to be a way of translating consistently *between* them. Are culture and civilization overlapping or even synonymous, or are cultures always subdivisions of civilizations? Can two civilizations exist in the same place, or is there only one in any given place? Are societies parts of civilizations or are they two names for the same thing? What is the dividing line between religion and culture? Can a civilization have multiple religions in it? Can a culture also have multiple religions? Can a religion span multiple cultures? As a formal matter these questions have no answer, or too many answers.

Furthermore, not only is it difficult to properly theorize such words, but it is also practically impossible because of the nature of academic specialization. Suppose scholars in the field of religious studies were finally able to establish some sort of consensus about the category of religion. They would be able to do so by describing what religion is, what it *includes*, but of course a concept is what it is not only by virtue of what it includes but also what it *excludes*. That means that a category such as "religion" is defined by the territory it claims but also, and necessarily, by the boundaries forced upon it by neighboring categories like science, art, ethics, culture, tradition, society, and so on. The scholar of religion is obligated to define "religion" against things like "culture" but has no control, or little control, over what constitutes the definition of "culture." The scholar of religious studies could, and typically will, define culture for the sake of defining religion, but do other scholars who lay claim to the authority to define "culture" (i.e., anthropologists) endorse such definitions? The problem is mirrored in fields such as anthropology, which will define "culture" and then have its own provisional definition of "religion" for the sake of establishing one of the boundaries of "culture." Will scholars from other fields accept the definition of "religion" that was formulated for the sake of defining "culture"? For every concept there is a field that claims it as its own, and multiple other fields that cannot do without that concept to define theirs, and the jostling to establish stable boundaries never ends and consensus never arrives.

The result is a proliferation of definitions for each of these terms, and no referee to tell us where the boundaries really ought to be. Without some universal rubric, one runs into a version of the "folly" that the philosopher Donald Davidson identified in the case of defining truth: "You worry about the concept of truth when it is the focus of your attention, but you pretend you understand it when trying to cope with knowledge (or belief, memory, perception, and the like). . . . It is all right to assume you have an adequate handle on intention and convention if your target is meaning. I could easily go on."[31] A similar folly affects ideas such as religion, culture, civilization, tradition, and related ideas such as society, system, secular, scientific, philosophical, artistic, and so on. When scholars focus on a particular term like "religion" they treat it as ambiguous, malleable, mercurial, and difficult, but treat the concepts that are being used to explain the ambiguous concept as if they were clear and well established, even though those very same terms are just as ambiguous, malleable, mercurial, and difficult. It is not fully within the power of religious studies scholars to define religion, because their subject matter's definition is at the mercy of scholars in other fields whose subject matter's definition is similarly at the mercy of other scholars . . . and so on and so forth.[32]

Some scholars might argue that this is no serious predicament, and that these terms are clear enough to go on using them. That has been the prevailing spirit in most academic scholarship, and serious observers have long noted the definitional problems with these terms and continue to use them as usual. Braudel, as noted above, discusses the definitional problem with "civilization" in the very first paragraph of his *History of Civilizations*, and then proceeds as if the problem were trivial. In reality, the intellectual stakes are greater than one may realize. The question of "conceptualizing Islam" ought to be seen as an episode in a larger history, a particular example of a more general philosophical and indeed metaphysical problem. One's use of our tetrad of terms decides and communicates one's positions on underlying questions of truth, rationality, and goodness without staking out those positions explicitly or connecting those positions with the selection of those concepts—whether this happens consciously or not. In other words, not only are these terms used to say what Islam is or what Islamic is, they are also used more generally in modern intellectual culture to express what reality is, what rationality is, and what goodness is, but without saying so in so many words. These questions will be explored thoroughly in later chapters.

Logical Dimensions

Let us dwell on the logical dimensions of this question. When called upon to be explanatory in relation to Islam, this tetrad of religion, civilization, tradition, and culture function as "animal" and "biped" do in relation to "human being" ("rational animal" or "featherless biped"). If human beings are a kind of animal or a kind of biped, then clearly one must already understand what makes a thing an animal or a biped and what excludes a thing from those categories. Without a clear conceptual demarcation between animals, three-dimensional bodies, and growing things (human beings are all of these things), nothing theoretically useful can be gained from identifying human beings as a kind of animal. One would be seeking to clarify one idea ("human being") using an idea that is more obscure ("animal"). Put another way, if one did not know how to define the difference between animals and plants, or between bipeds and quadrupeds, of what use would it be to classify a human being as a "rational animal" or "featherless biped"?

By analogy, in the case of placing Islam into some implicit classification scheme, one had better have as solid a grasp of religion, civilization, culture, or tradition (or whatever one says Islam is) as one has of the difference between animals and plants when one classifies human beings as rational animals. Otherwise, one is doing little more than relabeling Islam and pointing to it from different vantage points. One is not *conceptualizing* it. Rather, Islam remains in that undertheorized state of "I know it when I see it." Without a good grasp of these ideas on their own and in relation to each other, referring to "the civilization of Islam" on the one hand and "the religion of Islam" on the other is little better—analytically speaking—than referring to it as "Islam" here and "Mohammedanism" there. It amounts to mere stylistic variety flowing from one's intuitions, or at best, different folk concepts that usually reflect hidden presuppositions about the nature of the world.

Since these concepts are not going to go away, one needs a way in which the terrain—the terrain that seems to have intelligible features that call upon us to draw lines around them and call whatever falls on one side of that line "civilization" or "culture" or "religion"—can be rendered more intelligible. One needs parameters that can give the already existing practice of describing and demarcating civilizations, cultures, religions, and traditions a more analytic character. There ought to be a way of mapping out the intuitions of thinkers regarding what does or does not count as civilization, religion, tradition, and culture using a consistent and coherent rubric—something that has thus far been lacking.

Remember that, logically speaking, things are grouped together into a kind or a set because of certain common features that nevertheless vary from individual to individual. Sometimes the common features are fully intelligible as parameters that can be described and modulated explicitly and consistently, and at other times the commonalities are known intuitively rather than being fully theorized or analyzed. In order to understand how the concepts of civilization, religion, culture, and tradition all belong to an intelligible category called metaphysical institutions, let us first look at some simplified analogies to make it more clear what is meant here by parameters and theorization.

Consider the question of conceptualizing a rhombus. One knows that a rhombus is a quadrilateral, a polygon, a kite, and a parallelogram. Each of these categories is well-defined in itself, and each is clearly defined in terms of all the others. There are parameters such as "number of sides," "angles," "length of sides," "perpendicular lines," and "parallel lines" that are consistent between them.

Now consider the fabric patterns tartan, gingham, paisley, and tattersall. Unlike the geometric categories just mentioned, these patterns are not typically known through an analytical definition or theoretical procedure. Rather, one knows them when one sees them, and in this respect they are similar to the concepts of religion, civilization, tradition, and culture. Knowledgeable people know how to spot paisley or tartan but not how to fully *define* them in relation to each other. There are no formulas to make sense of tattersall in terms of paisley, or gingham in terms of tartan. Nor does anyone need such formulas, because the common sense of those people who are reasonably well acquainted with fabric patterns is reliable enough.

The several categories into which a rhombus fits are marked by their complete mutual translatability and by being fully analyzable: they have clear definitions on their own, and they are definable in terms of each other. When one describes a rhombus as a polygon here, and as a quadrilateral there, and a kite elsewhere, it generates no confusion or ambiguity because one could further point out that a kite is a kind of quadrilateral, or that a quadrilateral is a kind of polygon, that only some kites are rhombuses, and so forth. The definitions of such terms are fully stipulated as part of a logical procedure where those people using terms such as "rhombus" and "quadrilateral" have complete control over what such terms denote. They can say, "Let a quadrilateral mean . . ." and that is all it can mean for the purposes of the procedure (in this case, geometry). The parameters are obvious, and there are no competing conceptions of these concepts.

Definitions for the types of fabric patterns cannot be stipulated as can those of geometric shapes. These patterns remain undertheorized in this sense, and one depends on the ability of the right people to spot and classify them. Quite simply, it is paisley if the right people say it is. Even though the parameters may be somewhat opaque, nevertheless the use of these pattern names tends to *converge* on a common understanding. Modern sartorial life is not trapped in a multigenerational enterprise of conceptualizing and reconceptualizing with questions like "What really *is* paisley?" There are not hundreds of definitions for tartan.

Now, there is no reliable way of translating between civilization, tradition, religion, and culture using parameters that can be held constant between them, unlike the case with polygons, quadrilaterals, kites, and parallelograms. One cannot define civilization in terms of tradition, religion, and culture, or define culture in terms of religion, tradition, and civilization—and so forth and so on—in a way that maintains a constant set of parameters that allows one to avoid equivocating or falling into I-know-it-when-I-see-it arguments. Indeed, one typically finds oneself in a definitional circle in which these terms are all loosely defined in terms of each other, with post-hoc rationalizations rather than clear conceptions. Scholars rely on each other's reasonableness and common experience, as all people must do in the case of natural language. But since it is in fact *theoretical usefulness* that is being sought after, mere idiomatic competence in using these terms is far from enough. Moreover, the concepts of civilization, culture, tradition, and religion do not crystallize according to a common understanding (neither in terms of a clear concept nor in idiomatic usage), unlike the case with fabric patterns. They diverge.

So, on the one hand, the meanings of our tetrad of terms cannot be merely stipulated like geometric figures. We cannot just make them mean what we want them to mean since they are rich folk ideas that are inherited, continue to be widely used in everyday language and in different areas of intellectual life, and, in the case especially of religion and tradition, have a history of usage reaching back many centuries. Yet on the other hand their use does not converge on a broad consensus as we have in the case of the fabric patterns. Even so, scholars will comfortably assert, in all sorts of contexts, that Islam is one or more of these things, or all of them at the same time. Worse yet, it is on the basis of such classifications that they say that this or that idea or practice has the attribute of being *Islamic* or not, a point that will be discussed at length in later chapters.

One is thus dealing with two related analytical questions: (1) Are the things we are interested in well-theorized? (2) Do the conceptions of these things converge when used by the relevant authorities?

When it comes to polygons, quadrilaterals, kites, and parallelograms, the things are well-theorized, and almost unavoidably they therefore converge on a common understanding. We can use these terms without concern for misleading ambiguities. In the case of tartan, gingham, paisley, and tattersall, the things are undertheorized, but they still converge on a common understanding. Even in the absence of theorization, these terms are still fully adequate to the uses we conventionally assign to them. But in the case of civilizations, cultures, religions, and traditions, the things are undertheorized, and their conceptions continuously diverge and fragment into mutually exclusionary definitions. These terms are thus useful only to a certain point (e.g., to register the presuppositions of the community using them), but beyond that point—for example when they are used as if they were analytically clear conceptions that help to illuminate other concepts— they become useless and misleading.

Now, if polygons and quadrilaterals are kinds of geometric figures, and tartan and paisley are kinds of fabric patterns, are civilizations, religions, cultures, and traditions kinds of anything at all? A main argument of this book is that in fact they denote different configurations of a single reality that is left unrecognized or poorly understood, as if one tried to conceptualize individually the ideas of "mountain lion," "cougar," "panther," and "puma" but lacked the concept *Puma concolor* or even simply "cat." To adequately theorize culture, civilization, religion, and tradition will thus require identifying the general category to which they all belong.

But simply *naming* such a category will not do, because that would simply take the logical and definitional problems and transfer them to a higher level of generality. Instead, one needs a set of explanatory parameters that does not change drastically according to the biases of the individual scholar but that can be universal and be used to analyze these concepts individually, in relation to each other, and also in relation to other related concepts. Moreover, each of these invariant parameters should allow for empirical or contingent variation. As in the example of the polygons above, what is desired is not only a folk definition but a set of intelligible parameters such as number of sides and measure of angles that do not only define one thing but also can be used to define related things. For example, a folk definition of a circle would be something like "shaped like the full moon," but a proper theorization would define it in terms of parameters such as "points," "lines," "distance," and "plane," all of which are used in the definition of *other* related shapes. Since existing definitions of religion, culture, tradition, and civilization resemble the "like the full moon" definition rather than the geometric one of "a set of points in a plane a given distance from a given point," one must establish the parameters and framework to more fully theorize them, a task that will be carried out within the general rubric of the concept of the *metaphysical institution*.

This book's argument concentrates on this tetrad of civilization, culture, religion, and tradition, even though there are other related terms about which some of the same points can be made. Whatever can be said of "society" that is philosophically interesting can be said just as well about "culture," while other terms, such as "system" and "structure" and "discourse," are subcategories of the more capacious concepts that make up our tetrad. As we will see, other relevant terms, such as "community," "practice," "legacy," "identity," "hierarchy," "rules," "norms," and "values," are constituent aspects of the general model of institutions that will be developed here. Beyond this tetrad there is only blue sky. That is what makes them *metaphysical* institutions.

Institutions

Some remarks are necessary about the use of the concept of "institution" as a general category that will be used to include these ideas.[33] First, like the concepts of civilization, culture, religion, and tradition, "institution" itself has been inadequately theorized as a formal matter in the scholarly literature, a claim many might find surprising. One will search in vain for an agreed upon definition either in philosophy or in social science. "Institutions are as mysterious as they are ubiquitous. . . . Social ontology has been characterized for decades by a Babel of different approaches."[34] "In the institutional literature there is still an unclarity about what exactly an institution is. What is the ontology, the mode of existence, of institutional reality?"[35] "Definitions of institutions abound . . . none of them has yet become firmly institutionalized in the social and political sciences"[36] (the appearance of "institutionalized" in the statement itself is noteworthy) or "In everyday language and in the social sciences, the term 'institutions' is used in a broad and sometimes amorphous way"[37] or "A term frequently used loosely to refer to established ways of behaving or, more formally to major social systems or structures which organize the primary social practices, roles, and relationships within a culture."[38] To take a particularly telling example, nowhere in the over five hundred pages of *Introduction to Sociology*, edited by a major figure in the field, is a straightforward definition of "institution" offered, nor does one appear in its massive glossary wherein the word "institution" appears only as part of the definition of other words or with an adjective in front of it for special cases, for example, "total institution."[39] "Despite, or perhaps because of, its wide acceptance, institutional theory is associated with intense, unresolved debates around key constructs and issues. The meaning of the concept of an institution, for instance, is considered by many researchers, particularly from realist traditions, to be *overly ambiguous and thus lacking in terms of being a reasonable construct for research.*"[40] Indeed, most often "institution" is defined in much the same way that our tetrad (religion, culture, civilization, tradition) tends to be, namely, for the purpose of registering authoritative usage but without clarifying or demarcating the idea for those who do not already know it when they see it. One must already grasp what an institution is, both in general and in particular, before one defines it, and one's audience must grasp it too. In sociology, for example, one already knows that one is interested in institutions and what counts as one and what does not, while at the same time there are competing visions for what counts as an institution and there is no arbiter for deciding it. Furthermore, these definitions also tend to suffer from certain logical circularities, such that terms that are defined in terms of institutions (e.g., government, economy, politics) are then used in the definition of institutions. Part of the difficulty, as with the tetrad discussed above, is the boundary of "institution" with other closely related terms such as "system" and "organization." It should be emphasized that being undertheorized formally does not mean being under*studied* materially (a caveat that can also be made with respect to the tetrad of concepts discussed above). Within the sphere of consensus determined by the idiomatic "we know it when we see it," the different kinds of institutions, as well as their origin, change, and effects, have been widely and carefully studied especially in sociology and in other fields such as economics, but the absence of a formal consensus definition remains, and is noteworthy. Even so, the various notions of "institution" diverge far less than a term like "religion" or "culture," and is less sensitive to the metaphysical assumptions of the researcher (though not entirely so).[41]

For practical purposes, "institution" gets one into roughly the right domain of experience and brings to mind more or less the right examples, which is why it is suitable to be used in connection with our tetrad. Popper, for example, said "traditions and institutions are in most respects strikingly similar"[42] and indeed was at pains to truly differentiate them except through idiomatic connotation, while Toynbee described civilizations as "institutions of the highest order—institutions, that is, that comprehend without being comprehended,"[43] a statement that can easily be extended to many uses of "culture" as well. Religion, for its part, is commonly named as one of the basic forms of social institutions. For example, the historian H. A. R. Gibb used "institution" in this way when he spoke of "the Islamic religious institution" as opposed to Arab or Persian social traditions, also using the term to designate subcategories such as Sunnis, Shīʿis, and Sufis.[44] The definition of "institution" that will be developed in this book will not depart in spirit from any of the existing definitions but ought to be seen as synthesizing and regimenting them while expanding the concept's applicability.

One alternative approach to naming the encompassing category of our tetrad, rather than using an idea such as "metaphysical institution," would have been to take one of the existing terms—either religion, culture, civilization, or tradition—and expand its meaning to encompass all the others. "Tradition" is a good candidate for this extended technical usage, but the more generic term "institution" is more advantageous for a few reasons. "Tradition" is frequently polarizing and is often used either as a term of abuse or of praise depending on who is saying it. One of the main arguments in this book is that all of the terms in this tetrad carry strong presuppositions about right and wrong, true and false, rational and irrational, and that what is necessary is an invariant rubric in which to situate them all. The concept of "institution" is flexible and neutral enough to sustain the parameters that are going to be laid out here, but at the same time carries little of the baggage or emotional resonance of any of the terms in our tetrad. For example, it will be argued that the Modern Project is indeed a metaphysical institution, which many might be willing entertain who at the same time would balk at being categorized as part of any "tradition."[45]

In any case, since there is no broadly accepted definition of "institution" in the first place, neither in terms of its essential nature nor in terms of its applicability to various domains of life, the conception of institution to be developed here, and its subsequent extension to cover metaphysical institutions, will not depart from any standard view because no such broad consensus exists. Even so, this book will not be seeking to displace existing definitions or descriptions of the various fields in which the concept of "institution" arises, which provide official or quasiofficial usage or communicate the general view of the scholar offering them—sociologist, political scientist, economist, et cetera. Rather, the goal is to refine and develop the definition of the general category "institution" and to expand its scope to include those that can be rightly labeled as metaphysical.

It is hoped that the reader will come to realize, as the argument unfolds, that even a concept as familiar as "institution" defies easy conceptualization and upon exploration is a veritable enigma when it comes to establishing a definition. Those realities in the world that come to be called institutions are made up of entities (individual human consciousnesses) that themselves are mysterious and inscrutable, and therefore it ought to come as no surprise that the unique interaction of such entities that come to be called institutions should also be difficult to theorize—not only in metaphysical institutions but in all such special instances of human beings thinking together. In that sense, this book is not an attempt at domesticating religion, culture, tradition, and civilization in order to make them fit into a conventional concept like "institution," but instead to understand the mystery of what people call "institutions" and to free the concept from certain metaphysical and logical bonds that have kept modern intellectuals from understanding the true nature of social reality. Paradoxically enough, it is only through the acknowledgment of the mysteries involved that analytical clarity can be achieved.

Metaphysical and Ultimate

The term "metaphysical" also needs some explanation. How can an institution be *metaphysical*? To understand this, one can begin from the obvious fact that there are institutions corresponding to various important domains of collective human life: politics, law, education, family. Metaphysics concerns ultimate questions of what is real, what is possible, and what is good—the domain of first principles, or ultimate presuppositions, or what one is always already always thinking as a conscious being. Conventionally, institutions in the domain of politics are called *political* institutions, those in the domain of law are *legal* institutions, and so forth. Such institutions are intelligible features of the general topography of what this book will call *shared thinking*, which also includes the political, the legal, the educational, and the familial. Metaphysics stands astride the horizons of that terrain, and the hitherto unclassified institutions corresponding to this ultimate horizon are, to follow the idiomatic pattern, *metaphysical* institutions. The term "metaphysical" has long been highly polyvalent and difficult to define,[46] and it is therefore important that the modifier of "metaphysical" connected with "institution" not be misconstrued. A metaphysical institution is not itself "metaphysical" the way a cause or substance is. Rather, an institution is metaphysical the way the "natural" sciences are natural—that is, it *concerns* the metaphysical. Metaphysics *as such* cannot be captured by or reduced to an institution. To call an institution "metaphysical" can be confusing because a metaphysical institution itself might claim to reject metaphysics, or might not consider itself to even be an institution in the first place, which is not the case with most examples of institutions. A philosophical resistance to metaphysics and the failure to recognize the institutional nature of one's own ultimate presuppositions, which is so characteristic of the modern world, is a major theme addressed in this book. Indeed, the central difficulty plaguing the conceptualization of institutions is metaphysical—a failure to deal properly with the ultimate. As will be argued in later chapters, without breaking free of the metaphysical constraints that operate in most of academic philosophy and social science, the ambiguities and definitional dead ends in conceptualizing social reality will continue to proliferate. A prerequisite for this endeavor is to provide a fully theorized framework for our tetrad—civilization, culture, tradition, religion—which have hitherto existed at the level of folk usage and have been encumbered by persistent ambiguities and inconsistencies.

Before moving on, however, it might seem necessary to justify the category of "metaphysical institutions" as a relevant or actual domain in the first place. After all, the whole problem with religion, culture, civilization, and tradition is that people cannot agree on how to delineate the boundaries of these ideas that bundle together enormously complex facets of human experience. If no one has hitherto been able to demarcate each one separately, how can one justify attempting to theorize an encompassing domain into which they all belong *together*?

It is hoped that the full sweep of this book's argument will answer this question convincingly, but for now, it might be useful to note that this work began as an exercise in surveying the literature about "conceptualizing Islam," which led to an inquiry into the nature of all those things Islam was said to be. There was no formula for discovering the ambiguities and incoherencies attached to the use of these terms and to their definitions, but the problems are impossible to miss. It could be said that a scholar inquiring into the case of defining Islam is in a unique position to expose certain logical difficulties with these ideas because in one way or another Islam is said to be all of them, leading one to examine how the terms religion, culture, civilization, and tradition relate to each other in a way scholars from specialized academic fields such as religious studies, anthropology, and history might not consider. In any case, a multigenerational failure to properly demarcate a relevant domain despite a strong desire to do so (which has been the state of affairs for religion, culture, civilization, tradition) is a good indicator that some larger picture is being missed or avoided. It became clear to the present author that what is necessary is a more comprehensive approach that will enable one to make sense of vexing terms like "religion," "culture," "civilization," and "tradition" as components of a more general framework. In the absence of a more universalizing concept like "metaphysical institution" such notions are always going to evade satisfactory theorization, and rather than understanding the nature of social reality in terms of sufficiently precise concepts one will remain mired in the mere exegesis of folk ideas.

Definitional Shortcomings

As mentioned above, one goal of establishing this framework is to avoid the ambiguities that have plagued previous attempts to define these terms. *Ambiguity* is going to be a major thread in the tapestry of this book.

Scholars have sometimes attempted *simple* definitions of our family of terms,[47] but these are often too general and hence analytically weak, and are sometimes closer to poetry or aphorism. They can have their value, but too simple a definition cannot be very useful in light of the enormous complexity of things that go under the label of culture, civilization, religion, or tradition.

A definition that is too *complicated,* however, can easily sprawl out of control and lose coherence, and become little more than a long register of the sundry things that the conceptualizer *already knows* belong in the definition by learned intuition, which is what most complex attempts at defining these metaphysical institutions turn out to be.

Consider an early (1889) and, for decades very influential, definition of "culture," that of Edward Tylor, who said it was "that complex whole which includes knowledge, belief, art, morals, law, custom, and any other capabilities and habits acquired by man as a member of society." Or recall the definition of "religion" by the anthropologist Clifford Geertz in 1966: "(1) a system of symbols which acts to (2) establish powerful, pervasive,

and long-lasting moods and motivations in men by (3) formulating conceptions of a general order of existence and (4) clothing these conceptions
with such an aura of factuality that (5) the moods and motivations seem
uniquely realistic."[48] As Nongbri points out, Bruce Lincoln critiques Geertz
by offering a conceptualization of religion:

> (1) A discourse whose concerns transcend the human, temporal,
> and contingent and that claims for itself a similarly transcendent
> status, (2) a set of practices whose goal is to produce a proper
> world and/or proper human subjects, as defined by a religious
> discourse to which these practices are connected, (3) a commu-
> nity whose members construct their identity with reference to a
> religious discourse and its attendant practices, and (4) an institu-
> tion that regulates religious discourse, practices, and community,
> reproducing them over time and modifying them as necessary,
> while asserting their eternal validity and transcendent value.

Do such sprawling definitions really clarify?

One ambiguity from which such definitions suffer is that they contain
closely related or near-synonymous elements that are not clearly differentiated
from each other. What is the difference between a *custom* and a *belief*, or
between *knowledge* and *morals* (Tylor)? What is the difference between a *mood*
and an *aura*, or between a *symbol* and a *conception* (Geertz)? What is the
difference between an *institution* and a *community*, between a *discourse* and
a *practice* (Lincoln)? These notions can be distinct or they can overlap, and
one is simply expected to know where these lines are, but that knowledge
is folk knowledge. They are not delineated in a well-theorized way. These
fuzzy boundaries can entail spillover out of the relevant conceptual space
(i.e., causing the concept to embrace things that do not belong) and also
incompleteness (i.e., failing to include things that should belong). This is
the basic problem of demarcation: does the definition include and exclude
the right cross-section of human experience, regardless of the level of generality or specificity? For example, does a given definition of culture leave
out obvious examples of culture,[49] or does it sprawl out such that too many
things qualify as culture, many of which would not belong, if one follows
the wording of the definition?

A second type of ambiguity arises from the fact that these definitions
contain elements from different logical and even ontological categories. If
one were to define blue, for example, by saying "a range of colors including

periwinkle, navy, aquamarine, teal, cerulean, and sapphire," each item in the list is logically speaking the same kind of thing and there is no question of explaining how they all belong together. But how do *capabilities* and *art* go together (Tylor)? What about a *symbol* and a *conception* (Geertz)? Or a *community* and a *practice* (Lincoln)? In order for logically disparate entities (e.g., a community and a practice) to belong together in the definition of a thing (not merely the experience of it), there must be an appropriate subject for those multiple kinds of predicates. Both size and mass can be attributed to a three-dimensional body because bodies have, and must have, both size and mass, and therefore both the size and the mass of a body can appear in a description of bodies without raising logical problems even though they are different categories of predication. Indeed, they fit together. But in logically fragmented definitions (i.e., containing elements of different logical categories) like those mentioned above, what gives the theorist the confidence to claim that all of these conceptually disparate elements—ranging as they do over people, actions, things, and ideas—all actually cohere? What is their ontological glue? We know the parts of a helicopter belong together because we can see them attached and we can witness the machine working or failing to work, but how is it that in the case of culture or civilization or religion we can draw a line around just this particular gigantic set of phenomena, both incorporating a great deal and excluding a great deal, without an explicit way of holding them all together meaningfully other than the reliable *we-know-it-when-we-see-it*? Scholars produce such sprawling definitions because they understand that one must have a sufficiently complex set of attributes considering how multifaceted these realities are, but they cannot manage to avoid articulating a list of properties that have no conceptual *fit* other than the fact that the conceptualizer decided to stick them all together because the conceptualizer *already knows* that they belong together. If "civilization" includes ideas, *and* ways of acting, *and* people, how do we know that there is a thing there in the first place? Is it a whole, or a bundle, or just a jumble? Why give this aggregate—culture, or religion, or civilization—a name unless we know it is a *thing* in the first place? And if that thing can be fully described only in terms of different *kinds* of things, one ought to provide an account of how those different kinds of things are attributes of a single meaningfully coherent reality. In other words, if these are the predicates, what is the subject?

The goal of chapter 2 will be to use the concept of the institution in part to overcome these logical and definitional problems. However, as mentioned earlier, when one turns to the conceptualizations and definitions relevant to the concept of institution one encounters some of the very same difficulties, although in the case of institutions one is dealing with a situation more akin to the example of fabric patterns mentioned earlier; that is, people generally agree about what counts as an institution but they are not able to adequately theorize just what that is. Consider the following list of recurring terms that appear throughout conceptualizations of the concept of the institution. Many of these terms are used somewhat differently by different theorists: actors, agency, agent, atomistic, autonomy, behavior, capabilities, collective, commitment, consensual, constitutive, constraints, conventions, duties, enforcement, equilibrium, function, game, goals, holistic, identity, individual, intention, interests, knowledge, legislate, mechanism, mind, norms, objectives, objects, obligation, officeholder, organization, pattern, practices, positions, regularity, regulative, rights, ritual, roles, rules, sanctions, social, social facts, stability, status, structure, system, teleological, values. These terms frequently overlap in their meaning and hence are ambiguous; they are not only different but in many cases are different kinds of things; and they are used to denote both institutions and noninstitutions.

Sometimes the conceptualizations in which they appear are simple and brief, as when Anthony Giddens, to use one important example, calls institutions "the more enduring features of social life."[50] In another register he characterizes institutions as "the most deeply-layered practices constitutive of social systems,"[51] which for him require the existence of "(a) knowledge— as memory traces—of 'how things are to be done' (said, written), on the part of social actors; (b) social practices organised through the recursive mobilisation of that knowledge; (c) capabilities that the production of those practices presupposes."[52] This latter, more complex articulation would be intelligible to a sociologist, but it raises the problem of what binds these entities together. Just what is it that makes it possible to speak of knowledge, practices, actors, and capabilities as aspects of one thing? One might reasonably presuppose that they belong together, but that is not the same as an account of what makes them cohere. Finally, there remains the question of demarcating institutions from other things: Giddens says he distinguishes institutions from "social systems" but is there some definition that would allow one to consistently draw that line? He seems to identify institutions as the "deepest" or most "enduring" aspect of social systems, but then just how deep or how enduring?

To sum up, one must avoid (1) overly simple and hence analytically weak definitions; (2) definitions that exclude the right things or include the wrong things; and (3) hodgepodge definitions that bundle logically disparate features. Instead, one must strive for a theorization of institutions that is complex, coherent, and correct in scope. One must especially be on guard against an increasing complicatedness that comes at the cost of a proliferation of ambiguities that tend to pile up with the addition of component upon component to the definition. Simple theorizations are intelligible but weak, while complicated theorizations are rich but typically obscure and confusing. The goal is a theorization that is rich, clear, and targeted. This task can be accomplished only by thinking about metaphysics metaphysically, and it must begin from the fact that the matter at hand involves conscious beings relating to each other across time and space.

Synopsis

- The primary terms used to define Islam conceptually are *religion, civilization, culture,* and *tradition.* One or more members of this tetrad remain ultimate in all significant conceptualizations of Islam.

- In the several fields that have been devoted to their study, none of these four terms has an agreed upon definition, neither on their own nor in relation to each other.

- A lack of formal definitions for important ideas is not intrinsically wrong and is inevitable, but one should not use such unclear terms to make *other* ideas (such as Islam) more precise. Definitions are only as good as their most ambiguous term.

- Culture, civilization, religion, and tradition, which are the most central terms used to define Islam, remain folk concepts whose definitions at best serve to register received opinion by certain scholarly authorities.

- The existing definitions for this tetrad do not help scholars to classify phenomena into the categories of religion, culture, civilization, and tradition. They fail to include or exclude on their own but are changed on an ad hoc basis in keeping with a given scholar's views.

- In light of this general definitional chaos, scholars need a general rubric or concept that allows one to discuss this tetrad (and related terms) in a way that overcomes previous definitional obstacles. That rubric will be the concept of the *metaphysical institution*.

- The concept of the institution itself remains poorly defined and undertheorized but is still useful because it brings one to the right domain of ideas and is neutral to many of the normative commitments that plague the terms of our tetrad.

- The realities we call institutions are much more paradoxical and mysterious than they may at first appear, which is why they persistently defy attempts to define and conceptualize them.

- To call an institution "metaphysical" is akin to calling a science "natural," meaning it pertains to the metaphysical but is not itself metaphysics, which in all cases has become a difficult word to define and work with even though no better options currently exist.

- Metaphysics concerns ultimate questions of what is real, what is possible, and what is good—the domain of first principles, or ultimate presuppositions, or what one is always already always doing as a conscious being.

- Institutions of all kinds, in order to be correctly conceptualized, must be studied metaphysically, meaning, in terms of ultimate questions of what is real, possible, and good. Otherwise, one will remain mired in the same generations-long definitional dead ends.

- Different modes of ambiguity have plagued previous definitions of our tetrad of concepts. Such conceptualizations have either been too simple, too complicated, or poorly demarcated.

- One must therefore strive for theorizations of religion, culture, tradition, and civilization that are rich, clear, and targeted, not to replace these ideas by a single mono-concept but to make existing discussions more clear and future ones more fruitful.

Chapter 2

The Nature of Institutions
and Shared Thinking

Every human being thinks on his or her own, but human beings also always think together. The thinking that belongs to every living human being receives from, imitates, and trusts the thinking of other human beings, and therefore the *content* of thinking is transmitted *between* human beings while at the same time constituting an essential dimension of individual consciousness *within* any human being. While shared thinking—a technical term whose scope this chapter is meant to delineate—has no separate faculties of its own apart from the individual thinkers that make it up, it is nevertheless misleading to treat each individual human being as an atom that could exist without the sharing that is essential to the reality of any individual's thinking. The perception, memory, reason, imagination, love, and will of each human being is autonomous, but the growth, nourishment, and contents of these faculties and powers are not. How one's own thinking and the thinking of others are constitutive of each other is not easily pictured through metaphor or theorized by definition or procedure, and analytically speaking can be adequately expressed only in terms that are inescapably paradoxical for reasons that will be discussed later.

To state it using the imagery of the first person: There is everything one can perceive, remember, understand, reason, imagine, love, and appreciate for oneself. Call this the *I*. One says "I know" and "I believe." But no one can simply do these things oneself. In one's acts of consciousness one also relies upon others and guides others, meaning that thoughts are expressed and understood between people, and are bequeathed and inherited across time and space. That is the difference between saying "I know" and "we know," between "I understand" and "we understand," "I value" and "we value," "I discover" and "we discover," "I love" and "we love."

The relationship of *I* and *we* is a question of consciousness—of meaning and understanding—for which no mechanical or structural metaphor is fully adequate. The *we* is not an aggregate of which each *I* is a mechanical part. Nor is the *we* a kind of "organism" or "organic whole" if the basis of such a metaphor is the modern biological notion of nodes and functions in a mechanistic or "systems" sense. No *I* can be or become an *I* without also consciously participating in a *we* (in many different ones, in fact), and there can be no *we* except by virtue of the many realities in it who say *I*. The *I* is not merely the *we* at a smaller scale, and the *we* is not the *I* merely multiplied and aggregated. The *I* is not simply constructed by some *we*, and neither is any *we* merely a collection of beings who say *I* with some shared attributes. An *I* is not an algebraic product of its relationships, and a *we* is not a mere archipelago. Human beings are not islands, but they are not mere intersections either.

A significant part of this book's overall argument will concern a meaningful minimum of metaphysics, in particular the nature of consciousness and meaning. In order to properly understand anything about the metaphysics of the *we* one must sufficiently know the metaphysics of the *I*. Otherwise, one is left with a mere folk understanding of the *we* that does not comprehend the true nature of that thing of which the *we* is a collectivity. But since no human being can think without the thinking of other human beings, it should also be obvious that in order to fully theorize the *I* one must sufficiently theorize the *we*—one must know how it is that human beings actually relate to each other in real life in terms of their consciousness, meaning, and understanding. In other words, while one's conception of shared thinking will only be as good as one's model of individual thinking, one cannot have a full account of individual thinking without an account of how one shares thinking with others.

This relationship of *I* and *we* is not a trivial matter. Even the most comprehensive description possible (one could say, *ontology*) of individual human thinking will not amount to a description of what happens in shared thinking, and neither will the most ambitious conceptualization of collective consciousness amount to an account of individual human thinking. Human beings are never fully determined by their social relationships because such relationships are constituted by human beings themselves, but neither are human beings fully autonomous (that is, free from reliance upon that which is outside of themselves) in their thinking at any point in their lives. To be a human being is to think for oneself, but one cannot think for oneself without others human beings thinking for themselves too. This relationship changes over time, but it never goes away. One is born into it, and one dies with it. No amount of detail about some collective human reality will be enough to explain what it means to be an *I*, because human thinking is not merely an aggregate of relationships. One cannot merely extrapolate from the outside in—from *we* to *I*. But human thinking relies upon the thinking that come from other human beings in order to grow, live, survive, and thrive. Therefore, in order to understand shared thinking or we-thinking, to comprehend the nature of *we*, one cannot rely merely on introspection. One cannot merely extrapolate from the inside out—from *I* to *we*.

The metaphor of *structure* is frequently used—indeed, overused—to describe how agents operate within various kinds of social relationships, with a strong emphasis on the way that the individual is constrained, as if from the outside, by a certain *system* of thinking, akin to the way the various parts of a device are determined by their place within the design of the machine. In this image, one starts from a *we* and goes down to the level of the *I*, as if beginning from the *we* and finding the *I* inside of it, a container shaping its content.

But it is also true that the *I* is the container, and the *we* is the content. Picture individual thinkers and imagine a field of interactions stretching from within human beings reaching within other human beings, the way magnetic fields exist between (and inside) magnets because of what exists *within* the magnets. The *we* is inside of the *I*. After all, what are relationships if not interactions between realities that must exist on their own such that a relationship between them can be established in the first place? The structure metaphor has limited applicability in the case of a true *we* because the relationships that make up a *we* exist only if the realities that are inter acting *know how* to be in that particular relationship. That awareness has to exist *within* the consciousness of the human beings who are interacting.

In general one must take great care with such imagery as "inside of," which, after all, is a spatial metaphor for something that is not itself spatial. Indeed, the container-content relationship in these two cases—the *I* within the *we*, the *we* within the *I*—amount to slightly different metaphors, and one needs to keep track of that difference (and analogous ambiguities and equivocations that plague other metaphors) with great care. "Within" or "inside" can mean many things, as can phrases such as "part of." Saying, for example, that an individual is *part of* a system and also that a system is *part of* an individual are related claims that nevertheless equivocate on the phrase *part of.* One must recognize how consequential the choice of metaphors such as "structure" and "construct" and "part" can be when it comes to conceptualizing how human beings think and how they interact with each other. Another such metaphor, highly relevant in this regard, is the notion of "system," an idea taken so much for granted, so seemingly neutral, unladen, and precise, even though it implies a definite imaginative picture of the reality being thus represented, and with no theoretically precise definition despite its ubiquitous use. To call something a system is to analogize it to a physical complex or a network of cause-and-effect nodes, or otherwise is a way of naming a collection of rules, principles, methods, or procedures that human beings implement—an if-then formalism or recipe. As will be seen later, the very notion of human thinking and social reality as "structure" can often be deeply misleading.

This chapter endeavors to establish the *concept* of the institution with as much precision as possible. Subsequent chapters will deal with the metaphysics of institutions.

Section 1: Necessary and Universal Parameters

Let us begin by offering the first of three rudimentary definitions of an institution:

> *Institution*: an instance of shared thinking in a relationship of community, practice, and legacy.

At a first level of approximation these concepts can be described quite simply. A *community* is a group of conscious beings defined by a common practice and common legacy. A *practice* is a set of conscious actions carried out by a community using its legacy as input and also producing a legacy as output. A *legacy* is bequeathed and inherited by the right conscious beings (community) carrying out conscious acts in the right way (practice).

It is precisely by knowing the right things (legacy) and being able to do things the right way (practice) that a group of people constitutes a *community*. A community's authority to carry out its practice and thereby to bequeath and inherit its legacy is intrinsic, and that authority exists precisely in terms of the community's relationship to that practice and that legacy. An act can be a *practice* only when it is done by the right people (a community) making use of and leaving behind the right kind of thinking (a legacy). A *legacy* must be validated by the right group of people (a community), and it must be produced the right way (its practice).

One could think of this triad as consisting of *who* an institution is (community), the things an institution *does* (practice), and *what* an institution has (legacy). An institution is constituted by thinkers, thinking, and thoughts, or thinkers thinking thoughts. The nature of this thinking will be discussed extensively in later chapters.

Take the example of modern science as an institution. There is the community (scientists), the practice (the correct way to "do" science, or doing things "scientifically"), and the legacy (the scientific knowledge that is bequeathed and inherited by the community carrying out its practice). Science (scientific knowledge) is science only when it is produced by the right kinds of people in the right way. Scientists are only scientists (the right people) only if they *know* or *have* the right knowledge and if they do things the right way. And the *right* way (one might call it the "scientific method") is determined precisely by an authoritative community working on the basis of established knowledge and producing that knowledge.

Or consider a medieval blacksmith guild. There are the guild members (community), the right way to work iron (practice), and the right things one has to learn, know, and pass on as a blacksmith (legacy). One cannot be a member without knowing how to work iron and without the knowledge proper to the guild; the right way to work iron can be established and taught only by authoritative and reliable smiths who know the right things; and the knowledge necessary to be in a guild can be passed on and received only by the right kind of people producing that knowledge the right kind of way.

Natural languages are particularly significant institutions (although that is not all they are). There is a community of speakers, the actual expression and understanding that takes place between them, and the knowledge they bequeath and inherit. To be a speaker of English requires knowing certain things and being able to speak and understand; the knowledge of what constitutes English is completely determined by English speakers who using their language the right way; and the correct use of English is determined completely by whether it is carried out by English speakers who know the right things. What makes an English speaker an English speaker? His or her possession of a certain legacy and the practice based on that legacy. What makes English practice English practice? Native speakers using their legacy to speak (practice) their language. What makes the English-language legacy the English-language legacy? The fact that English speakers speak it the way one is supposed to speak it. This language analogy will be expanded upon in chapter 6.

❧

There are key *logical relations* between each element in this triad of community-practice-legacy. These logical relations are crucial to avoiding the pitfalls of simplistic or convoluted definitions mentioned in the previous chapter (that is, including too much or too little, using ambiguous terms that are not clearly distinct, and using terms ranging over different logical categories that are simply piled together without justification).

These three logical relations that bind together the elements of the triad of community, practice, and legacy are (1) mutual irreducibility, (2) mutual distinctness, and (3) mutual implication.

That means that first, the concepts of community, practice, and legacy, *taken together*, fully account for and correctly "map" the conceptual space of institutions—they leave neither empty space nor do they spill over its boundaries. Second, these three notions of community, practice, and legacy are conceptually clear and distinct from each other. Third, community, practice, and legacy imply and presuppose each other.

Consider, as an analogy, how the three axes of bodily space relate to each other and to the space they define:

1. One has three values x, y, and z for every location in the space. The three spatial dimensions are not reducible to each other, and having only two values would leave a location or set of locations underspecified, but having four could only repeat information. The three values exactly account for locations in bodily space.

2. Each value for an axis or dimension is analytically distinct. To be an x value, for example, is to necessarily not be a y or z value. Each dimension is conceptually distinct from the others without overlap or remainder. There is no possibility of confusing up-down with left-right or front-back. One cannot reduce any one to a combination of the others. These three parameters are mutually distinct.

3. The presence of an x is meaningful only in the presence of a y and a z. In bodily space, the three values imply each

other; to speak of an x value in space means there has to be a y value and a z value. They are co-implicative.

Another way of saying this is that x, y, and z are comprehensive in relation to the domain they cover, they are different from each other, and taken together they constitute a genuine whole and not a mere aggregation.

One could again exemplify these relationships in a related metaphor, that of an aircraft's latitude, longitude, and altitude:

1. Latitude, longitude, and altitude account for an aircraft's location. There is no fourth parameter, and two parameters are not enough.

2. Latitude, longitude, and altitude are distinct when it comes to locating an aircraft. A latitude is by definition not a longitude or altitude, and mutatis mutandis for the other two. No possibility exists for confusing any one with the other two.

3. Latitude, longitude, and altitude imply each other and presuppose each other when it comes to locating an aircraft. Having a latitude presupposes having a longitude and an altitude—and mutatis mutandis for the other two. In a world of latitudes and longitudes, for example, there are necessarily altitudes.

Latitude, longitude, and altitude—in terms of an aircraft's location—cover the entire relevant domain of bodily space. When it comes to locating an airplane in bodily space, there is nothing outside of latitude, longitude, and altitude. No single one of them can be confused with either of the other two. Any plane that has an altitude, or latitude, or longitude necessarily has both of the other two. Locating *two* airplanes by finding their respective latitudes, longitudes, and altitudes allows the air traffic controller to know where they are in relation to the tower but also allows the airplanes to know where they are in relation to *each other* using the same coordinate system. This latter point is significant, because it is desirable not only to conceptualize religion, culture, civilization, and tradition individually but also to be able to situate them—as concepts—in relation to each other.

Taking these relationships and applying them to how community, practice, and legacy explain the concept of an institution, one arrives at the following:

1. Mutual irreducibility: An institution consists of legacy, practice, and community. Two of them would be insufficient, but a fourth parameter can only repeat already existing information or go outside of the conceptual space.

2. Mutual distinctness: Legacy, practice, and community are conceptually distinct. A legacy is by definition not a practice or a community, and the same holds mutatis mutandis for each of the other two.

3. Mutual implication: A legacy can be a legacy only in the presence of a practice and a community, and the same holds mutatis mutandis for each of the other two.

In other words:

1. Community, practice, and legacy fully and exactly account for what one calls an institution.

2. Community, practice, and legacy are distinct from each other (conceptually).

3. Community, practice, and legacy, in an institution, imply and presuppose each other.

These three concepts of legacy, practice, and community cover the whole of the relevant conceptual space, while at the same time remaining unambiguous in relation to each other, meaning that at a first level of approximation or analysis one can describe everything an institution is in terms of legacy, practice, and community and can do so without creating ambiguity between them, and in terms of understanding institutions it is only in terms of *each other* that one can talk about a legacy, a practice, and a community. Insofar as one is conceiving of something as a legacy, one is necessarily conceiving a practice and a community—if not explicitly, then as a necessary presupposition. When one is conceiving of something as practice, one is necessarily conceiving of legacy and community (again, either explicitly or implicitly). And when one is conceiving of something as a community, one is necessarily presupposing a legacy and a practice. This further means that in the context of conceptualizing institutions, the concepts of community, practice, and legacy are definable in terms of each other and are *only* definable in terms of each other: One demarcates the community (who is a member, who is outside) always and only as a function of its practice and its legacy. One demarcates the practice (what one does, what one does not do) always and only as a function of the community and its legacy. One demarcates the legacy (what one bequeaths and inherits) always and only as a function of the community and its practice. There can be no community without its legacy and its practice, no legacy without a practice and a community, and no practice without a community and a legacy.

In chapter 5 the significance and benefit of these principles, as ways of regulating definitions of things like institutions, will be made more clear.

&.

Now, let us think about institutions in terms of another triad, and offer a second rudimentary definition of an institution:

> *Institution*: an instance of shared thinking characterized by stability, dynamism, and purpose.

Once again, one uses three parameters to define the conceptual space of the institution: *stability*, *dynamism*, and *purpose*. For a concrete metaphor, consider the image of a cottage in the woods. The cottage must stay the same—it is not much of a cottage if every part of it is moving. But since the environment around it changes, it too must change (Will the heat or air conditioning be on? Are the windows open or closed? What kind of repairs and adjustments are needed to keep up with the encroachments of the natural world?) But in order to remain the same and to change in the right ways it must have a known reason for being there. There is no way of understanding the stability of a cabin without understanding its dynamism and purpose, no way of understanding its dynamism without its stability and purpose, and no way of understanding its purpose without its stability and dynamism. As an object in the realm of shared thinking, an institution can remain the same institution only if it is also able to make changes in light of the changing world as determined by its purposes. Those changes can exist only against the backdrop of an enduring reality oriented toward certain outcomes. And the goals of an institution can be realized in the world only if the institution is stable enough but also able to change with the world in certain respects.

The English language, for example, necessarily remains stable and is reproduced across time and space; but it is also necessarily dynamic as the language gains and loses speakers and encounters a changing world; and there is necessarily always a right way to speak it and wrong ways to speak it. In a living institution these three aspects are always present.

In the institution of modern science, the scientists, the way of doing things scientifically, and the knowledge of science cannot drift from instant to instant but remain stable. But also, by the very conditions of its existence, the people change (both inwardly, and also in terms of change in population), the practices will be modified, and the knowledge will be tended through keeping and discarding. Furthermore, and necessarily, this sameness and change is not directionless or purposeless.

If an institution were constantly in flux, it could not persist from one moment to another, or exist across geographic expanse. If it were never to change, the world would change around it and render its original relationship to the things around it transformed anyway. If it had no direction or purpose, no way of being fulfilled, then the very standard or measure of its stability and growth would be missing.

In an institution it is impossible to conceive of one of these three aspects—stability, dynamism, or purpose—without presupposing or implying the other two. That is, its dynamism and purpose are part of its stability, its stability and dynamism are part of its purpose, and its stability and purpose are part of its dynamism.

As in the case of community, practice, and legacy, stability, dynamism, and purpose also fulfill the three logical relations mentioned above:

1. Institutions are always stable, dynamic, and purposive.

2. This stability, dynamism, and purpose are conceptually distinct from each other in institutions.

3. In institutions this stability, dynamism, and purpose presuppose and imply each other.

꒰ꔫ꒱

These two rudimentary formulations, based upon the two different conceptual triads, are relatively simple but nevertheless each possesses a certain analytical strength and theoretical coherence, for the reasons mentioned above. The elements within each triad are not merely placed together; they clearly fit together. Now, since the goal here is not only coherence but also sufficient complexity and nuance, let us take these two rudimentary definitions and *combine* them. The resulting complex conceptualization based upon combining these two triads will still maintain the three analytical principles above: mutual irreducibility, mutual distinctness, mutual implication. This combination is accomplished not by merely appending one definition to the other, but by crossing the two triads with each other.

Verbally, this results in the following definition: an institution is an instance of shared thinking in a relationship of community, practice, and legacy that is characterized by stability, dynamism, and purpose. However, unlike other long definitions of complex realities, this formulation is not a mere laundry list but instead maintains the same clarity and logical relations as the first two rudimentary definitions mentioned above.

By multiplying, as it were, each triad by the other, or refracting each one through the other as if through a prism, one produces nine elements. Community can be viewed through the prism of stability, dynamism, and purpose; practice can be viewed through the prism of stability, dynamism, and purpose; and legacy can be viewed through the prism of stability, dynamism, and purpose. But also, that which is stable can be viewed in terms of community, practice, and legacy; that which is dynamic can be viewed in terms of community, practice, and legacy; and that which is purposive coordinate can be viewed in terms of community, practice, and legacy. The result, using each triad as a kind of prism for the other, is a more complex set of concepts or coordinates that can be used to analyze the concept of the institution.

Because these aspects of the institution (community, practice, legacy; stability, dynamism, purpose) are not mechanical parts or discrete slices but constitute a parameter for every point in the entire conceptual space of shared thinking, when they are combined together they do not *fragment* the conceptual space but instead further specify each point in that space, the way that a photograph can have increasingly high levels of resolution, increased range of discrete colors, and more gradations of lighting all at the same time. That is to say, every point in the conceptual space of institutions or shared thinking has a community coordinate, a practice coordinate, and a legacy coordinate; *and* every point in the conceptual space has a stability coordinate, a dynamism coordinate, and a purpose coordinate.

As mentioned above, when these triads are "multiplied" by each other (or "refracted" through each other), the resulting nine elements have the same internal relations as each triad did before, except that instead of three elements or dimensions there are nine. The nine cover the whole space, they are distinct from each other, and each presupposes and implies the existence of the other eight. One increases complexity without a new proliferation of ambiguities.

Stated another way, when one analyzes or unfolds the verbal formulation "shared thinking in a relationship of community, practice, and legacy characterized by stability, dynamism, and purposiveness" one arrives at nine necessary parameters of an institution (see table 2.1).

That means that community, practice, and legacy each can be defined in terms of three important attributes. Community members possess the right *memory*, *mastery*, and *moral authority*. The practice is *communicative*, *creative*, and *corrective*. And the legacy is *available*, *intelligible*, and *valuable*.

It can also be read as institutional stability, dynamism, and purpose each having three main attributes. Stability is understood in terms of *memory*, *communication*, and *availability*. Dynamism is understood in terms of *mastery*, *creativity*, and *intelligibility*. And purpose is understood in terms of *moral authority*, *correction*, and *value*.

Let us turn to these results of combining the first two rudimentary triads in more detail:

- *Memory*: Community members must know how to access the right sources and remember the right ideas. They must have

Table 2.1. Combining the triad of community, practice, and legacy with the triad of stability, dynamism, and purpose

	Stability	*Dynamism*	*Purpose*
Community	Memory: Human beings who remember and perceive	Mastery: Human beings who reason and imagine	Moral Authority: Human beings who judge and care
Practice	Communicative: Transmission and communication taking place	Creative: Creation/ modification/ ramification taking place	Corrective: Keeping/discarding, regulating, refinement
Legacy	Available: Things that are available across time and space	Intelligible: Things that are adapted and intelligible	Valuable: Things that are valued and promoted

the right lore, vocabulary, and recall. Community members are custodians. Community members bear the forms of thinking across space and across time. It is in the community members that these forms of thinking exist and subsist. It is within them and between them that meaning and understanding take place. They know the right things.

- *Mastery*: Community members have the ability to extrapolate and to create and discern patterns from the legacy they inherit. Community member possesses the *abilities* and *capacities* (faculties and intuitions) that enable them to generate novel iterations in the relevant domain that can become part of the legacy they bequeath. A community member does more than merely repeat. Mastery is the capacity to create the new from the old, understanding its possibilities as well as its impossibilities, necessities, and probabilities, and how forms of expression fit into novel situations. Community members know how to navigate and manipulate their own legacy. Community members know how to *iterate* new forms on the basis of existing ones. They reason and imagine the right way.

- *Moral Authority*: Community members are the arbiters of the right way to do something, making them intrinsically trustworthy and reliable. A community, or a member thereof, has intrinsic *authority* to inherit and bequeath and to follow its practice. A community member arbitrates the *right* way to do things. The community member chooses the right paths to navigate the terrain created by the forms of thinking in order to arrive at the right destination. The community member governs and determines the legacy. They love the right things, and are entrusted with them.

- *Communicative*: A practice consists of communication and transmission. It is interpersonal in space among a living group of people, and also is interpersonal across time, as when people speak the same language with each other and from generation to generation. Practice is characterized by replication, repetition, and conveyance. There is *bestowal* and *reception* between people across time and space.

- *Creative*: A practice consists of the creation of the new, of modification and novel iterations—as in the way novel utterances are used in day-to-day natural language. Institutional practice is never purely mechanistic, deterministic, or random. Practice must include *possibilities* of expression and not only necessities, as well as new ramifications, and these novel possibilities are intelligible to others when they appear in different contexts, since it would be of little value to generate what cannot be understood by anyone. The practice *grows* over time and across space.

- *Corrective:* Practice consists in keeping and discarding. Certain things are upheld and enforced, while others are demoted and displaced. There is a refinement and correction that always takes place. There is always at least one right way to do or make something, and always at least one wrong way. To practice is to understand what to do (how to be) and what *not* to do (how *not* to be) in such and such situation. The practice is *pruned* and *tended* across time and space.

- *Available:* An institutional legacy endures and abides. It has a certain robustness and fixity, a degree of permanence. It is therefore and thereby accessible. A legacy is bequeathed and inherited, and cannot be hidden or lost. A legacy is by definition enduring and usable as the material for new iterations in the relevant domain. One can do or make new things with a legacy—practically, intellectually, emotionally, socially, spiritually.

- *Intelligible:* A legacy consists of adaptations and applications, made possible by the fact that the legacy is intelligible and meaningful. A legacy contains within it intelligible and meaningful change made possible by the fact that it is *interpretable;* its meaning can be discerned. The elements of a legacy must mean something and not mean something else, or most probably or definitely meaning *this* and improbably or definitely not meaning *that*. The legacies present certain possibilities of meaning and usefulness, but not others. As a necessary and important corollary, there must be something a legacy cannot mean, and a place in life it must not take up.

- *Valued:* A legacy is loved, valued, and respected. It is important. It consists of that which is considered worthy of being kept and not discarded, remembered and not forgotten. Legacies are worthy. They are *chosen* or *preserved*. Not everything that can be a legacy actually becomes one. Someone has to *care* about it.

SHARED ACCOUNTS, SHARED HEURISTICS, SHARED NORMS: THE CONTENT OF SHARED THINKING

Let us now turn to a third triad and add a final rudimentary definition:

> *Institution*: an instance of shared thinking constituted by accounts, heuristics, and norms.

This triad answers to questions raised by the concepts laid out above: Memory of *what*? Mastery of *what*? Moral authority regarding *what*? *What* is communicated? *What* is created? *What* is corrected? *What* is available? *What* is adapted? *What* is valuable?

The answer to these questions is a third triad: accounts, heuristics, and norms.

Account is used here as a technical term that includes *descriptions, representations, facts, premises, axioms, presuppositions,* and *assumptions,* whether they are simple or complex, isolated or combined with heuristics and norms. An account is an expression, a form conveying a meaning, about what is *given.*

Heuristic is used here as a technical term, and it can include *methods, templates, guidelines, techniques, theorems, procedures, processes, logics, recipes,* and *rules,* whether they are simple or complex, or isolated or combined with accounts and norms. A heuristic is an expression, a form conveying meaning, about how to connect an *if* with a *then.*

Norm is used here as a technical term and it can include *values, standards, imperatives, maxims, purposes, goals, ideals, exemplars,* and *objectives,* whether they are simple or complex, or isolated or combined with accounts and heuristics. A norm is an expression, a form conveying meaning, about what one *ought* to care about and deem worthwhile.

This triad could be thought of as three kinds of knowledge:

- Accounts are expressions of an institution's *know-that* or *know-what.*

- Heuristics are expressions of an institution's *know-how.*

- Norms are expressions of an institution's *know-why.*

Every human being has a way of knowing what reality is, which is a combination of what one experiences and remembers directly for oneself and also what one trusts to be the case based upon what other people show or tell, and what one reasons or imagines to be the case. That part of this dimension of thinking that is shared as forms of thinking between individuals in an institution is an *account*. Accounts are the institution's shared forms of thinking regarding what there is, what is the case, the state of things. It is the descriptive aspect of shared thinking. One could call it, for lack of a better term, the factual. In a sense, accounts are the encoding of "our" memory.

All human beings are rational and imaginative. They can extrapolate from the known to the unknown, from the present to the absent. Human beings can detect patterns and regularities and place things into groups, and see parts in terms of wholes, and think of and iterate new things based upon these abilities. But human beings cannot reason and imagine unrestrictedly such that at every moment a human being extrapolates all possible outcomes and sees every possible pattern or whole in his or her experience. Rather, human beings use techniques and procedures and habits and emulation to deal with new experiences. Human beings all have problem-solving and pattern-making procedures, methods, reflexes, and habits that they inherit and sustain, since the innate faculties of reason and imagination cannot do all that work all the time. One cannot extrapolate and create all new ideas and forms on one's own. That part of this dimension of thinking that is shared as forms of thought between individuals in an institution is a *heuristic*. Heuristics are the institution's shared forms of thinking that serve to help human beings to get from an *if* to a *then*, how to iterate new from old, how to discern patterns, how to perceive wholes, how to solve problems, how to navigate what is necessary, possible, and impossible.

Every human being also has a sense of good and bad, right and wrong, beautiful and ugly. They also all have maxims and articulated values by which they live, which they have on their own but at the same time they all need *exemplars* for their behaviors. They all feel "I know what is right" but also depend on others to know what is right. It is not possible for a human being to actively care about everything worth caring about, or to formulate an idea of the value of all things that are actually valuable. That part of this dimension of thinking that is shared as forms of thought between individuals in an institution is a *norm*. Norms are the institution's shared forms of thinking pointing to what is good, beautiful, valuable, worthwhile, desirable, purposeful, and fulfilling. Norms are forms of thinking shared between human beings concerning what *ought* to be the case.

All shared thinking (meaning as a technical term of that which constitutes an institution) is either an account, a heuristic, or a norm, or some combination of these three dimensions of forms of thinking. Anything outside of these three dimensions is not shared thinking in the sense considered in this book, and nothing other than these three is necessary to understand the content of shared thinking. These three dimensions are distinct from each other, and they presuppose each other. Accounts are, in part, the products of the inferences and extrapolations of the heuristic dimension, and they are also given by the norms that enable us to trust the testimony of other sources. Without heuristics and norms an institution could have no accounts. Heuristics depend upon accounts as their starting point, and they require norms in order be directed toward something. Without accounts and norms there are no heuristics. Norms depend upon accounts to know what they are about, and they require heuristics in order to establish the possibilities that are ranked from good to bad. Without accounts and heuristics there can be no norms. Put in simpler terms: facts require trust in sources as well as methods of verification, procedures require inputs and an outputs toward which they are directed, and goals require possibilities that are established by what is the case. There is an entire metaphysics of consciousness implied here, which cannot be explored comprehensively in this book, but a certain minimum will be discussed in the next chapter.

Terrain, Route, Destination: The Journey Metaphor

One can visualize the nature of shared accounts, heuristics, and norms using the allegory of a journey that a group of human beings take together. Any journey can be thought of as always having three dimensions: a *terrain* to be traversed, a *route* to be discerned, and a *destination* toward which one is directed.

The dimension of *terrain* is where one is, what one is presented with, the facts of the situation. The dimension of *route* is the discernment of the ways in which it is possible, impossible, easy, and difficult to navigate that terrain. The dimension of *destination* is the sense of where one is headed, the kind of place one desires to be, the ultimate end of one's efforts, the good environment that one hopes for. In other words: *through what* is one traveling, *how* does one travel through it, and *why* is one traveling at all? To get from here to there, one has to know what here is, how to get there, and why one wants to go.

On this journey *I* know the terrain for myself, but I also have to depend on others to know what the terrain is, and others depend on me.

Each traveler needs the others for knowledge about that terrain from a different point of view or to know about terrain that one could not possibly have direct knowledge of oneself. Thus *we* know the terrain differently than any *I* can know it.

I can discern the route myself, but I also need others to help find the route, and others depend on me. Each traveler relies upon others' competence and abilities in seeing and understanding all the possible, inevitable, and untenable routes. Thus *we* discern the route differently than any individual *I* can discern it.

I know where I hope to go and to end up, but I also depend on others to know where I want to go, and others depend on me. Each traveler relies upon others to enrich and nourish one's sense of what place was most desirable on that terrain, being therefore guided by others' sense of what part of the terrain is desirable as a destination. Thus *we* know where we want to go and where *we* want to be in a way that is different from how any individual *I* can want to go or desire to be.

Thus, *I* journey because *we* journey, but also *we* journey because *I* journey. An institution can be imagined as many people on a journey whose terrain is traversed together, whose route is discerned together, and whose destination is chosen together—thus constituting a *we*.

This together-journey requires forms by which such sharing of thinking can take place and through which a *we* can be realized, because the innate abilities of human beings to individually know the terrain, discern the routes, and care about destinations are not the same as how these states of consciousness are to be conveyed from one traveler to another. The forms that the travelers use to share knowledge of what the terrain is are here called *accounts*. Those forms that they share in order to navigate the possibilities, impossibilities, necessities, and probabilities of the route are here called *heuristics*. And those forms that they use to share understanding of the worth, desirability, and value of the destination are here called *norms*.

These three dimensions are always present together. Anywhere or anytime there is one, there are always the other two. The journey as a whole is made up of a terrain, a route, and a destination, but each part of the journey has its own terrain, its own route, its own destination no matter how large or small the portion of the journey one considers. Whether one looks upon the whole journey or a small part of it, whether one sees it from the sky or from close up on the ground, whether one zooms in or zooms out, the relationship between terrain, route, and destination remains constant. No matter how wide or close a view one adopts in relation to one's route, for example, there will always be a corresponding terrain and destination. No matter how wide or narrow a focus on terrain, there will always be route and destination. No matter how wide or narrow one conceives of one's destination—the next step or the ultimate goal—there is always a terrain and a route.

That means that whenever travelers share an account of the terrain they do so in light of the route and destination. Whenever they share a heuristic by which to navigate, they do so in light of the terrain and destination. And whenever they share a norm that expresses the value of the destination, they do so in light of the terrain and how one navigates it. We will return to this journey metaphor in section 2 below.

§◦

A three-by-three table was used to express the crossing of community-practice-legacy with stability-dynamism-purpose (see table 2.2). If one incorporated the new triad of accounts-heuristics-norms it would look like this:

Table 2.2. The triad of accounts, heuristics, and norms combined with the other two conceptual triads

	Stability	*Dynamism*	*Purpose*
Community	Human beings remembering and recalling shared accounts, heuristics, and norms	Human beings reasoning and imagining shared accounts, heuristics, and norms	Human beings judging and caring for shared accounts, heuristics, and norms
Practice	Transmission and communication of shared accounts, heuristics, and norms	Modification/ ramification of shared accounts, heuristics, and norms	Keeping/discarding, regulating, refinement of shared accounts, heuristics, and norms
Legacy	Shared accounts, heuristics, and norms enduring/ available across time and space	Shared accounts, heuristics, and norms that are adapted and intelligible	Shared accounts, heuristics, and norms that are valued and prioritized

How can one add this third triad of accounts-heuristics-norms and represent it visually? If one crosses this triad with the other two, one arrives at twenty-seven elements whose most realistic visualization might be a three-by-three-by-three cube, with each of the twenty-seven subcubes representing a particular combination of three. Since that is not practical in a book, we will need to be content with a list of these twenty-seven dimensions. Visual metaphors such as the above table or three-dimensional cube are in any case a double-edged sword; they guide and mislead. The boxes of a table are discrete areas of a page, and the pieces of a cube are discrete portions of space, but the whole spirit of this model is that every point in the conceptual space has *all* these elements in it. Also, each of the twenty-seven items would ideally have its own name but that would require inventing dozens of terms.

So, combining the three triads, framed from the starting point of the triad of accounts-heuristics-norms, here are the necessary features or universal facts of any institution:

1. *Accounts* existing as stock and store in the memory and recall of people.

2. *Heuristics* existing as stock and store in the memory and recall of people.

3. *Norms* existing as stock and store in the memory and recall of people.

4. Community members having mastery over *accounts*, knowing how they fit into patterns and wholes, and knowing how to navigate new situations using them.

5. Community members having mastery over *heuristics*, knowing how they fit into patterns and wholes, and knowing how to navigate new situations using them.

6. Community members having mastery over *norms*, knowing how they fit into patterns and wholes, and knowing how to navigate new situations using them.

7. There are people into whose care is entrusted *accounts* who are the arbiters of what they are and who have the proper solicitude and care to manage these things.

8. There are people into whose care is entrusted *heuristics* who are the arbiters of what they are and who have the proper solicitude and care to manage these things.

9. There are people into whose care is entrusted *norms* who are the arbiters of what they are and who have the proper solicitude and care to manage these things.

10. *Accounts* that are portable and transmitted between individuals across space and time.

11. *Heuristics* that are portable and transmitted between individuals across space and time.

12. *Norms* that are portable and transmitted between individuals across space and time.

13. *Accounts* that are iterated and reiterated in different ways, and are modified, recast, and used in novel contexts.

14. *Heuristics* that are iterated and reiterated in different ways, and are modified, recast, and used in novel contexts.

15. *Norms* that are iterated and reiterated in different ways, and are modified, recast, and used in novel contexts.

16. *Accounts* that are kept and reinforced and repeated, while others are discarded, stopped, and abandoned.

17. *Heuristics* that are kept and reinforced and repeated, while others are discarded, stopped, and abandoned.

18. *Norms* that are kept and reinforced and repeated, while others are discarded, stopped, and abandoned.

19. *Accounts* that are able to survive and endure from time to time and from place to place.

20. *Heuristics* that are able to survive and endure from time to time and from place to place.

21. *Norms* that are able to survive and endure from time to time and from place to place.

22. *Accounts* that are comprehensible and intelligible such that when they are changed or adapted over time they remain true to their meaning.

23. *Heuristics* that are comprehensible and intelligible such that when they are changed or adapted over time they remain true to their meaning.

24. *Norms* that are comprehensible and intelligible such that when they are changed or adapted over time they remain true to their meaning.

25. *Accounts* that are treated as important and deemed to be worth attention and care.

26. *Heuristics* that are treated as important and deemed to be worth attention and care.

27. *Norms* that are treated as important and deemed to be worth attention and care.

These twenty-seven aspects continue to relate to each other in terms of the logical relations mentioned throughout this chapter—mutual irreducibility, mutual distinctness, and mutual implication. In light of the complexity and scope of the realities that are sometimes spoken about (a world religion, for example), twenty-seven turns out to be a relatively small number, and this does not even take into account the empirical variability of each of these twenty-seven features.

The resulting definition of an institution is the product of three triads that are combined to create a definition that is complex, coherent, and clear:

An institution is an instance of shared thinking in a relationship of community, practice, and legacy; characterized by stability, dynamism, and purpose; and constituted by accounts, heuristics, and norms.

In particular, the definition applies to each configuration or member of the set called metaphysical institutions:

A culture, civilization, religion, or tradition is an instance of shared thinking with respect to ultimate questions, existing in a relationship of community, practice, and legacy; characterized by stability, dynamism, and purpose; and constituted by accounts, heuristics, and norms.

Section 2: Empirical Variation

The concepts outlined in section 1 describe the *universal* or *necessary* features of institutions. Every institution will have them, and any reality that has them is, in that respect, an institution, although it may not be *only* an institution, as will be expanded upon in subsequent chapters.

But institutions are clearly not all the same within these parameters, and their particular or contingent variability should be accounted for and rendered explicit. Returning to the geometric metaphor: although any three-dimensional object necessarily has a shape, a size, and a location in space, one still must specify what the object's particular shape is, how large it happens to be, and where it is located specifically. Analogously, the particular configuration of an institution—the way it occupies the space of shared thinking—will also vary along the parameters it shares with all institutions. That is to say, while conceptualizing the necessary features of any institution one must also theorize how those parameters can vary from institution to institution, even as that variation does not alter the necessary conditions of the conceptual space in which all institutions exist.

For *community* the empirical variation one can choose to look at is the distribution or concentration of its memory, mastery, and moral authority. Within the community there are relationships of guidance and reliance that give rise to the shape, as it were, of the institution's *hierarchy*. Is the community egalitarian or stratified? Who guides whom, and who relies upon whom? How concentrated or distributed among the members of the community are memory, mastery, and moral authority? Is there a clearly delineated elite, and is that elite large or small? Or are there instead many elite populations that overlap in different ways? How reliant are some community members upon others with respect to being community members? How much does each member carry the moral authority of the institution within himself or herself?

In a language, for example, the community's memory, mastery, and moral authority will be widely distributed, whereas in a guild the community will be more hierarchical, and in modern science one will have multiple overlapping hierarchies. There can be different elites in the same community when it comes to memory and recall as opposed to mastery and creativity. Orchestral conductors, for example, are among the ultimate custodians of the repertoire of classical music, but they are not the ones endowed with the ability to create and iterate new music.

For *practice*, one can choose to observe the variable balance or the relationship between old and new—between replication, repetition, and imitation on the one hand, and innovation, modification, and originality on the other. Practice necessarily encompasses the old and the new, but how much old is there and how much new is there, and what is the balance between them? How heterogenous is practice across space and across time? How much of the old gets recapitulated? How much that is new comes into the picture in relation to the old? How much new and old is retained?

For example, some words in languages remain relatively stable over time, whereas others are relatively more mutable, and similarly in some languages the vocabulary is relatively homogenous over geographic expanse while in others it is more variable. Some artistic techniques such as Quranic calligraphy are much the same as centuries ago, and novelty is not easily tolerated, whereas certain traditions of painting rely far less on what is old.

For *legacy*, one can choose to observe the variable modalities by which meaning is conveyed in form. What *kinds* of media and technologies are used to encode, and thereby bequeath and inherit, what is meant and understood in an institution? Is it oral or written? Is it encoded in artifacts or enacted by people?

Some languages, for example, have been transmitted almost entirely orally, while others are a mix between oral and written, and the media of the written language changes over time: manuscript, print, electronic. Such things are dependent upon available materials and the environment, and the media in which things can be encoded differs from place to place and time to time.

In the case of *stability*, the salient variable is degree of longevity, resilience, endurance, and robustness. How strong is the memory and recall of the community? Are the forms of thought communicated or repeated across time *intact* or in a degraded form, and across space *intact* or in a degraded form? Do the forms of thought have longevity over time and constancy over geographic expanse?

A small institution like a local club will not have the kind of forms of thought that remain intact over long periods of time the same way a religion would, for example, and over time might essentially become a different institution altogether, whereas religions can retain stable aspects for centuries.

In the case of *dynamism*, the salient variable is between rigidity and flexibility, the spectrum of elasticity. In short: How wide is the scope for change and growth? How generative or powerful is the faculty of imagination and reason in the community? How wide is the range of new forms in the practice over time and across space? What is the variety or the quantity of new forms in the practice?

In a religion like Islam, for example, certain forms of spiritual expression will take on a large diversity of forms and be open to new possibilities, whereas a discipline such as Quranic exegesis allows for a much slower growth and elasticity when it comes to new forms.

In the case of *purpose*, the salient variable is degree of care: sincerity, attentiveness, and prioritization. Are the community members sincere in how they govern and judge or are they indifferent or cynical regarding the purpose? How disciplined and attentive is the practice—the activity or even concentration of the keeping and the discarding? How important or crucial or essential is it, how central to one's purpose—is it knowledge of the means or of the end itself? How central or peripheral to one's *overall* purposes in all of life is the legacy? Where does some particular aspect of legacy fit in the totality of one's legacies altogether?

Some institutions become hollowed out over time and retain only their outward aspects, and people, as it were, go through the motions. Since institutions are not simply impersonal objects but are constituted by *shared thinking*, the attention and wholeness of purpose that each community member bring to it will be of great significance. One can see the difference between sincere solicitude and cynical indifference in institutions like religion, politics, and education. How disciplined and attentive the community is to keeping the correct balance of old and new, for example, is highly significant. Another factor that is important, of course, is how the legacy and practice of the institution fit into the total collective life of its members, and understanding that role. One must not mistake an ultimate teaching (say, a metaphysical teaching) and deem it to be secondary. Nor should one raise a secondary idea to the level of the ultimate when thinking about an institution like a religion or a culture.

There are in fact many possible variable parameters, but these are arguably among the most significant ones, and they are useful for being able to account meaningfully for a wide variety among institutions.

As for the variability of accounts, heuristics, and norms, it consists of a spectrum whose two ends one can call, for simplicity's sake, *showing* and *telling*. One can think of the spectrum between forms that communicate by *showing* versus those that communicate by *telling* as being characterized by the difference between the *concrete* and the *abstract*; the *imaginative* and the *rational*; the *symbolic* and the *verbal*; the *allegorical* and the *logical*; or the *exemplary* and the *instructional*.

Communication by *showing* (concrete, imaginative, symbolic, allegorical, exemplary) functions by the analogy of wholes to wholes, while communication by *telling* (abstract, rational, verbal, logical, instructional) works through some kind of language or language-derived code (e.g., mathematics). Forms of thinking that *show* have a harmony, rhythm, a balance of parts, but cannot be broken down into a grammar or grammar-like system. Forms of thinking that *tell* have a set of steps that are to be followed in order to be understood. Forms that *show* are intelligible in the manner of an allegory, a metaphor, a symbol, an artwork, or an image, while forms that *tell* are intelligible in the manner of a language, a code, a procedure, a rule, a convention, or an argument.

An institution will always have accounts, heuristics, and norms, but where these forms of thinking fall on the spectrum between *showing* and *telling* is an empirical or contingent parameter that varies from configuration to configuration of shared thinking. A blacksmith guild will lean heavily toward the concrete, imaginative, symbolic, and exemplary in their accounts, heuristics, and norms, while the field of organic chemistry will lean toward the abstract, rational, syntactical, and instructional in theirs, but without either one being purely one modality or the other. Indeed, there is no such thing as purely concrete or purely abstract in the realm of shared thinking. They always go together in various combinations, although the balance between them is not necessary or constant.[1]

One can think of this variability in terms of the journey metaphor mentioned earlier: An account that *shows* or *depicts* is like a pencil sketch or gesture from one traveler to another describing some part of the terrain, while an account that *tells* or *describes* is real like a verbal explanation or written note from one traveler to another of some part of the terrain. A heuristic that *shows* or *depicts* is like a pencil sketch or gesture from one traveler to another of different routes to take and different kinds of obstacles to be avoided in the terrain, while a heuristic that *tells* or *describes* is like a verbal explanation or written note from one traveler to another of those different routes and obstacles, or turn-by-turn directions. A norm that *shows* or *depicts* is like a pencil sketch or gesture from one traveler to another of a destination or the qualities of the place one wishes to end up, while a norm that *tells* or *describes* is like a verbal explanation or written note from one traveler to another of that destination or kind of place.

A person might stand atop a hill and gesture down to you that there is sharp drop on the other side. Or they might call down and tell you. These are *accounts*. An account is neither your direct consciousness of the terrain, nor the personal consciousness of the person communicating to you, but rather an account is a form of shared thinking in the context of the journey. As you come to a stream you have never crossed you might imitate the person who went before you in stepping on certain stones at a certain rate, or that person might already be on the other side and call out to you how to do it, or they might even act it out for you. These are *heuristics*. A heuristic is neither the teacher's nor the learner's ability to extrapolate outcomes but instead is a form of shared thinking in the context of the journey. Perhaps you have never gone on such a long hike and you feel unusually tired, and you see someone go sit on a rock under a tree and get comfortable doing it and you then do it too, or that person tells you that in order to feel more comfortable you need to sit down under the shady tree on a flat rock. Or you see a traveler pick up a thorny branch from the trail and toss it aside, and indicate that you should do the same, or tell you that one should move dangerous obstacles out of the way for other people. These are all *norms*. A norm is neither the teacher nor the learner's care or love for a good destination or environment but instead is a form of shared thinking in the context of the journey. These three different forms of thinking get remembered and then passed down from traveler to traveler. They are various ways of *showing* and also *telling* of what there is, how to make your way through it, and where you should want to be.

The relationship between forms that show and forms that tell, and how they relate to meaning and understanding in different modes, will be discussed in detail in chapter 4.

Table 2.3. Empirical variability within institutions

	Strength, resilience, longevity	Elasticity, flexibility, growth	Care, solicitude
Hierarchy	How hierarchical or stratified is memory of forms of thought? * How strong/robust/ keen is recall/ memory of those forms? * Do the forms of thought *show* or *tell*?	How hierarchical or stratified is mastery of forms of thought? * How prolific/ generative of forms of thought is iterative/creative faculty? * Do the forms of thought *show* or *tell*?	How hierarchical or stratified is moral authority over forms of thought? * How sincere/ solicitous is the care of forms of thought? * Do the forms of thought *show* or *tell*?
Old-new	How much of old or existing forms is communicated? And *what* that is old is communicated? * How faithful or intact is the signal that is communicated? * Do the forms of thought *show* or *tell*?	How much of new/ novel forms of thought are ramified or iterated? And *what* is new that is created? * How diverse/varied is the ramification? What is its scope? How quickly does it happen? * Do the forms of thought *show* or *tell*?	Which old and which new forms of thought are kept or discarded? And how much variation is allowed? * How attentive/ active/disciplined is the refining? * Do the forms of thought *show* or *tell*?
Modality of media	Forms of thought are available in what kind of media? * How durable are the forms of thought? And what is their propensity to be inherited? * Do the forms of thought *show* or *tell*?	Forms of thought are adapted and intelligible within what kind of media? * How variegated are the adaptations of forms of thought? * Do the forms of thought *show* or *tell*?	Forms of thought are valued in what kinds of media? * How central or peripheral are forms of thought relative to other forms? * Do the forms of thought *show* or *tell*?

The Example of Modern Medicine

To make this discussion more relatable, let us turn to a familiar example of an institution—modern medicine. Its accounts, heuristics, and norms can be referred to for simplicity's sake as medical *knowledge*, medical *skills*, and medical *ethics*. In the institution of modern medicine, knowledge would include things like a grasp of human anatomy, pharmacology, and published research. Skills would include physical exams, surgical procedures, and differential diagnosis. Ethics would include knowledge of what medicine is for, what role a physician plays in society, and what the place of health is in the good life.

Medical practitioners must have memory and recall of such medical knowledge, skills, and principles; such things need to be in their possession in some way. Practitioners must also have mastery over their knowledge, skills, and principles, meaning they have the ability understand how and in what circumstances they could be used, or must be used, or mustn't be used, or might be used, and so forth, being able to skillfully modify and apply them in novel situations. They must have moral authority regarding knowledge, skills, and principles. It is medical practitioners who are most trustworthy when it comes to medical knowledge, skills, and ethics. They should care most about medical knowledge, skills, and principles and be most reliable about it, deferring to no other moral authority.

Medical knowledge, skills, and principles are transmitted from generation to generation and between people living at the same time. They are also *iterated*, meaning they are added to, subtracted from, placed into new contexts, and ramified and adjusted in many different ways. And they are also *refined* in that there is a constant process of keeping and discarding.

Medical knowledge, skills, and principles endure across time and space and are therefore available within medicine. They are also *intelligible* in that as they can exist in new iterations and ramifications while remaining understandable as intended. And they are necessarily valuable and important, being necessarily worthy of keeping and cherished rather than discarded and forgotten.

Consider a particular bit of medical knowledge: "Red blood cells carry oxygen throughout the body." A community member necessarily knows this and remembers it. He also has mastery of it in that he understands how it fits into broader patterns and can use this knowledge rationally and imaginatively. And he carries the moral authority to care about and be reliable when it comes to this knowledge. This knowledge is necessarily transmitted and communicated, but it also exists in various ramified and iterated forms, which is to say that the knowledge in that statement can be reframed or recast or resituated in many different ways, and among the different ways in which that knowledge is iterated some are kept and some are discarded. That form of knowledge is necessarily available to modern medicine, and it is also intelligible in its various forms, and must also be deemed worthwhile and valuable because otherwise it might be discarded like humoral theory.

Likewise consider a certain medical skill or method: the procedure of administering a physical exam on a new patient. A practitioner has to remember its steps but also must be able to use the relevant procedures and techniques for every new patient, who will always present a different case, and of course it is medical practitioners who are most reliable by virtue of their moral authority and their care when it comes to such skills and procedures. The steps and guidelines are transmitted and communicated, iterated and modified and adjusted in many ways, and some iterations are kept while others are discarded. Such skills are always available, must remain intelligible in their various forms, and are deemed valuable.

Finally consider an ethical principle of medicine such as "Do no harm." It is something that practitioners must remember, that they must be able to manipulate and modify in their reason and imagination, and about which they are reliable and trustworthy. Such principles are always communicated; they ramify and are iterated in different ways and combinations; and there is always a process of tending and refining such principles. They necessarily endure and are available, are intelligible in their various forms, and are considered important.

Finally, if one considers the relationships between knowledge, skills, and ethics in modern medicine, one can observe the following: one's knowledge in medicine is a function of various intellectual procedures and practical skills as well as reliance on trusted sources of authority. Procedures and skills such as performing an exam depend on knowledge of the body and also ethical and epistemic values that guide the procedures of thinking and doing. And ethical principles or beliefs about what is good depend on what the relevant reality actually is and also what possibilities and ramifications arise from that reality, from which one is obliged to choose the best option.

Thus one can see how these various dimensions of the institution of modern medicine all fit together but at the same time are distinct, and one can also observe how twenty-seven turns out to be quite a modest number of parameters to analyze even the commonsense aspects of a familiar institution.

Furthermore, one can think about the variability of these twenty-seven parameters. Modern medicine has different forms of hierarchies, such that certain kinds of knowledge, skill, and trust are widely distributed (taking blood pressure) while others are much more concentrated (surgery). The practice always includes old forms combined with innovations that are always kept in the right balance through disciplined and ethical refinement, but in some cases there is much more reliance on continuity and old forms (e.g., pediatrics), whereas in others new iterations have greater scope (e.g., cosmetic surgery). Legacy also varies in terms of the medium used: textbooks give way to e-books, hand painted anatomy gives way to computer-generated visualizations, in-person instruction is supplemented with video courses, et cetera. And the accounts, heuristics, and norms are transmitted by example (e.g., students doing rounds with practitioners observing them actually practicing on patients) and by instruction (e.g., reading from a textbook or sitting in a lecture).

Section 3: The Outside of Institutions

IDENTITY, ROUTINE, HEIRLOOMS

OSSIFICATION, PLASTICITY, INTERESTS

ASSERTIONS, REFLEXES, DEMANDS

Thus far, this chapter has dealt with what is inside the boundary of the concept of institution, both its necessary features as well as its important parameters of variability. But it is also important to distinguish institutions properly understood from those realities that are very close to them in their various aspects but from which they must be kept distinct. These are the important conceptual contraries of the elements of an institution. Not all shared life is shared thinking.

Let us start from the triad of community-practice-legacy. When some human population is definable in terms of its practice and its legacy, they constitute a community. But once the moral and intellectual conditions of practice and legacy no longer apply—that is, once what is good and what is true become irrelevant to demarcating the group—one has at best a mere identity.[2] When some human doing/making/thinking is definable in terms of its practitioners and its canon, one has a practice. But if that practice becomes disassociated from a source of authority that guarantees its correctness and allows it to adapt, and if it ceases to be nourished by a legacy and no longer feeds a legacy in its turn, it becomes a mere routine or behavior. When human works are bestowed and received by people who understand how they work with fidelity to the methods that produced them, those works are a legacy. But when that which one receives becomes unusable according to its original purpose and is not truly intelligible to its possessor, it becomes a mere heirloom.

A community can decay into an identity, a practice can decay into a routine, and a legacy can decay into an heirloom, but not all identities, routines, and heirlooms are simply results of such degeneration. There are identities, routines, and heirlooms that are what they are and could not be otherwise, for example, certain ethnic groupings, many everyday activities, and ordinary keepsakes, respectively. Identities, routines, and heirlooms are not bad things on their own—if that is in fact what they are. The point here is not to erase one set of concepts in favor of another but rather to adequately define the differences between them and to give the concept of shared thinking or institutions both scope and limits.

The mere simultaneous presence of heirlooms, routines, and identities does not make an institution, and to reify such a coincidence of disparate factors by conceiving of them as a unified reality is to commit a basic confusion. Identity, routine, and heirloom do not relate to each other logically the way the community, practice, and legacy do—through mutual irreducibility, distinctness, and implication. That is, there are no wholes corresponding to identity-routine-heirloom. Arranging them together in different ways does not result in any intelligible category of realities as we have in the case of metaphysical institutions that can be theorized as different configurations of the same parameters (see above). There are only different identities, different routines, and different heirlooms. It is the difference between three sides of a triangle as opposed to three unattached line segments.

Conversely, to take a true institution constituted by community, practice, and legacy and to think of it as a mere aggregate of identities, routines, and heirlooms is to fragment it. When one conceives of an actual community as a mere identity, one removes legacy and practice from the picture; when one conceives of an actual practice as a routine, one removes community and legacy from the picture; and when one conceives of an actual legacy as an heirloom, one removes practice and community from the picture. An institution is not merely the *coincidence* of community, practice, and legacy or of stability, dynamism, and purposiveness—any more than bodily space is the mere coincidence of width, height, and depth.

Now let us turn to the triad of stability-dynamism-purpose. When shared thinking's stability is bereft of dynamism and purpose, it becomes paralysis or ossification. When its dynamism or growth is bereft of stability and purpose it becomes mere plasticity or hoarding. And when its purposiveness has no stability or dynamism it is nothing more than impulse and appetite.

Of course, some things ought to be rigid, some things ought to be plastic, and impulses are not necessarily bad. But ossification should not be mistaken for stability, plasticity should not be mistaken for dynamism, and impulses and desires should not be mistaken for purposiveness. A group of people characterized by a mere aggregate of rigid conformity in one respect, ceaseless change in another respect, and the pursuit of some desires in yet another respect does not make an institution or any kind of whole. And neither should a true institution be viewed as such an aggregate of ossification, change, and impulse in cases where it is more appropriate to speak of that reality's stability, dynamism, and purposiveness of shared thinking.

That is, on the one hand, community, practice, and legacy as well as stability, dynamism, and purposiveness fit together and *belong* together, while on the other hand, identity, routine, heirlooms, rigidity, change, and impulse are just things that exist on their own.

Finally, one comes to the triad of accounts-heuristics-norms. When accounts are isolated from the dimensions of heuristics and norms, they can only be assertions or biases. When heuristics are isolated from the dimensions of accounts and norms, they can only be mere reflexes or compulsions. And when norms are isolated from the dimensions of account and heuristics, they can only be mere demands. The triad of accounts, heuristics, and norms constitute a whole, whereas the mere coincidence of assertions, reflexes, and demands are just fragments that might happen to be found in the same group of people.

Let us look at these differences in more detail:

COMMUNITY VERSUS IDENTITY

A community without true practice and legacy is just an identity. A community can be studied *as* an identity but is not reducible to one.

An identity is a population of human beings grouped according to biological filiation, gender, sexuality, national origin, ethnicity, or geographic ancestry (a religion can be the basis for identity but only when it is conceived of as a cultural marker without any moral or intellectual conditions). What distinguishes a community from an identity is that an identity requires no legacy or practice in order to remain an identity. An identity places no moral or intellectual conditions on the beliefs, behaviors, or attitudes of those who belong to it. The sole fact of biological filiation or physical attribute does not place two people in a community with each other, because one does not have to do or think anything in particular to be of a race, a gender, a national origin, or phenotype. Some types of "religious" belonging are also de facto identities, because to the degree that a religious affiliation does not actually require any particular actions, abilities, or beliefs, it becomes a mere identity—but only under that condition. If the wrong behaviors or beliefs can eject a person from an identity, then it is not merely an identity in the first place but rather is a community or perhaps a quasicommunity that is a community in one respect and an identity in another. A community is a mode of belonging that ought to be sharply distinguished from those groupings that are not conditioned by any normative element—a woman is no more or less a woman by being a criminal or a being saint. One can enter and exit a community but not an identity.

While an identity does not have a practice or a legacy, an identity can nevertheless be crystallized around an heirloom or a routine. For example, a nationalist in Europe or America can invoke or identify with something called "Western civilization" or build monuments with ancient Roman columns but that does not mean that they are participating in a true practice. A legacy or a practice is different from a badge of solidarity. Muslims will sometimes make what appear to be traditional practices into markers of identity with a very tenuous link to their principle. When a long beard is motivated by a desire to stick a thumb in the eye of the dominant culture, it is not a practice but a mere impulse answering to no principle (at least, to no Islamic principle—it could be a Marxist act of resistance). It is not comprehended or understood but serves to say, "This is something with which I identify." In such cases the identity is already there (racial, national, geographic) and it instrumentalizes an heirloom or a relic.

There can be overlap between an identity and a community, even though they are conceptually distinct. For example, Black Americans can be classified as an identity, but they are also a community. In America one cannot cease to be Black or choose to be, which is why it is an identity, but there is also a Black American community (or communities) with practices and legacies and community members with authority or legitimacy. In other words, the community of Black Americans can be distinguished conceptually from the identity of being Black.

Identities are typically chiseled from the outside, as it were, by relationships of power. They have no moral or intellectual legacy. What sets aside one identity from another is precisely some particular situations of control in which some common attribute has an important effect on one's life. Left-handed people do not constitute an identity, despite left-handedness being a natural feature without moral or intellectual conditions, because no significant relationships of power crystalize around handedness (no wants or fears are satisfied in terms of left-handedness), and thus left-handedness is not seen as being a determining factor in any relationships of control or power. A proper understanding of purposiveness as distinct from mere desire or want (see below) is crucial in understanding how power shapes what come to be called today "identities."

PRACTICE VERSUS ROUTINE

A practice without community and legacy is a mere routine. A practice can be studied as a routine but is not reducible to one.

No community acts as the arbiter of a routine, and a routine neither inherits nor bequeaths a legacy. A routine is way of doing or making something that is a pattern of actions or beliefs arising not as the creative application of a principle but as a spontaneous response to stimuli or as habits acquired from one's identity group, or a quasimechanical and effectively deterministic process.

Routines register as mere patterns in life, mere behaviors. One does things because that is how things are done by whoever does them. Routines and habits are not truly rational or imaginative, bordering on the pointless—being neither faithful to a purpose nor in conformity with a principle. Mere routines are never creative. A routine is reflexive, mechanical, passive, rote, habitual—again, a mere behavior. The mere fact that two people happen to do something the same way does not mean they share thinking.

Unlike a routine, a practice (in the sense used in this book) has a history and a present, and potentially a future. A practice is consciously *preserved* and deemed worthwhile by a community that also discards and deems unworthy other possible ways of doing that practice. A routine, on the contrary, can be done neither correctly nor incorrectly.

LEGACY VERSUS HEIRLOOM

A legacy without community and practice is just an heirloom or a relic. A legacy can be studied as an heirloom but is not reducible to that. A legacy is an heirloom, yes, but that is not all it is. All legacies are in a sense heirlooms and relics of the past, but not all heirlooms are legacies in the sense meant in this book.

An heirloom or relic, unlike a true legacy, is not inherited and bequeathed through a practice by a community but simply changes hands. Unlike a legacy, an heirloom is a form of thinking that is not put to use in new contexts according to its original meaning. An heirloom is something whose meaning and use is different from its original purpose, and which is not fully understood or usable by the person who possesses it, unlike a legacy, which is put into practice by those who know how to do so and why.

Heirlooms are mere givens that one simply possesses and that are bereft of their original purpose because they are not able to take up their original place in life. The possessor of an heirloom does not fully understand it. An heirloom has at most only a past, not a present or future. An heirloom is simply *had*, whereas a legacy is practiced by a community. A text or an idea becomes an heirloom when it is not understood according to its original meaning.

To use an analogy: most people know what an anvil is but would not know what to do with one. Only blacksmiths and their apprentices truly inherit and pass on anvils as a legacy, and crucially what they pass on and inherit *as blacksmiths in a guild* is not the physical object per se but the *thinking* (a point that will be expanded upon in chapter 4). A guild of blacksmiths, for example, would inherit and bequeath anvil knowhow (along with the anvils). An antique collector might acquire and bequeath a medieval anvil, but it would only be a family heirloom in the shape of an anvil. It would not be part of a guild's legacy.

STABILITY VERSUS OSSIFICATION

Stability in shared thinking without dynamism and purpose is just group repetition, or conformity, or ossification. In an institution people have to do/think things the same way to greater and lesser degrees, but not all instances of people doing/thinking things the same way is institutional stability. The neck of someone with whiplash is not stable but simply stiff.

Being stuck is different from being stable. Stability in shared thinking is not the same thing as a group of people who do and think the same thing over and over because they do not know any better and really could not imagine doing anything else. Stability without dynamism or purpose is just being trapped, perhaps even being afraid to do anything different, or simply being too ignorant of the past or too weak-minded to comprehend that something else is possible. Ossification means one thinks the same thoughts for no meaningful reason.

DYNAMISM VERSUS PLASTICITY

Dynamism in shared thinking without the presence of stability and purpose is just drift, momentum, or overgrowth—meaningless change, accumulation, or variation. In an institution people have to do new things to lesser and greater degrees, but not all instances of people doing new things together is institutional dynamism. The wind can blow patterns in the sand, but that is not dynamism. Institutional dynamism is different from pure plasticity. Not being able to stay in one place, or being unable to say no to anything new, or being unable to hold to a norm, or being reflexively antitraditional, revolutionary, or rebellious are all things that should not be confused with true dynamism in shared thinking. Unchecked growth and accumulation in ideas and practices is not dynamism but a kind of metastasis or even hoarding.

PURPOSE VERSUS INTERESTS

Purposiveness in shared thinking without stability and dynamism is just drive, impulse, egotism, tyranny, fear, and even the will to power. In an institution people must have goals, but not all instances of people working toward what they want are instances of institutional purposiveness. One can have tyrants or mobs, or even simply ad hoc organizations (e.g., commercial ventures), which are not institutions in this sense. In America one can establish a limited liability corporation quite easily, for example, but it is not thereby an institution—it is not shared thinking as theorized here. A political entity can have goals or desires that are shared, but without the stability and dynamism in shared thinking it is either a mob or a tyranny, or at least something less than an institution. In a company or government there are of course ambiguous things such as the "culture" of the place, but one must discern whether that so-called culture is institutional or just a superficial set of repetitions and expectations.

With mere impulses one can have an *organization* but without the stability and dynamism of shared thinking it cannot rise to the level of a true institution. There is of course ambiguity in terminology here, but using this rubric one can understand that boundary. A mere organization's leaders do not have *moral authority* per se, but rather different forms of coercive authority. In an organization one has mere *motives* or *interests* of different kinds, but there is a difference between restraining the passions with interests (essentially balancing passion against passion) and dominating over them in light of purpose. Groups of animals can have motives and systems but not purposes. An institution might *have* a bureaucracy or organizations, or even a government or governments, but it cannot simply *be* any of these. That is, an institution is not a system, but it *has* a system or systems. Moral authority might entail certain forms of coercive authority, but mere coercion never bestows moral authority.

ACCOUNTS VERSUS ASSERTIONS

Accounts severed from heuristics and norms unavoidably become mere group assertions or biases. It is precisely through having the right processes and procedures, as well as the right trusted sources of information, that accounts can be right instead of wrong. After all, on what basis can one justify refining or changing accounts? Not on the basis of other accounts, since no sheer accumulation of facts or descriptions can ever provide its own standard for judging whether those descriptions are true. Rather, one must be guided by heuristics and norms in order to judge which accounts are right and which are wrong. An account is never true simply by virtue of itself but also by virtue of what we already trust to be reliable as well as by virtue of what we understand to be possible, probable, necessary, or impossible.

For example, how does a piece of medical knowledge such as "stomach ulcers are caused by acid" (the previous consensus) relate to another such as "stomach ulcers are caused by bacteria" (the present consensus)? How does the institution of modern medicine maintain one as true and the other as false? Without reference to the relevant medical procedures (e.g., double-blind studies, clinical recordkeeping) and medical norms (e.g., the belief that one should understand how to heal stomach ulcers, that one should follow certain kinds of evidence), there would be no way to justify preferring one account to the other and one would be making mere assertions.

HEURISTICS VERSUS REFLEXES

Heuristics severed from accounts and norms unavoidably become mere group reflexes or compulsions. It is by having the right inputs and being geared toward the right outputs that a process or rule or guideline can be right instead of wrong. On what basis can heuristics be refined? It is not on the basis of other heuristics, since no heuristic or grouping of heuristics, no matter how complex and rich, can ever decide its inputs or the nature of what problem it is there to address (its output). Rather, one must use accounts and norms to judge which heuristics work to properly connect an input with an output and really connect the right *if* with the right *then*, and which ones do not. A heuristic does not work only by virtue of itself but also by virtue of how it relates to what is given and what is worthwhile.

For example, it was once a common protocol that postmenopausal women would be given hormone replacement therapy, but that general if-then heuristic (*if* a woman is postmenopausal, *then* she should receive hormone replacement) was abandoned and now those treatments are much more selective. Such revision in procedures can be justified only in the context of an institution with reference to certain accounts (e.g., an increased understanding of the effects of such hormone replacement) and in light of certain norms (e.g., the importance of other aspects of women's health). Practitioners who carry on automatically prescribing HRT for all women after menopause would not be following a heuristic but operating on mere reflex.

NORMS VERSUS DEMANDS

Norms severed from accounts and heuristics unavoidably become mere group demands or impulses. It is precisely by having the right sense of what is real and what is possible that one can be right about what is good. On what basis are expressed norms refined? Not on the basis of other norms, because norms can proliferate and pile up, but without a sense of what is real and what is possible one cannot decide which norms and which stated destinations are the right ones. Rather, one must rely upon accounts and heuristics in order to judge which norms actually lead to the good. Norms are not right simply by virtue of themselves but by virtue of what reality is and what possibilities exist by virtue of what is taken to be given.

For example, physicians now work within a framework of norms that includes an increased emphasis on "patient satisfaction," which can even affect their pay. "There should be shared decision making between a doctor and patient and a physician's income should partly be a function of patient satisfaction" is a new norm that replaces older norms such as "the doctor knows best." How can such a change in norm be justified in the institution of modern medicine? It would have to be on the basis of certain accounts (e.g., about the outcomes of doctor-patient interactions) and also on the basis of certain heuristics (e.g., procedures for exploring and categorizing evidence). Otherwise, it could only be a mere demand that the role of the doctor be changed, since that role would not be changed in light of any facts or arguments that would justify it as a new norm within the context of an institution.

Concluding Comments

Let us note certain broad ramifications or implications of the conceptualization thus far:

1. Institutions are what they are, and are not what they are not. Following the parameters outlined above, an institution is any reality, large or small, long-standing or short-lived, that fulfills the conditions of being "an instance of shared thinking in a relationship of community, practice, and legacy; characterized by stability, dynamism, and purpose; and constituted by accounts, heuristics, and norms." That thing is an institution in that respect, regardless of whatever it happens to be called or even if it happens to be called nothing at all. But also, something that does not fulfill the necessary parameters of an institution should not grouped together with realities that do fulfill them, which is why it is necessary to understand the near neighbors to the above conceptualization as discussed in section 3 of this chapter. And of course no institution or aspect of one should be demoted (e.g., a community should not be treated as a mere identity).

2. The term "institution" is contingent. The concept of "institution" was chosen for the reasons cited in chapter 1, but in fact it does not matter whether one calls this conceptualization "institution" or something else. The contours of the definition developed here are meant to be free of dependence upon the idiomatic connotations or emotive associations of the word "institution" and instead rest firmly upon the way that the constituent concepts are defined and relate to each other. That is why this model emphasizes the conditions of mutual irreducibility, mutual distinctness, and mutual implication at each stage of the development of the definition. (These relations will be discussed again in chapter 5.) In theory it should be possible to discuss *all* these parameters without even using the word "institution" or "institutional." This conceptualization is meant to minimize reliance upon mere idiomatic or everyday understanding of the terms involved.

3. Institutions can be nested or overlap in the general conceptual space of shared thinking. Institutions can be made up of many smaller institutions, and furthermore they can be overlapping in one or more of their features. Such conceptual overlaps are problematic only when the nature of the overlap is obscure. When their character is clear, overlaps create no conceptual traps. Different quadrilaterals can have common or distinctive features, but since they are fully theorized their overlaps and differences generate no ambiguities.

One can have institutions within institutions, and indeed an institution could be seen as the aggregation of its constituent institutions as long as the integrity of the parameters is maintained as one scales up or scales down. In other words, if one can "add up" several institutions, each of which fulfills the parameters of the model, then it is possible (though not inevitable) to be able to combine them together conceptually and speak correctly about a "megainstitution" so long as that aggregate also fulfills the necessary parameters. Each subinstitution, or conversely each megainstitution, will differ in terms of its empirical/variable parameters.

Let us return to the example of modern medicine. One could analyze "modern medicine" as an institution itself but also analyze each institution that is part of it—medical education, medical research, clinical practice—each of which also fulfills the conditions of being an institution but with empirical variations (e.g., the shapes of their respective hierarchies). One could further see "modern medicine" itself as an institution within "modern science," which as a whole itself (including medicine) could also be analyzed using the definition of institutions here. Further, modern science is an institution within the larger institution of the Modern Project, as is modern philosophy and modern art/culture. But it is not only a question of institutions within others. There can also be partial overlap between institutions. Medical education is also part of the institution of modern higher education, which latter has undergraduate athletics within it, which latter itself has an overlap with art/culture, and so on.

4. This definition of institutions scales up or down, and can be used as a whole or in part, and still maintain its integrity. In thinking about institutions or shared thinking, one can isolate each triad of community-practice-legacy, or stability-dynamism-purpose, or accounts-heuristics-norms, and still have a handy way of analyzing and thinking about institutions that does not fragment them fundamentally. A black-and-white photo and a color photo are both, in a sense, complete pictures, but one of them has more information and parameters.

Indeed, as a practical matter it is highly unlikely that a twenty-seven-dimensional model will be frequently used in every respect, but it is very practical and useful to be able to use each triad as a heuristic or key to the entire rubric. For example, when one's question pertains most directly to a community reality, the parameters of practice and legacy will be present themselves as clarifying concepts. Or if one is focused on the dynamism of a community, then asking questions about its stability and purpose will be useful. Likewise, when studying some kind of norm, it becomes handy to understand it in light of the background accounts and heuristics. Using each triad, or even a triad of triads (such as the two triads that result in memory-mastery-moral-authority, communicative-creative-corrective, available-intelligible-valuable) without resorting to the full rubric still captures logical and analytical virtues of the model. How this definition can be broken apart without resulting in fragmentation, and maintain its analytical integrity when used in parts, has everything to do with the metaphysics of social reality, which will be discussed in chapter 5.

Synopsis

- While shared thinking has no separate faculties of its own apart from the individual thinkers that make it up, it is misleading to treat each human being as an atom that could exist without the sharing that is essential to any individual's thinking.

- No *I* can be or become an *I* without also consciously participating in a *we* (in many different ones, in fact), and there can be no *we* except by virtue of the many realities in it who say *I*.

- The first of three rudimentary definitions of an institution is the following: an institution is an instance of shared thinking in a relationship of community, practice, and legacy.

- A *community* is a group of people defined by being those who know the right things and who do things the right way.

- A *practice* is defined by inheriting and bequeathing the right things and by being carried out by the right people.

- A *legacy* is that which is bequeathed and inherited by the right group of people doing things the right way.

- The three elements of community, practice, and legacy are mutually *irreducible*, mutually *distinct*, and mutually *implicative*—in a way that is conceptually akin to the three dimensions of bodily space.

- Mutual irreducibility means that all three terms are necessary to cover the conceptual space. Mutual distinctness means that the three do not conceptually overlap. Mutual implication means that each presupposes and implies the others.

- The second of three rudimentary definitions of an institution is this: an institution is an instance of shared thinking characterized by *stability*, *dynamism*, and *purpose*.

- Stability means that shared thinking is remembered, communicated, accessible. Dynamism means that shared thinking is created, changed, adapted, and intelligible in different contexts. Purpose means that shared thinking depends on moral authority, is tended, and is valued.

- An institution's stability presupposes and requires dynamism and change; its dynamism presupposes and requires stability and purpose; and its purpose presupposes and requires stability and dynamism.

- A third of three rudimentary definitions of an institution is this: an institution is an instance of shared thinking constituted by certain accounts, heuristics, and norms.

- *Account* is a technical term that can include descriptions, representations, facts, premises, axioms, presuppositions, or assumptions. Accounts are the institution's *know-what*.

- *Heuristic* is a technical term that can include methods, templates, guidelines, techniques, theorems, procedures, processes, logics, recipes, or rules. Heuristics are an institution's *know-how*.

- *Norm* is a technical term that can include values, standards, imperatives, maxims, purposes, goals, ideals, exemplars, or objectives. Norms are an institution's *know-why*.

- Accounts, heuristics, and norms can be seen as analogous to a group of travelers (1) sharing knowledge of the journey's terrain, (2) sharing the ability to navigate its route, and (3) sharing a sense of its worthwhile destination.

- These three definitional triads can be combined into a conceptual ennead in such a way as to maintain the qualities of mutual irreducibility, mutual distinctness, and mutual implication, even after each triad is refracted through the others.

- This multidimensional model of an institution is complex and coherent, demarcates the relevant domain, and can scale from simple to complex institutions while maintaining the same logical principles.

- The full formulation of the features of an institution is thus the following: an institution is an instance of shared thinking in a relationship of community, practice, and legacy; characterized by stability, dynamism, and purpose; and constituted by accounts, heuristics, and norms.

- Each of the nine necessary features of institutions is also a parameter that can vary empirically from institution to institution. All institutions have these features, but institutions vary empirically along many parameters.

- Within the parameter of community, institutions vary in terms of the kind of hierarchy they embody, ranging from relatively egalitarian to relatively elitist.

- Within the parameter of practice, institutions vary in terms of the balance between old and new expressions.

- Within the parameter of legacy, institutions vary in terms of the modality—the media or substrate—by which the legacy is bequeathed and inherited.

- In the case of institutional stability, the relevant variation is longevity and resilience.

- In the case of institutional dynamism, the relevant variation is how rigid or flexible the range of possibilities is.

- In the case of institutional purpose, the relevant variation is the kind of sincerity, solicitude, and prioritization people have for that institution, and its place in the entire lived life of human beings.

- When it comes to the triad of accounts, heuristics, and norms, the variation to be considered is between "showing" and "telling," or between communicating by example and by instruction.

- Institutions must also be distinguished from what they are not. Other notions lie at the conceptual borders of institutions. These are nine ideas that are close to the ennead of concepts but that are not part of what makes an institution.

- A community disconnected from a practice and legacy is only an *identity*. Identities, unlike communities, do not place moral or intellectual conditions on the people who constitute them.

- A practice is done by the right people according to the right inheritance, but when severed from authority and legacy one has at most a *routine* or a mere *behavior*.

- A legacy that is not legitimized by a practicing community is only a *relic* or an *heirloom*. Heirlooms, unlike true legacies, can only change hands and are not truly inherited or bequeathed as part of a practice.

- Stability in an institution, severed from its dynamism and purpose, is mere *ossification* or the inability to do anything else.

- Dynamism in an institution, severed from its stability and purpose, is pure *plasticity*, hoarding, metastasis, or a compulsion toward change.

- Purpose in an institution, severed from stability and dynamism, is nothing more than *motives* or *incentives* of various kind—whether tyranny, egotism, greed, or another kind of impulse.

- Accounts severed from an institution's heuristics and norms are mere *assertions* or passive biases.

- Heuristics severed from an institution's accounts and norms are mere *reflexes* or *compulsions*.

- Norms severed from an institution's accounts and heuristics are mere *demands*.

- Given the nature of this model, the term "institution" itself is contingent and can be replaced by any other placeholder. The key to the model is not the idiomatic sense of institution but the logical relations between its constituent concepts.

- Institutions can be nested or overlap in one or more of their features. One institution can be found entirely or partially within another, and when properly analyzed the combination of one institution into a larger one does not violate the conceptual rules of the rubric.

- Because of the way the three triads relate, using one of the triads instead of the full ennead retains many of the virtues of the definition. Each simple triad is a useful heuristic that enables one to access the entire complex multidimensional model.

- A culture, civilization, religion, or tradition is an instance of shared thinking with respect to ultimate questions, existing in a relationship of community, practice, and legacy; characterized by stability, dynamism, and purpose; and constituted by accounts, heuristics, and norms.

Part II

Metaphysics

Chapter 3

The Metaphysics of Antidualism

The concept of institution in the previous chapter is a portrait of a special kind of "we" that is more than simply a collectivity of human beings, but this book's conceptualization of the nature of shared thinking or we-thinking requires a certain inquiry into the nature of human consciousness insofar as it is necessary to discuss how individual thinking and shared thinking relate to each other. It will be necessary to understand the place of metaphysics in relation to other modes of human thinking and practice, and also in a certain measure to actually think metaphysically—that is, to both understand the place of ultimate presuppositions about what is real, possible, and good, and also to navigate those presuppositions correctly as conscious living beings. The previous two chapters were largely an analytical or conceptual exercise meant to define the scope, limits, and internal relationships of concepts, so let us now explore what kind of being and what kind of world is presupposed such that this conceptualization of an institution makes sense.

Antidualism and the Soul

Alfred North Whitehead noted that modern philosophy "oscillated in a complex manner between three extremes. There are the dualists, who accept matter and mind as on an equal basis, and the two varieties of monists, those who put mind inside matter, and those who put matter inside mind."[1] Those who Whitehead called monists formulated their monism on the basis of the dualistic model's basic division: nonmaterial but nevertheless objectively real human minds trying to make sense of a world that operated more or less mechanically and that could be understood more or less mathematically as described in modern physics, a conceptual division that has endured in various forms since the introduction of substance dualism by early modern figures such as Descartes and Galileo. The presumption throughout the centuries-long monism/dualism debates has been that the real or apparent boundary between the two substances is intelligible enough to be the basis of discussion. That is, even for the two kinds of monists Whitehead identified, the nature of the appearance of two substances and the basic problem of how to reconcile mind and matter remain the same. By analogy, think of the famous Vedantic allegory in which a stick is mistaken for a snake, not a bird, which means that the object is a snake or a stick, or even both in some way, but the discussion is about the conceptual line—taken for granted—between snake and stick (not mirage and water). The debate Whitehead refers to is analogous: it is a question of real or apparent mind, real or apparent matter, and the real or apparent line between the two substances as normally conceived in the philosophy and science of the modern period.

But the terms of debate as Whitehead described them no longer truly apply, because as a matter of ontology the Modern Project has thoroughly expunged dualism, but not because it lost out to one of the two types of monism. Instead, the agreed upon terms of debate between mind and matter (whichever one was real) simply broke down. The waxy mechanically manipulable stuff envisioned by the first substance dualists, the res extensa, could not survive successive discoveries in physics—starting from Newton's mechanism-free theory of gravitation and culminating in contemporary quantum mechanics and relativity with their indeterminacy, wave-particle duality, nonlocality, and space-time distortions, just to name a few nonmechanical and indeed paradoxical features of reality as conceived of by modern physics. For its part, the mind, res cogitans, as an independently existing spiritual and immaterial thinking substance, could not survive Darwin, who gave permission to many thinkers to assume that everything human beings are results from the deterministic or random behavior of whatever that stuff was that the physicists and chemists study. Dualism lost out, while neither brand of monism won: the intelligibility of matter was destroyed by physics, and the status of the mind by biological evolution. The result is that there are no dualists anymore, but there are no monists either. What emerged from the collapse of the dualist/monist debate in modern thought are various forms of *antidualism*.

Why use the term "antidualism" instead of monism, materialism, phys-icalism, or naturalism?[2] Few thinkers really think of themselves as "monists," and instead rely on the idiom of "physical reality" or "material reality" or "nature" or the like, and they typically frame their position as a declaration of allegiance to the methods of modern science that they imagine to be well demarcated, or as reliance upon a trustworthy community of scientists as arbiters of truth. The problem with terms like "materialism," "physicalism," and "naturalism" is that no one knows what "material," "physical," and "nat-ural" mean beyond general folk concepts. One relies upon what scientists do, not upon knowing exactly what *the stuff* is. The Cartesian line between mind and matter required a very distinct kind of matter—mechanical, deterministic, and quantifiable, where all physical objects were the kinds of things an artisan could fashion. In modern physics, not only are physical entities not anything an artisan could fashion, but they are also literally things one cannot even imagine. The "matter" of modern materialists is far stranger than the invisible forces and substantial forms the early modern philosophers sought to distance themselves from. One cannot really "put mind inside matter" or "matter inside mind" because matter has become literally unimaginable. (This unimaginability of what is called "matter" will be discussed in chapter 5.)

Today, in place of a genuine monism, one has a general stance or posture that presupposes that reality is whatever physicists study or consider to be real, where "physical" or "material" or "natural" mean nothing fundamen-tally different from simply real or actual as understood by the authoritative community. As Bas van Fraassen writes, "I propose the following diagnosis of materialism: it is not identifiable with a theory about what there is but only with an attitude or cluster of attitudes. These attitudes include strong deference to the current content of science in matters of opinion about what there is. They include also an inclination (and perhaps a commitment, at least an intention) to accept (approximative) completeness claims for science as actually constituted at any given time."[3] Yet even though modern science may not have a precise definition for the stuff of reality, there is only *one* such stuff, and this attitude is why one needs a concept like "antidualism." Despite not embracing an explicit substance monism, upholders of this view nevertheless remain adamant that there can be no return to the dualistic conception that assumed that there was an *independent* substance completely outside the realm of the stuff that scientists alone are authorized to describe. (Recall that once upon a time scientists like Galileo affirmed that the soul was real and that it was the domain of things like morality and that scientists did not study *that* but rather studied the *other* substance.) This antidualism is outright hostile, not only to the particular conceptions of mind or spirit that have appeared and disappeared throughout the history Western thought but to any reality that would violate belief that modern science alone can know what is real in any domain whatsoever. Some varieties of panpsychism that have become fashionable (have gone in and out of fashion for a long time) are in no way a departure from antidualism, and in fact constitute an entrenchment of it. They do not allow belief in a soul but offer rein-terpretations of the descriptions of reality given out by physicists. There is nothing outside of what physicists (a community and a legacy, not only a method) can study. Commonly, one refers to this attitude as scientism, but antidualism will be used in this book for the sake of greater precision. Antidualism is both postdualist and pseudomonist. It cannot be avowedly monist because it does not know what the "stuff" is, but it cannot be dualist either, because that would be to accept a reality beyond its domain or to "allow a Divine Foot in the door." Adherence to antidualism is important because it rules out, both as idea and stance, anything resembling a soul, spirit, mind, or intellect that is not completely explainable in terms of the rules governing the one stuff. The soul or mind can be spoken of as met-aphors, never as real things.

The Structure within and the Structure Between

There are two significant modes of the antidualist stance to be discussed here as it relates to shared thinking and institutions.

Some conceptions of human consciousness are antidualist by virtue of an explicit mathematical-mechanistic description of nature, in which the rules governing galaxy formation and the rules governing states of consciousness are precisely the same. Whether one thinks of human consciousness as an illusion, as an emergent phenomenon, or as an epiphenomenon, there is no rupture, leap, or move up a hierarchy when one reaches human conscious-ness. From the galaxy to the solar system to the biosphere to the species to the community to the family to the body to the brain there is a single continuum of the one stuff behaving as the one stuff. No stuff stands above any of the other stuff. All the stuff moves and likewise is moved. One can call this stance objective or ontological antidualism.

An example of this stance can be seen in this passage from John Searle: "How can there be an objective world of money, property, marriage, governments, elections, football games, cocktail parties and law courts in a world that consists entirely of physical particles in fields of force, and in which some of these particles are organized into systems that are conscious biological beasts, such as ourselves?"[4] The way that objective-ontological antidualism relates to institutions (human beings thinking together) can be visualized by means of a computer server farm in which many individual machines are linked together to overcome certain physical limitations related to processing power. As a practical matter, an individual computer processor can process only a certain amount of input without being physically destroyed (by heat, for instance). A single desktop computer might take tens of thousands of years to render a modern animated film, while a server farm might accomplish the same task in a matter of months.

Despite the superficial appearance of multiple entities interacting, the structure *inside* one computer and the structure *between* multiple computers is really the same unitary structure. Drawing boundaries between machines is arbitrary in terms of the actual *computing*. When you link up two thousand individual computers to run a climate simulation, the entire arrangement is really just *one* processor—a single system. There is just input, processing, and output—nothing else. There is no inside and outside, no above and below, no between and among. There is no ontological leap anywhere.

Objective-ontological antidualism sees human beings linked up in an analogous way, at least implicitly. The structure between and within each node (each human being) is the same. There is no separate consciousness that modifies or determines what happens between the human processors; it is all just physical stuff being physical stuff. Pile a billion human consciousnesses together and you simply get a larger interaction of physical stuff. The individual human being is a small pile of the stuff, and the group (a culture, let's say) is a big pile of that same stuff. Complexity and unpredictability do not change the ontological nature of the situation. The activity of ten thousand marbles in a jar is complex and unpredictable, but no one thinks that such complexity and unpredictability bring the marbles closer to consciousness and free will. There is no ontological break between one marble and many.

Each individual human being is an antidualist system of biochemical activity, and multiple such individual human systems interacting with each other will add up to a larger aggregate antidualist system of biochemical activity. There is no equivocation on the term "system" here. There is no ontological difference between a bag of a thousand marbles and a thousand bags of a thousand marbles each all in a giant jar.

The second version or iteration of the antidualist stance sees human subjects as constructed and determined by social structures of domination and control, so much so that the subject is not merely hemmed in by outside constraints but rather is intelligible only in terms of those conditions—constructed and constrained by culture, language, or other social factors. Here the structure is not mechanical and ontological but rather psychological and sociological—often framed as linguistic but extending to culture and politics. There is no individual self that is free of or that operates independently of that "structure" (a particular spatial metaphor, let us not forget). The *I* has no wiggle room inside or outside of the structure—not psychologically, not socially, not ethically, not cognitively, not linguistically, not emotionally. The subject does not navigate the world but is made by it. Actually, the constraints go even deeper than that: the very *I/we* distinction as an idea is—indeed, would have to be—a construct of the structure. Where else could that idea that there is an *I* and a *we* come from? Instead of being analogous to a farm of mechanical computers linked up by the very same rules that govern each computer, this psychosociological antidualism posits deterministic cultural conditions that make each subject into the aggregate sum of the *relationships* in which that subject participates. All subjects taken together are, therefore, really just an aggregation of relationships. The relationships *between* agents (that is, "structure") create the relationships *within* agents (the subject itself). "Language speaks us," as Heidegger said.

Needless to say, those who espouse this *subjective* antidualism also accept, if only by quiet deference (sometimes accompanied by performative protest), the objective antidualist account. Whether one starts from objective-ontological or subjective-sociological antidualism, one ends up at a pseudomonistic conception in which a structure or set of rules governs both the relationship between nodes as well as the internal structure of the nodes themselves. There is no space left for a real *I*.

And yet, crucially, both modes of antidualism are *methodologically dualist*—a folk dualism, as it were. Thinkers who are adamant that human beings are something like moist robots are equally adamant that this mechanical nature in no way undermines free will or rationality. Those who declare that the human subject is constructed by power nevertheless carry on and try to convince others of their own moral and intellectual rightness as if they were free to be wrong or to be right. The Modern Project is populated by different amalgams of de facto dualism and performative antidualism.

Sociologists will often posit a total reality divided between agents and structure, with some giving more power to the structure and others to the agency of individuals in it. But what is the nature of this totality such that one can meaningfully differentiate between structure and agent in the first place? One must have a definite metaphysical assumption about the nature of that totality such that it makes sense, given what human beings are, to see the line between structure and agency as being important or even discernible. Yet against the backdrop of antidualism such a demarcation between agent and structure has to be ultimately arbitrary and nonexplanatory. Since "agents" are human beings, it is self-evidently important to have a minimally correct account of their nature. One must ask: is it even possible, in an antidualist account, for what are called "agents" to have agency? If what the antidualists say is true, an "agent" would just be an arbitrary cross-section of the total "structure" broadly conceived. Under antidualist assumptions, differentiating between agents and structure is like asking, What is more important, the structure of the server farm or the operations of the computers that make it up? It is clear that the question and its answer are meaningless (or trivial) as formulated. Within such assumptions, the "agent" is a reification of antidualist processes, reflecting a manner of speaking that is useful for discussion but names no real border or joint in reality. (Recall Searle's assumption that such agents are "entirely . . . physical particles in fields of force.") One could, for example, assert that a satellite "wants" to fall toward the earth but is kept in orbit by its velocity, but that does not mean that the object has something called "agency" that exists in tension with the structure of the physical system. Do any of the atoms in a satellite know that they are in orbit? Would any collection of them know? Why attribute a fictional attribute of "agency" to an arbitrary cross-section of a giant antidualist system?

Nevertheless, antidualists will make arguments *as if* they possessed a consciousness that can operate freely in relation to the structure of the physical reality or the power structure of social relationships—this is methodological (or folk) dualism. This clash between how people theorize human thinking (mechanical, deterministic, random) and how they as human beings actually think (freely, meaningfully, rationally) is one of the most remarkable features of the Modern Project as it stands today.

The Transcendental Limit and the Impossible Scales

Some philosophers have been willing to grapple with the tension between metaphysical antidualism and methodological (or folk) dualism, and will argue that the *rightness* and *rationality* of what we think and say cannot (or ought not) be denied. To deny rightness and rationality, they correctly observe, is to presuppose both of them; these presuppositions are sometimes called basic validity claims. That is, one cannot say we *ought* to believe in the absence of morality, or *argue* that rationality does not exist, because these assertions presuppose what they are denying. Such transcendental-style arguments for the validity of claims to truth and rightness are not new, but some who accept them will nevertheless assert that this acknowledgment—that is, acceptance of the conditions that must be in place to make any kind of truth or morality claim—can nevertheless say *nothing* about metaphysics (at least as far as they conceive of metaphysics).[5] Karl-Otto Apel, the philosopher who perhaps paid the greatest attention to the universal validity conditions of communication, says, "My method ascertains only what it itself relies on as a method of foundation; it ascertains only those kinds of presuppositions that it itself cannot dispute if it is to avoid performative self-contradiction. It can provide no ontological-cosmological explanation of the whole world; rather, it provides solely for the self-ascertainment of argumentative reason. But to the extent that it leads to indisputable statements, does it lead to trivial or insignificant statements?"[6] What Apel seems to miss is that to claim that certain presuppositions cannot be disputed is already to presuppose a world in which this very claim can make any sense, and to exclude worlds in which it cannot. Moreover, it may indeed be true that one cannot fashion an *entire* ontology and cosmology from transcendental arguments in favor of the validity of rational and moral claims, but Apel's method of ascertaining presuppositions itself *presupposes* both a being capable of understanding presuppositions as well as a world that is hospitable to the existence of just such a being. A method of thinking (which is Apel's interest here) that relies on certain unavoidable presuppositions can only *arbitrarily* refuse to take a position on whether there exist beings who can make such presuppositions. Once such an assumption about the existence of such presupposers is made—and indeed it *must* be made—one has made a metaphysical claim and one has no choice in the matter. Apel says that his method—ascertaining the presuppositions his method cannot dispute— can provide "no ontological-cosmological explanation of the whole world," but that statement leaves too much unanswered. What *would* count as an explanation, and why does it have to be the *whole* world, and does not the invocation of the "whole world" mean that one already knows the basic contours of what the "whole world" is and isn't? The assumptions embedded in these parameters go far beyond mere method.

Charles Taylor goes so far as to say that establishing such presuppositions of thought cannot disprove the mechanistic picture of the world, an argument that is incomplete unless one can first point to what *would* count as evidence against that mechanistic picture, which Taylor does not provide. He says that "there remains an ultimate, ontological question [that transcendental arguments] can't foreclose."[7] But what does it mean to "foreclose"? In what way is the ontological question "ultimate"? If I discover a handwritten note in the forest, I cannot "foreclose" the question of who wrote it, when, and where, but I can know that it was not written by a turtle. Providing an alternate full-fledged ontology-cosmology of everything, which modern science itself certainly does not possess, is not a reasonable condition to place upon those who would reject the mechanistic picture (really, just the antidualist stance),[8] which, after all, is not common sense but a highly speculative view that is far from self-evident. If it was so obvious, why did figures such as Descartes and Galileo have to invent it and why did no one do so before?

This acknowledgment of certain validity conditions for human reason, meant to avoid the logical traps of certain brands of "performative self-contradiction," is as far as most modern philosophers are willing to go, and even they seem to be in a small minority. Apel considered himself a "white raven" among contemporary philosophers for his quite modest antirelativism and antiskepticism.[9] Apel's and Taylor's views highlight an important line—on the far side of which lie metaphysical questions that they claim cannot be "foreclosed" or "explained." On the near side of the boundary, one is allowed to establish the necessary conditions for communication so as to avoid self-refuting stances that undermine the very enterprise of thinking and argument. Beyond the line there lies the dreaded dualism, the belief that there exists some entity not fully bound by the rules of the one stuff that scientists study.

This antidualist stance is simply untenable as far as consciousness is concerned, and renders the understanding of social reality impossible. The real reason that one is not allowed to tread beyond the transcendental line articulated by Apel and Taylor is that, according to the unwritten rules of the Modern Project as it stands today, only physicists are allowed to say what is actually real, while philosophers must limit themselves to what questions one can ask and how to think clearly. This division of territory between scientists and everyone else is not established by God or reason but is a social fact and a historically contingent situation (as will be taken up in chapter 7). It was not always the case the science and philosophy were so dogmatically separate, even in the Modern Project, a history that cannot be explored here. If today's scientists do not want us to move beyond the mechanistic picture, then that is their self-imposed limitation, and no one is obligated—again, except by social pressures—to obey their philosophical proclamations.

One simply cannot carry on believing that we will understand social realities while assuming or pretending that human beings are machines or social constructions (two versions of the same view) or that they can be understood as if they were. One can collect mountains of data, write long books, and find out many interesting and even insightful things about human affairs—but this only goes so far. If one wants to understand *shared* thinking, one cannot have a completely blinkered notion of what thinking is in the first place. We must cross the boundary Apel and Taylor seem to treat as inviolable, a limit that does nothing but perpetuate the flawed notion that only modern scientists are allowed to speak about what is real.

The picture of the "I" and "we" that one must avoid is precisely the one that sees the "I" and the "we" as merely different instantiations of a monistic structure. Any full conception of institutions—and especially metaphysical institutions such as culture, religion, civilization, and tradition—must overcome the obstacle of antidualism. Otherwise, one will remain mired forever in the domain of folk concepts.

In fact, far from being a horizon, the boundary that Apel and Taylor present as the limit of what philosophers are allowed to say metaphysically about rationality and communication is actually the minimum starting point.[10] What good is it to argue that human beings' moral and rational claims are valid if one is forbidden to describe a being actually capable of morality and rationality? The situation is akin to arguing for the precision and accuracy of certain physical measurements while being forbidden from making any claims about the nature of the measuring equipment, or by insisting upon a description of a measuring device that would be patently incapable of measuring anything.

If one believes a weighing scale will read one hundred grams regardless of the object that is placed on it, or that the scale's reading depends on the prevailing temperature and not the weight of the object placed on it, or that the scale simply reads different values at different times chaotically, then it is a form of madness to use the scale as if it gave accurate and precise values for the weight of objects. Such a belief constitutes madness especially if the scale *typically works*. If human beings are bound by deterministic physical or social processes (like the scale stuck at one hundred grams), or if one's true nature is simply illusory (like a scale reading weight based on temperature instead of mass and gravity), or if one's thinking is just random, then it is certainly possible to function day-to-day as if human beings actually can think and reason (this is methodological dualism), but one will be doing so with an account of one's own nature completely at odds with it. That is the Modern Project's strange tension regarding consciousness: rationality and morality are taken to be real, and one acts as if they were real, but one must adhere to an account of human nature that renders rationality and morality absurd.

Whatever that structure (and it is always a "structure") of human consciousness is taken to be in the antidualist stance, if one took the discovery process far enough and filled out the picture of the structures that give rise to structures that give rise to structures, one would reach down to the structure of the biological system, straight into the question of the so-called hard problem of consciousness. That is simply a fact. It is not enough to be sentimentally uncomfortable with straightforward reductionism. One can think here of the philosopher Hilary Putnam, who believed one could "reject both relativism and semantic materialism"[11] but who, despite embracing theism at the end of his life,[12] prohibited what he called "reactionary metaphysics,"[13] which seems to mean any metaphysics that departs from antidualism.

One cannot refuse to defy antidualism while saying things like, "Yes, minds are really nothing but the physical, but that doesn't mean that the mental isn't *real!*" Modern philosophy is littered with such bare assertions, and they never make sense. They are simply declarations of a willingness to live with a belief at odds with one's own experience of one's self, or at most a vague hope that somehow in the future it will make sense.[14] That willingness (indeed, demand) to hold an outright contradiction or utter a vague hope is not an argument. If one gets the metaphysics of consciousness completely wrong, there is no chance of understanding the nature of social reality, which is constituted by shared thinking.

Synopsis

- It is important to explore not only the analytical features of institutions but also the metaphysical reality that makes them possible as real things in the world.

- Modern views toward consciousness are most precisely characterized as *antidualist* as opposed to monist, physicalist, materialist, or naturalistic when it comes to the reality of consciousness.

- Antidualism is a stance that is not doctrinally monist but rather stands against the possibility of any reality that stands outside the domain of whatever it is scientists study and deem to be real—often euphemistically called "material" or "physical."

- The first of two kinds of antidualism is ontological or objective antidualism, which is an explicit description of human thinking as one ripple in a pattern of physical interactions, an arbitrary part of a larger structure.

- The second kind of antidualism is psychosociological or subjective antidualism, which sees human thinking as determined and constructed by cultural and social conditions à la Heidegger's "Language speaks us."

- Some philosophers have recognized the epistemic implications of antidualism and have attempted to formulate certain necessary validity claims for truth and meaning, but these almost always stop short at rejecting the metaphysical claims of antidualism.

- Antidualism must be abandoned and rejected in order to make any sense of the actual experience of shared thinking. The coupling of metaphysical antidualism and a methodological or folk dualism must be recognized for its consequential incoherence.

Chapter 4

The Metaphysics of Meaning

The previous chapter discussed "the structure within and the structure between." Now let us turn to the topic of *meaning* and "the structure behind structure."

The antidualist stance denies the simple fact, experienced by all human beings, that one means what one says, and that one can understand what is meant by what is said by others. *To mean what one says* is to have an intention to communicate something and to then use the appropriate forms to do so. *To understand what is meant by it* is to be able to interpret the spoken forms to understand the intention of the speaker. Almost all modern philosophy bends itself into pretzels trying to say anything else but this is because of the metaphysical implications.

Ontological antidualism posits a structure hidden deep in the human organism that gives rise—the details of which can never be laid out—to sensible structures of utterances, some of which somehow "have meaning" or are "bearers of meaning" in a narrow jargony sense often incomprehensible outside of academic philosophy. Psychological/subjective antidualism, for its part, would have us believe that there is no human subjectivity outside of the forms or structures of language or culture no matter how deep one goes into consciousness; it is linguistic structure all the way down. It is impossible, in any variety of antidualism, to first mean something and *then* say it ("then" considered logically or temporally), or to hear something and then understand what was meant by it. That would not fit into the "structure." There is no entity that could *mean* anything, and no entity that could understand *what is meant*, thus rendering actual thinking and communication an absurdity to which we cling for lack of a better coping mechanism. There is only the apparent part of the system on the one hand and its hidden workings on the other.

The concept of "meaning," so crucial to understanding the nature of institutions of any kind, is a broad and difficult concept in modern philosophy because of how pervasive it has been and how many mutually exclusive ways it has been deployed as a technical term in various systems. In contemporary thought on the subject of meaning one will come face to face with a bewildering array of ideas and theories: structuralism, positivism, hermeneutics, poststructuralism, semantics, and other philosophical currents (within not only philosophy but also linguistics, anthropology, and sociology). These intellectual currents all have varying takes on what "meaning" is and how it works, but this variation is entirely downstream of the more basic question of the metaphysical framework in which they exist and which they take as a given—namely, antidualism. What these differing perspectives on meaning argue about is not whether there is a hidden structure beneath the apparent structure of language and other forms of expression: they all accept that there is a single overall system and that beneath the apparent structure there is a hidden structure that needs to be discovered (let us remember, I do not use terms such as "physicalist" or "materialist" because no one knows what "physical" or "material" mean). They disagree only about what the best approach is to study that underlying structure and to what degree it can actually be discovered and understood. Put simply, the disagreements are only methodological, not metaphysical.

Within antidualism the demarcation of something called "meaning" amounts to drawing or presupposing a line somewhere in the entire within-and-between system and labeling as "meaning" (or "sense" or "content") what falls on one side of the demarcation and nonmeaning (or "context" or the "unsayable" or "nonsense") on the other. Studying the structure on the meaning side of the line is sometimes called "semantics" by those who take the objective antidualist approach, and "hermeneutics" by many of those who take the subjective approach. The "semanticists" and "hermeneuticians" are at odds with each other at a certain level, but the opposition is relatively superficial. One can think of semantics as the study of meaning by those who aspire to provide some kind of objective or scientific account of how meaning actually works (dominant in analytic philosophy and in the field of linguistics), and hermeneutics as the study of meaning by those who seek to explore the presuppositions and limitations of interpreting various forms of human expression (dominant in continental philosophy and in the humanities and social science fields that concern themselves with such questions). Semantics is a kind of extension of science (or is simply part of it), while hermeneutics is a kind of extension of artistic and literary criticism (or is simply part of it). Their differences are not unreal, of course. Hermeneuticians will point out that semanticists are insufficiently critical of their own concepts and ideas and that they are mistaken in assuming a kind of standpointless or universal position in studying meaning, while the semanticists will point out that the hermeneuticians' claim that one can never escape one's historical conditions and get to the meaning of a text is a claim that undermines its own validity. The multifarious configurations of semantics and of hermeneutics will not concern us here, but suffice it to say that there is no strict dividing line between them, and even within each camp there is no consensus position on any issue—except of course on antidualism, which is an almost universal dogma.

Determinism, Randomness, or Something Else

What kind of causal nexus can exist between the underlying or hidden "structure" that means and understands and the apparent structure of things like linguistic expressions if antidualism is true? One possibility is that the two structures are linked deterministically, like a microphone and a loudspeaker, and another is that their connection is random, like the shape of lightning as it connects the sky to the ground. Alternatively, the nexus between the two structures might be some combination of deterministic and random, like a roulette wheel. Put simply, if that part of a human being that *means* and *understands* is a kind of structure—a biological, computational, linguistic, or other kind of system—and if the expressions of language are another kind of structure, then those two structures must be related to each other in some way, and antidualism allows only two real options: determinism and randomness.

The goal of this book is not to offer yet another way to cope with this situation, or to be existentially authentic, or imagine a technologically advanced future in which antidualism will make sense of consciousness. Modern philosophy, in its various stripes, has done these things plenty enough, and others are welcome to pursue those avenues of inquiry, which thus far have led to little more than the renaming of the same old concepts for generations. The question is *right now and here*, is a metaphysical one: How do meaning and expression relate if antidualism is true? The answer to this question has to be a point somewhere on the spectrum between determinism and randomness. These are the options. It does no good to sit up straight and place one's hand firmly on the table and declare, "Just because I believe that I am entirely subject to physical laws does not mean that meaning is simply physical!" Yes, it does. If someone wants to say that submarines swim, they should at least not say that submarines *mean* to swim.

Indeed, it is necessary to register something important about contemporary philosophy when it comes to consciousness. Every metaphysics one encounters that (1) does not affirm the existence of *something* like a soul, (2) remains loyal to the Darwinian conception of human beings, and (3) *also* tries to avoid "reductive" materialism/physicalism always turn out to be differing versions of the same incoherent assertion. Philosophers create many different ways of declaring (never demonstrating) that one cannot or should not reduce mental properties to physical properties *even though* the mental is ontologically exhausted by the physical. The physical is all there is, they say, and yet for various and sundry reasons it is *important* (why?) to maintain some kind of distinction between the physical and the mental. These assertions are all versions of what was outlined above: a metaphysical antidualism combined with a methodological/folk dualism. Whether one uses terms like "nonreductive" or "functionalist" or "compatibilist" or "non-eliminativist" or "emergentist" the basic position is the same:[1] the mental or the conscious is always rendered into an epiphenomenon that is somehow "real" because we experience it, but what we experience as consciousness has *no causal role*. What happens physically is all that happens. One has seen enough assertions of the form "Just because I'm a reductionist does not mean I'm a *reductionist*." Ideas like "nonreductive physicalism" are just words smashed together, like "nonround circle." What differentiates philosophers on these issues is not their metaphysics but the attitude or heuristics that they use to deal with it. To declare that individuals have "agency" (defined in some narrow technical sense) rather than saying they are causally determined is simply word play if one's account of what a human being is remains exactly the same. When reading the literature on this subject it is unclear whether what is sometimes called "voluntarism" means human beings are *actually* free or whether analytically it simply makes most sense to treat them, methodologically, *as if* they were free.[2] It seems to always be the latter. Essentially, one is arguing over whether or how much "causality" to attribute to the wiring *between* the computers on the one hand and the wiring *inside* of the computers on the other.[3]

Without some affirmative acknowledgment that what the physicists study cannot be all that is real, it's just antidualism. Only very rarely do philosophers crack open a window to let something beyond antidualism inside. In a very cautious and caveated passage the philosopher Paul Grice, for example, considered it "metaphysical snobbery, a reluctance to be seen in the company of any but the best objects" to exclude "such 'queer' or 'mysterious' entities as souls, purely mental events, purely mental properties and so forth." Grice did not affirm any particular entity of this kind, but he did leave open the possibility that a kind of reality that is established through "some form of transcendental argument, may qualify for the specially favoured status of *entia realissima* [real beings]."[4] This hypothetical possibility, stated as mildly as one possibly could, is a giant leap beyond what most modern philosophers are willing to even mention in writing, whatever they may believe privately.

Therefore, in the various permutations of antidualism, to speak about form and meaning is to speak about what amounts to two stages of the same system. "Form and meaning" really amount to something like "a structure translating another structure" in a way analogous to the way a microphone translates vibrations into electrical impulses and how an amplifier takes those impulses and retranslates them back into vibrations using a loudspeaker. The air vibrations constitute a structure, and the electrical impulses constitute another structure, and both together constitute a single system. Thus, the notion of the "meaning of an expression" amounts logically to "the structure behind a structure" or "the hidden and visible aspects of the system." Some expression has a certain structure to it (e.g., a linguistic one), and what gives rise to it is another underlying type of structure—perhaps the computational structure of neurons or the linguistic forms of society. What one calls "understanding" or "comprehension" is *another* structure interacting with the structure of the expression—again, a different structure of neurons or the like. This "structure behind structure" is the true logical form of phrases like "the meaning of the sentence" or "the intention behind an action" or any other similar statement describing utterance and interpretation, if one is unwilling to violate antidualism.

It is very important to escape from this antidualist stance, which is a dead end philosophically and has been so for a long time. One cannot passively acquiesce to it any longer. The simple act of *rejecting* what consciousness *is not* and *cannot be* is far from trivial. Ruling out the purely deterministic and/or random as a way of understanding how meaning and understanding take place is not a mere reduction of possibilities but the overcoming of a major barrier to coherence. Indeed, the deterministic/random conception of human consciousness is not common sense or self-evident but a highly restrictive and doctrinaire interpretation of human experience that renders the possibility of shared thinking or institutions (and indeed consciousness itself) inexplicable. The gap between what human beings experience themselves to be and what modern science tells them they must describe themselves to be is called, in philosophy's greatest euphemism, the "hard problem of consciousness." It is not even a problem at all. The account of human consciousness generating the "problem" is simply wrong, but there are all sorts of nonscientific reasons to pretend it is right. By rejecting the antidualist view one rescues the possibility of describing consciousness or at least approaching it without the absurdities entailed by the antidualist stance, and in so doing one loses very little except the socially constructed monopoly of scientists to proclaim philosophically on matters wherein they have no special wisdom.

What must be affirmed is something real that accounts for consciousness that does not fit into the antidualist stance. Call it a soul, call it a mind, call it a mystery, there must be *some* affirmation that modern science does not study all that is real about human beings. One must have at a minimum a conception of human consciousness that punctures antidualism.

In earlier chapters the three triads (community, practice, legacy; stability, dynamism, purpose; accounts, heuristics, norms) were discussed without reference to any particular position concerning their metaphysics. Instead, the conceptualization focused on the logical relationships between the various elements of shared thinking as well as the empirical variations within those parameters. At this point the analysis will be taken further and explore what human beings are and what shared thinking must itself actually *be* so that these features of institutions—which it is hoped will have been established at the conceptual level at least—can even be real at all. Among other things, we will see how any antidualist metaphysics renders all the necessary features of shared thinking impossible. In particular, the "structure behind structure" vision of meaning, which implies either a deterministic or a random connection between expressions and their speakers and audience, cannot coexist with any coherent notion of what makes social reality possible in the form of institutions.

Accounts, Heuristics, Norms: Ambiguity and Context

Our triad of accounts, heuristics, and norms and their empirical variation between the concrete and the abstract will allow us to identify six clearly identifiable modes of ambiguity in expression, which in turn can serve as a key for understanding the problem of ambiguity and context in general, and more specifically can help us toward understanding the implications of a "structure behind structure" metaphysics.

A main overriding question that will concern us will be the following: how can one make sense of the fact that ambiguities in expression necessarily exist (as is in fact implied by the model of shared thinking presented in this book) and that, despite that fact, meaning and understanding still occur, as is evidenced by the fact that the reader can understand the sentences in this book and sufficiently overcome its ambiguities? No deterministic/random causal nexus between meaning and expression can explain how human beings overcome ambiguity to accomplish meaning and understanding.

Let us consider each element of the triad in turn.

Accounts expressed imaginatively and accounts expressed rationally can communicate similar or overlapping meaning. They can be two sides of a similar act of description. In modern science, for example, an imaginative model such as the electron cloud is a way of representing a certain reality, and a corresponding theory or formalism such as the wave equation is the process by which the same reality is mathematically or procedurally described. Generally, in science an imaginative model is never lacking an abstract/instructional formalism for describing that model, and a formalistic or rational theory is never separate from a concrete way of imagining the theory or seeing it in a larger context or framework.[5]

A *heuristic* expressed imaginatively (such as the metaphor in philosophy of the "foundations" of knowledge, or the "structure" of an argument) allows one make inferences or to point to patterns and possibilities according to a certain modality, and it can correspond to a rationally or procedurally expressed heuristic such as formal logical arguments (deductions, inductions, extrapolations, inferences). As with descriptive accounts, the two modalities of heuristics can overlap in terms of the meaning they communicate. A philosophical metaphor such as "the structure of knowledge" captures a certain set of "arguments" in a concrete image, while a conceptual argument is a logical form that does similar problem-solving work but through a stepwise formalism. These two kinds of forms are frequently closely related to each other and in fact are never completely absent from each other. For example, the image of a structure implies a certain way of arguing about what kinds of arguments depend on which other kinds (the way a roof depends on walls and walls depend on solid foundations). Philosophical metaphors always imply an argument, and arguments always require a way of being visualized.

A *norm* that is expressed imaginatively (such as slaying a dragon, or the image of standing against the tide) enables one to think about the good, the worthwhile, and the beautiful; it conveys normative content. An allegorical expression can correspond to or overlap with rationally expressed heuristics such as maxims (e.g., "Overcome your fears" "Take the road less traveled by") and philosophical descriptions of virtues. A concrete or imaginative form (a work of art, or an exemplary heroic act) is a way of capturing a value or a preference in an image, and the rational form can be a maxim or an explanation communicating that same value or preference. The two modalities are interrelated: cultural and artistic symbols and allegories imply a way of being talked about, while maxims and moral teachings require a way of being visualized. ("Visualized" is a matter not only of color and shape but of any concrete imaginative form.)

These two modalities raise a key point about meaning and understanding: because imaginative and rational forms of thinking can have overlapping content but are expressed in different modes, as in the examples given above, it is easy to assume that the abstract form directly explains the concrete one, or that the concrete form directly explains or represents the abstract one. Indeed, this is often what one form is called upon to do with respect to the other. But one must be very careful when identifying the agent for the verb "explain" or "represent," because neither kind of form (imaginative or rational) is really an explanation or representation of the other kind of form in a *direct* manner. Rather, each is directly intelligible in its own mode, and it is only by virtue of each being understood as each was *meant to be understood* that one can speak of a concrete form "explaining" an abstract form or vice versa. The forms themselves do not explain or represent as if they were conscious agents. Rather, they are that *by which* human beings explain or represent, and that distinction is important even though it is very common for the two modes to exist together and to rely on each other, as in the examples used above: model and theory, metaphor and logical formalism, allegory and maxim.

Therefore, a verbal description of an image, for example, is not the very meaning of that image but is another modality of form whose meaning must be grasped on its own terms. Something is *meant* by the image (a scientific model, for example), and something is *meant* by the description (a related scientific theory). While that which is *meant* in both cases can have a close relationship, that connection is nevertheless not realized directly between the two forms—as if one were splitting white light through a prism to get a rainbow or recombining a rainbow with a lens to get white light. To use another example, formal logic is not a mere unfolding or disassembling of the image of a structure, and the image of a structure is not a mere projection of the concepts of formal logic onto an imaginative plane.

Or take the example of a lion as a symbol of a certain human virtue and contrast it with the verbal concept "courage." The lion is an imaginative form, and the concept "courage" is a verbal form with which one connects it. The concept of "courage" is not the meaning of the symbol of the lion, nor is the symbol of the lion a representation of the concept of courage. The concept of courage can be a *description* of what is understood by the lion symbol, but that description itself is a form with a meaning, just as the lion is a form with a meaning. The grasp of *what is meant* by the symbol of the lion is one thing, and the grasp of *what is meant* by the concept courage is another. When one talks about "courage" as a description of the lion symbol, one is really describing one's own understanding of that symbol. The symbol cannot just translate into the concept itself. When one talks about a lion as a symbol of courage, one is symbolizing or representing one's own understanding of that concept. A certain amount of common intelligible content (in Islamic thought, *maʿnā*) is understood both from the lion form and the courage formalism (although they do not share the exact same boundaries of meaning). *How* each form is intelligible, however, is different. The ability to associate a lion with the concept of courage is a connection made by virtue of the association of two *intentions* and not merely of two forms. There is no algorithm or rule to accomplish the explanation of an image in terms of a verbal description, but rather it happens by virtue of an intelligence that can grasp meaning in one form and also place that same meaning in *another* form.

Grasping of the meaning of a concrete form is an act carried out by a conscious being, not through a mechanical unpacking of one modality of form into another modality of form. Put simply, the *meaning* of a scientific model, for example, is not the verbal description of it (or the theory corresponding to it) but that which is grasped by human consciousness through the model as it was intended to be understood. The meaning is grasped, and then a human being might subsequently communicate that meaning in a verbal or syntactic form. The reverse can also happen—abstract ideas can be understood and then expressed imaginatively, being understood first through the abstract form, and subsequently being expressed by a human being through a concrete form.

In short, a symbolic representation of something is a form conveying meaning, and a verbal description is also a form conveying meaning. But neither form is downstream, as it were, of the other. Both modalities of form—concrete and abstract—are formal vehicles of mean-ing and under-stand-ing. A verbal description can help the understander grasp what is meant by a symbolic form, but the description is not that meaning itself. The meaning is what was meant by the mean-er, which is not a form but an intention that becomes expressed through a form.

❧

Not only are meanings not mechanistically or algorithmically translated between forms of one kind—such that a symbolic norm, for example, would be a mere mechanical translation of an instructional norm or vice versa—but the same forms can be used to communicate different *kinds* of meaning. That is to say, the same imaginative or rational form can be an account, a heuristic, or a norm.

Take the image of structure: one could use the image of a scaffolding as an account describing the arrangement of molecules in a metal, or as a heuristic for making epistemic claims, or again as a norm communicating the virtue of social cohesion. The very same form can be used in multiple modes and be intelligible in different ways, because there are different modes of analogy. Of course, a scaffolding might be roughly shaped like molecules, but molecules do not hang together mechanically like that and have completely nonoverlapping parts (think of how crude those stick-and-ball models are in chemistry); an argument is not *literally* a kind of spatially extended thing and the various elements are obviously not at all like the parts of a scaffolding; and the same for the symbolizing of the relationships between human beings. In each case, the form is the same but the mode of analogy is different.

One could repeat this exercise for many different kinds of form that can be deployed in descriptive, theoretical, and normative modes—for example, the images (as symbols) of a sphere, a dance, a river, a square, or a bridge all being deployed respectively as account, heuristics, and norms. The difference is not in the form but in the meaning of it and the understanding of it. Is the form being deployed to achieve descriptive truth, or is it acting like a handy processor (like some literal "rule of thumb"), or is it teaching a moral lesson—or even some combination of these? When something is *meant* by a form in shared thinking it will be meant in one or more of these three dimensions—descriptively, theoretically, or normatively.

The same holds true for rational forms as well. The sentence "That is true" could be said of something that is descriptively correct, or of something that is logically valid, or of a human action of great sincerity and loyalty. Which mode is it? To take another example, the sentence "A bird in the hand is worth two in the bush" could be a description of a state of affairs (describing how people think); it could be a problem-solving technique (a way of dealing with a workflow); and it could be a maxim (an instruction to be happy with what you have). There is no way, simply on the basis of each phrase standing alone, to judge whether it is an account, a heuristic, or a norm. If natural language is anything, it is ambiguous.

In sum, one can have *different* forms with the largely *overlapping* meaning (e.g., the lion and the concept courage), and the *same form* with *largely nonoverlapping* meanings (e.g., a spider's web as account, as heuristic, or as norm). The meaning does not deterministically lead to form, and form does not deterministically lead to understanding. But neither is the connection between meaning and form indeterminate or random. Meaning and understanding take place, because it is possible to overcome the ambiguity that this situation creates—if it weren't, you could not understand this sentence that you are reading. If constant disambiguation were not possible, communication could never occur. It should be noted that there are, of course, many different ways of classifying and analyzing ambiguity, and the present discussion uses the relationship between the three elements of the triad accounts-heuristics-norms understood in two modes in order to situate the discussion of ambiguity in the context of the model of shared thinking being established in this book.

How, then, is ambiguity overcome? *Context* immediately springs to mind as the decisive factor that enables one to navigate these ambiguities. But context is really just *more forms communicating meaning*. Context, indeed, is entirely made up of forms that one must also properly interpret in order for such forms to even be able to function as context. Any element of the context, whether it be a concrete or abstract form, would itself be ambiguous standing alone and would need its own context in order to be interpreted. A form that constitutes part of context needs context to be understood, and *that* context would need further context. How can context help one to understand what is meant by a form if the context itself is not intelligible and cannot be interpreted? Context cannot simply *be there*. The need for context is most familiar in the case of language (as can be seen in the very word "con-text" itself) but in fact applies anywhere there is mean-ing and understand-ing.

The seemingly endless process of context-requiring-context resembles the logical circle of a dictionary (as will be discussed further in chapter 6) in which every word is defined in terms of all the other words, in an ultimately closed network of loops. In the case of the dictionary, it is the lexicographer who has the moral authority to stand outside the network of loops, which is closed at the formal level but not at the meaning-and-under-standing level. The closed loop of the dictionary is a register or imprint of the ongoing activity of a language community mean-ing and understand-ing, and while it has the appearance of a closed logical circle it is in reality a part of the legacy of a community of language users practicing creatively and correctly. This is important because one understands that the dictionary could never, on its own, no matter how detailed, stand alone. There is no algorithm or rules, no sufficiently detailed if-then formalism that can enable understanding of meaning without the beings who mean and understand. When one reads a definition or a grammatical explanation, it is not like a car engine that has been disassembled and laid out. The common mistake is to imagine a definition as a direct translation of form to form. If one looks up the word "crimson" in the dictionary the definition one encounters would be its own form with its own intelligibility. If one instead asks a friend, "What is crimson?" the friend might show him a color swatch on his phone screen, which is also its own form with its own intelligibility. In both cases, one would then know what was *meant by* "crimson" by under-standing the meaning of a form.

A definition is, in fact, nothing but a specialized kind of context. "Context" is the general category to which definitions belong along with other kinds of forms that are used to disambiguate and interpret expressions. Indeed, if one were supplied with the right kinds of nonlexical context, one never would need dictionary "definitions." This is precisely how almost all language operates, since language has been around far longer than system-atic definitions have, and people learning their mother tongue almost never learn what is meant by words by consulting lexicons. Even with gigantic reference works, simply having verbal formulaic "definitions" or a registry of grammatical/syntactical rules would never be enough in the absence of all the other kinds of context in life. And each element of context must itself be interpreted as a form conveying meaning.

If the reality of meaning were a "structure behind structure" it would be impossible to properly understand how shared thinking can take place in the various modalities in which it clearly does: accounts, heuristics, and norms each existing on the spectrum from imaginative to rational. How do forms operate between the descriptive, the theoretical, and the normative? How do different kinds of forms communicate the same intelligible content (e.g., a model and a theory, a metaphor and an argument, a fable and a maxim)?

Remember that the structure-behind-structure metaphysics of consciousness allows only determinism or randomness. If the connection of meaning and expression are deterministic, then one runs into the problem of how it is that two different forms can mean the same thing, or that one form can mean two different things. If surface structure A (a form) always is linked with hidden structure B (a meaning), and if surface structure C (a form) also always links to hidden structure B (a meaning), then on what basis does one use A or C? If surface structure D (a form) links with hidden structure E (a meaning) half the time and with hidden structure F (a meaning) the other half of the time, how does one know in any particular instance if D means E or F?

If one takes recourse to "context" to break the tie in such cases, one simply defers the question, because each element of the context is itself a surface structure (a form or expression) connected with a hidden structure (a meaning), and one would have to know whether the relationship between form and meaning in the context is deterministic, random, or some combination. If one takes recourse in some further context, the problem just reappears over and over again.

Meaning Is Everywhere

If there is one thing that the Islamic tradition teaches about meaning it is that it is not just a single thing, like a single frequency of light, but reverberates along the whole spectrum. Different kinds of forms are conveying different kinds of meanings everywhere, all the time. It is really a purely philosophical choice to say that language, defined in a rigid technical sense, is the only conduit of meaning and that everything else is somehow secondary or even tertiary to what happens in the structure one calls "language." How does one draw a line around just these forms as "bearers of meaning"? The fact that philosophers cannot provide a stable demarcation between semantics and pragmatics, after decades of effort, is evidence of the fact that there is no such joint in reality as typically conceived of in modern philosophy.[6]

Consider what happens when a human being means or understands *anything*. Once one is free of antidualism, one can see that the *whole* human being means something when one expresses something and the whole human being is there when receiving and understanding and interpreting whatever form is expressed. (It might be somehow useful to pick out certain aspects of human meaning and understanding in order to study them, but that is a different question.) When you mean or understand something, the rest of you does not cease to exist but is right there at the moment of meaning and understanding. Of course, in Islamic metaphysics it is ultimately God who creates all forms, and thus all meaning is to be understood—whether in nature, or the works of human beings, or revelation—with that reality in mind. But even if one wishes to reject, metaphysically speaking, that there is meaning everywhere in that objective sense, nevertheless it is still true that a human being who intends to communicate something does not isolate that instance of meaning in some absolute way. One can (and indeed must) direct and redirect one's attention in many different ways, but one cannot detach oneself from one's own self. The whole of a human being is there where he is, even if not in his immediate consciousness. When a human being intends to say something, everything that is meaningful to him is going to reverberate in some way through the mean-ing of what he communicates. In the same way, whatever is meaningful for his audience is going to have a bearing on the understand-ing and interpretation of the thing that is expressed to him. So even if one believes, metaphysically speak-ing, that God did not create the world and that these things do not have meaning and there is no purpose or teleology in the world, nevertheless from the point of view, subjectively, of both the speaker and the audience, what sense does it make to isolate some particular factor or particular element called meaning from the rest of what is meaningful?

Essences in Light of Stability, Dynamism, Purpose

Let us now turn to a second triad in the conceptualization of institutions: stability, dynamism, and purposiveness, and see how they fare with respect to structure-behind-structure.

Without a stable connection between the form of expression and the intended meaning, no meaning could be reliably conveyed more than once. The philosopher who talks about the indeterminacy of meaning or claims to be anti-essentialist presumably means the same thing by "meaning" or "essence" with each use and relies upon a certain stability in the understanding of the audience, so claims to the contrary are logically self-undermining.[7] Moreover, context (which everyone takes to be necessary) would be of no help if the forms of the context were not also stable in *their* meaning.

Recall the "folly" discussed by Donald Davidson (chapter 1): one can pretend that a word or idea under consideration is hopelessly problematic or indeterminate only if one has the luxury of assuming that all the *other* words and ideas that explain it are clear and stable enough in their meaning, but then those very ideas are reframed as being hopelessly problematic when the philosopher's focus is turned to them. The presupposition that one can understand meaning cannot be separated from the presupposition that meaning is in some sense stable in forms, so the connection between meaning and form could not be arbitrary or random, because then it would be impossible to mean or understand anything.

But when it comes to meaning, "stable" cannot mean deterministic or mechanistic. If forms and meanings related deterministically and the relationship between the surface structure and the deeper structure remained always the same, nevertheless the world around this structure would always be changing. Think about how a language comes into contact with new vocabulary, and the turnover of old speakers and new ones, and the transformation over time of the speakers' consciousness of the world. The world is always going to be in flux, and in light of new experiences and new inputs the connection between form and meaning *has to change in order to remain the same*. Thus, if the connection between surface structure and hidden structure remained deterministically the same, it would actually cease to be stable.

Indeed, forms must also be revisable in light of meaning—that is, they must also be dynamic. Otherwise, one would be stuck in a rut of meaning, and could never say anything appropriate to a novel situation, which is what all situations are to greater and lesser degrees. That one can recognize meaning at all means that one could recognize that meaning in another form if the conditions were right. Otherwise, one has ruled out the very possibility of *re-cognition*—knowing again. Thus, the presupposition that one can understand meaning cannot be separated from the presupposition that forms are revisable in light of that meaning. If form and meaning were deterministically connected, it would be impossible to claim to understand anything new, because if something can mean only what it means and only that thing can mean that, one has not even entered into the realm of understanding at all. One is simply trapped in a mechanistic system, like a boulder rolling down a mountain.

It is obvious why a random connection between form and meaning—that is, between surface structure and deep structure—would make stability in meaning impossible, but is also renders true dynamism impossible, because it would mean that there is no constancy from expression to expression, and rather than true dynamism or creativity one would simply have random configurations following one after another, each with no connection with the last. Rationality and imagination are not the mere creation of the new or the mere possibility of change, but presuppose patterns, wholes, continuities, and constancy, all of which are ruled out by randomness or arbitrariness. If the surface structure and the hidden structure are related to each other randomly, rationality and imagination become nothing.

And unless there is a right and wrong in how forms communicate meaning—that is, fulfilling purposes—everything could mean everything, which is tantamount to saying that no meaning is possible. There would be no reason for meaning to remain stable or for meaning to change or for there to be a balance between stability and dynamism. Without wrong uses, right uses do not exist; and without right uses, there are no wrong uses. The presupposition that one can understand meaning cannot be separated from the presupposition that some forms are right and some are wrong. If the connection between form and meaning were random, or if it were rigidly mechanistic because of the "structure" underlying structure or some other metaphor describing a deterministic picture, then one would be caught either in a trap or in chaos—a clock whose hands cannot move or whose hands move randomly. In neither case is telling the *correct* time possible. Once again, the structure-behind-structure model of meaning makes real meaning and understanding impossible.

Neither Dualism nor Antidualism: Community, Practice, Legacy

An institution is nothing less than shared thinking, but it is also nothing more than shared thinking.

In chapter 2 the conceptual near neighbors of the necessary features of institutions were discussed (identity, routine, relic; ossification, plasticity, interests; assertions, reflexes, demands), but here let us speak about *metaphysical* near neighbors, especially with respect to the triad of community, practice, and legacy. Shared thinking, as an actual aspect of the world of human beings, exists between bodies and the greater reality of consciousness. Moreover, bodies and unrestricted consciousness are each in their own way necessary conditions for the realization of shared thinking. That is to say, institutions presuppose and cannot exist without bodily reality on the one hand and the full reality of consciousness on the other, which means that shared thinking cannot be reduced to bodies but does not fully encompass

consciousness either. This conceptual duality between body and consciousness is not meant to delineate some sharp metaphysical line, but rather to
make clear where shared thinking is differentiated at its "lower" bound (at
the level of bodies) and at its "upper" bound (since it does not exhaust the
reality of consciousness). Shared thinking as defined in this book is *more*
than simply bodies being bodies, but at the same time it is only an aspect
of consciousness as a whole. One does not wish to avoid one metaphysical reduction (antidualism, the notion that there is just one structure or
system some of whose parts are hidden) by committing another reduction
(the confining of consciousness to shared thinking, which winds up being
a version of substance dualism, most often a folk dualism). One therefore
must avoid both antidualism (or any material monism) and a crude substance dualism. But here one reaches a certain horizon beyond which this
book is not intended to go. The soul is where these forms of thinking exist
and where they come from, but the forms of thinking are not simply what
the soul is made of. They are an aspect of the soul but not as a rotor and
engine are parts of a helicopter. The soul as agent, the act, and the contours
of that act are not separable but neither are they reducible to each other.
Let us consider each part of this triad.

With respect to community, practice, and legacy, one can ask: What is
the mean-er or understand-er? What is mean-ing and understand-ing? And
what is the what-is-meant and what-is-understood? (What is the former
who forms the forms of thinking?)

On the one hand, the human beings who make up a community are
not simply bodies, but are realities that *mean and understand.* The relevant
aspect of this reality is the actual *faculty* or *(spiritual) organ* as opposed to
the whole human being—a conceptual separation, not a cut at the joints.
To say *thinker* is to speak in a technical sense of the aspect of human
beings that thinks. "Thinker" should not be used as a metonym for the
whole human being. The "thinker" qua participant in shared thinking is
a conceptual cross-section of the whole human reality that includes body
and consciousness.

To use the language of much of Islamic metaphysics, the "thinker" as
discussed in this book is a power(s) (*quwwah*) of the soul (*nafs*), and while
such powers may require the body to exist and function in the world, they
are not simply identical with the parts of the body qua body. While this
power does not encompass all of the faculties of human consciousness, it is
a part of consciousness and needs the rest of consciousness in order to be
what it is.[8] (The *thinker* can be thought of as a subset within the larger reality

of consciousness in a way analogous to how the "digester" is demarcated within the bodily system.) All communities coincide with groups of bodies but are not fully explainable as bodies, and it should go without saying that not all groups of human bodies are communities. Human beings need bodies to be members of a community, but thinking is not simply bodily.

Practice is also therefore an actual *act* or *activity* of *mean-ing* and *understand-ing*, and is also demarcated in two respects—between bodies and consciousness. A practice is not mere bodily change, although it coincides with it. The act of shared thinking is an aspect or dimension of a reality (human beings) that includes both bodily behavior and the unrestricted act of consciousness. Practice as thinking is not merely the bodily (visible and audible) transformations or experiences that are associated with it but is constituted by the *acts* of the thinker resulting in thoughts. It would not include, for example, bodily sensations such as pain or the desire to sleep; these are part of consciousness but not strictly speaking in the conceptual space of thinking. But also, not everything that happens in and by consciousness can be reduced to that aspect of consciousness that here is conceptualized as shared thinking. It is not enough to see human bodily behaviors repeated and modified. The changing tides are not the *practice* of the moon and sea. The precession of the stars is an example of repetition and modification, but it is not a practice. The repetition, modification, survival, reinforcement, and disappearance of certain patterns of bodily behavior cannot alone constitute the act of thinking. All practices are aggregates of behaviors—bodies moving and interacting—but not all collective behaviors constitute a practice. Yes, bodily movements need to happen for practice to take place (even if internal to one human being), but again that is not to say that practice is merely bodily. To conceive of human beings as giant clusters of mechanisms renders utterly arbitrary the demarcation of practice from nonpractice, or even behavior from nonbehavior.

A legacy must necessarily be made up of certain artifacts and products, but the *what-is-meant* or *what-is-understood* are not the objects, sounds, or glyphs themselves qua bodies, and at the same time not every object of consciousness is reducible to the forms of thinking as defined here as accounts, heuristics, and norms.

Once again there are two demarcations to be made. A legacy is conveyed between human beings through tangible and intangible bodily realities— writing, gestures, objects, buildings, sounds. Bodily artifacts or sounds or movements qua bodies are not in the space of shared thinking, regardless of the role that they play in the life of the institution. Artifacts come into the space of shared thinking when they are *understood*. To put it in Aristotelian terms, it is the *morphe* and not the *hyle* of the artifact that is bequeathed and inherited in the space of institutions. Bodies are passed from human being to human being and movements are echoed and repeated like waves in the sea across time and space, but these bodily facts are only a *condition* for the bequeathing and inheriting of a legacy in an institution, not the actual legacy itself. In this definition, a book is not part of an institution's legacy qua physical object but is so as an encoded communication between two human beings (although a book can also convey other meanings and purposes besides what is written in it, in its physical beauty, for example). It is the book as *thoughts thinkers think* that is the legacy. A mosque has the form of a mosque, but as a product or legacy of an institution it is not the stone or wood or the physical fact of the mosque that makes it an aspect of institution but rather its presence in the memory, imagination, and care of a community. But also, the entire content of consciousness (indeed the content of thinking) cannot be reduced to what is meant and understood as a social reality between human beings.

It should be clear that the very rejection of both antidualism and substance dualism amounts to a negation of the structure-behind-structure way of looking at form and meaning (or expression and meaning). The dimension or aspect of human reality where meaning and understanding (shared thinking) takes place is not a deterministic or random structure of any kind at all, and therefore could never fit the bill for what passes as that thing that underlies form in the antidualist picture. The structure-behind-structure idea is ruled out because neither determinism nor randomness can work, and so one must ask what can be left that can be characterized by neither antidualism nor substance dualism?

Synopsis

- In the various permutations of antidualism, "meaning" amounts to a hidden structure beneath the visible structure of expressions such as human language, constituting a "structure-behind-structure." Nothing outside this system can first "mean" or later "understand."

- The relationship between the underlying structure called "meaning" and the apparent structure of expressions is either deterministic, random, or a combination of those two causal patterns. No other possibility exists within antidualist constraints.

- This structure-behind-structure metaphysics of consciousness renders all the necessary features of institutions impossible, because no deterministic/random causal nexus between meaning and expression can explain meaning and understanding.

- Ambiguity is a necessary and unavoidable feature of the acts of meaning and of understanding, and yet this ambiguity is in fact sufficiently overcome, which antidualism cannot explain.

- Context is usually cited as that which overcomes ambiguities, but context is a tapestry of meaningful forms that requires disambiguation, and thus it does not help us to overcome the logical dead end of structure-behind-structure metaphysics.

- The structure-behind-structure model, and its deterministic and/or random causal nexus, cannot explain how institutions remain stable, how they change, or how they are oriented toward a purpose.

- Antidualism as a metaphysics and as a method must be rejected in favor of a metaphysics of consciousness and a methodological stance that is neither antidualist/monist nor substance dualist, i.e., which neither reduces thinking to bodies nor consciousness to mere thinking.

- Institutions exist in a realm—a cross-section of reality—that is more than mere bodies but less than the total reality of consciousness, while at the same time presupposing the existence of both and being metaphysically dependent upon both.

Chapter 5

The Metaphysics of Paradox

When it comes to saying anything affirmatively about that reality which means and understands, one runs up against perennial difficulties. There is something mysterious about human consciousness itself that makes it challenging to describe or to conceptualize in the straightforward way one might define a cat or a helicopter. More to the point for the argument at hand, those difficulties do not disappear or become trivial when one turns to the social realm. Indeed, these mysteries of consciousness do not go away, nor do the relevant ultimate presuppositions matter less, if one chooses instead to look at human beings interacting in large groups. Why should an aggregate of human beings' consciousnesses be less puzzling to understand than the consciousness of a single human being? Why should a "we" be more straightforward to conceptualize than an "I"?

Consciousness is indeed intrinsically mysterious and puzzling, and therefore no analytically or theoretically useful conception of it (if it is to be more than a mere idiom and is actually going to be explanatory with respect to other ideas or areas of thought) can exist that does not acknowledge some kind of paradox or mystery, and it follows that a proper conceptualization of social reality ought not ignore the problems related to imagining consciousness.

What Thinking Does versus What Thinking Is

Whether one calls it soul, spirit, intellect, mind, or something else, this reality of consciousness has commonly been conceived of by those who have taken it as a given as some kind of mystery, and it has typically been represented or symbolized as a "breath" or "spirit" or "light" or some other allegorical description that placed it outside the usual workings of everyday bodies. Such notions were recognized to be metaphors or symbols. Metaphysicians in various philosophical and religious traditions have had a lot to say about the soul but mostly have been concerned with what a soul *does*, and less with what a soul actually *is* except allegorically or symbolically, not uncommonly being reliant upon revelation or tradition.

Indeed, a great deal of metaphysics consists of refinements and taxonomies of the powers and abilities of this reality, but that kind of functional exploration is different from having a descriptive account or model of the soul of any detail or depth that is accessible directly to one's imagination. As an analogy for this difference between *does* and *is,* think of the "powers" of a smartphone. Many ordinary phone users can give a relatively sophisticated description of what a smartphone can do and how to use it, but how many can conceptualize the nature of solid-state storage, transistors, or even what the inside of a battery looks like? One can talk at length about the phone's software's powers and abilities without the slightest basic conception of what "software" is, never mind how it is written. Similarly, most talk about the soul has been about its powers, and descriptive accounts have tended to be explicit or implicit acknowledgments of its mystery, usually expressed in symbolic language. If one says, for example, that the soul is the "form" of the body, how different is that from saying that "software makes hardware work" or "the wind blows"? To imagine what it does is different from imagining what it is. Indeed, most of the intellectual work devoted to imagining what a soul might be (as a descriptive matter) is really about describing that horizon where bodily reality meets the soul (if it meets it at all). That means that a body conceived of as clockwork-mechanical will allow a certain kind of soul to be imagined, while a body conceived of as a paradoxical system of mutually entangled fields and indeterminate particles allows for another kind of soul to be conceived of.[1]

For antidualists, the philosophical gap between what consciousness *does* and what consciousness *is* has been essentially closed. They believe they already know much about what consciousness does, and in broad strokes it is not impossible to imagine. What remains is to work out the details of which neuron does what and how the brain is influenced by the surrounding biological and chemical structure. Antidualism does not see any mystery at all, nor any basic obstacle in imagining consciousness. Memory is *this* kind of cell interacting *this way,* happiness come from *this chemical* doing *this particular thing,* and so forth. One is told (or meant to assume) that one day soon human beings will be able to map the neuronal structure of the brain and upload our consciousness into a computer—perhaps not with current technology, but certainly at some future point through the triumph of human ingenuity and "artificial intelligence."[2] Consciousness is understandable the way complex machines are understandable. There is no insurmountable gap between what consciousness does and what it is. If there is any mystery, it is expressed in terms of "We do not understand it *yet.*" Something that one does not *yet* understand (in the manner of other things like digestion) is not a mystery or paradox but a mere problem. It may be that one does not have a fully-worked-out schematic of the "cognitive" or "linguistic" system, but that is a question of details, not principles. There is no essential paradox or mystery about "endocrine" or "vascular," and there is none about "cognitive" or "linguistic" either. These terms do not denote consciousness in the ordinary sense that you or I would think, but rather refer to a certain processing system with its inputs and outputs that is located mostly in the brain—not symbolically or allegorically but right down to the atom.[3] A few notable outliers lack the general optimism of this picture, but they are swimming against the tide of antidualism and tend to be marginalized within philosophy. Some postmodernists may not like the tone or overconfidence that sometimes attends to this erasure of mystery, but as noted earlier they remain staunchly antidualist all the same.

However, even with the tremendous optimism that many antidualists exhibit when describing individual consciousness, they can still put themselves in check by ideas like the "hard problem of consciousness" and other puzzles that still get attention in the philosophical literature about the mind. No such "hard problem" seems to arise in the realm of social reality, however, that might cause one to even lightly apply the brakes with respect to antidualism. In the social realm, metaphysics is a settled question or an ignored one. This uncritical attitude turns out to be highly consequential because the difficulties of conceptualizing consciousness at the individual level, which are already far greater than most are willing to accept, do not disappear at the collective level, and indeed many ways only become amplified and more intractable. Indeed, when it comes to thinking about or trying to imagine consciousness, certain conceptual problems pop up and keep popping up no matter how assiduously one tries to clarify them. Even within the confines of the antidualist stance, the conceptualization of human thinking presents genuine puzzles, and these turn out to be very important to the conceptualization of social reality.

Paradoxes

The exploration of the nature of human consciousness is the act of the conceptualizer conceptualizing the conceptualizer in its very conceptualizing, the definer defining the definer in its very ability to define, the theorizer theorizing the theorizer in the very attribute of theorizing. It is a scale being called upon to weigh and calibrate itself in its very act of calibration. Related to this eye-seeing-itself problem are certain logical difficulties in defining or even thinking about certain ultimate ideas. Think about where one finds oneself as soon as one sets out to define "knowledge" or "truth" or "goodness": one has to presuppose that the definition itself is an example of something known, or something true, or something good. If the definition is itself known, or true, or good (i.e., worthwhile), how does one know, or how is it true, or how is it good *before* one has a definition of knowledge, truth, and goodness? What makes the definition of knowledge *known?* What makes the definition of truth *true?* What makes the definition of goodness *worthwhile?* These kinds of puzzles do not arise in defining "cat" or "helicopter."

Some philosophers speak of the paradox of subjectivity, namely, that the subject can be aware of itself, about which Kant said, "It is simply impossible to explain, even though it is an undoubted fact."[4] Husserl identified "the paradox of human subjectivity: being a subject for the world and at the same time being an object in the world."[5] Whatever the relationship of subject to object, of knower and knowledge and known, is, it is not like any other relationship one can imagine between objects in the sensible world outside of us.

Consider also the so-called is-ought gap or the fact-value dichotomy. Hume famously said there is no way to get from the *is* to the *ought,* and in one sense he was right, but that is like saying there's no way to get from change to identity, or from self-as-object to self-as-subject, yet they are ever-present features of consciousness. It is typical to treat consciousness as though in the case of perception and memory it were like a photographic plate, and in the case of reason and imagination it were like a calculator, and in the case of ethics and aesthetic it were like a magnet pulled this way and that. But if one deeply examines the nature of these aspects of consciousness one realizes that they are not really like separate modules or parts of a system at all. Obviously the argument in support of this claim cannot be made here, but suffice it to say that the true nature of the so-called is-ought problem is not "How to derive an ought from an is?," since one has to define the nature of the "deriving," which is not at all settled, but rather "What is that reality that undeniably includes both the *is* and the *ought* such that they always seem to go together?" It might seem that things like "facts" and "values" are necessarily separate, and a lot of modern philosophy is built on that assumption that to the degree that one is believing or stating a fact, one cannot be believing or stating a value. In truth, even as a logical matter, the is-ought problem is better formulated as a triad of *is, can,* and *ought,* since the *can* has tended to be absorbed conceptually into either the *is* or the *ought.* But in actual thinking there are no pure is, can, or ought beliefs or statements. They presuppose each other at every level, and they can be considered separately only as a conceptual matter. This line of thinking cannot be fully pursued here, but my claim is that whereas *outside* of consciousness, as it were on the page, the *is, can,* and *ought* are mutually exclusive contraries, *inside* consciousness they are mutually implicative and copresent at every level.[6]

Yet another persistent mystery of consciousness has to do with the relationship of concrete and abstract, or between reason and imagination, between form and meaning in the technical sense that can be found in Islamic philosophy, which can also be seen in the perennial problem of universals and particulars. If universals are real, where are they and what are they? What are numbers? Are mathematical entities discovered or invented? When it comes to the bundle of closely related pairs such as universal and particular, abstract and concrete, imagination and reason, meaning and form, there is little that is meaningful that can be said briefly, but it is worth pointing out that Islamic metaphysicians usually assume that the soul has the ability to perceive, remember, and generate both formal essences having shape, color, and extension, as well as formless essences that have no extension but are nevertheless perceptible by the soul and are objectively real.[7] They are two different modalities of perceptibles. Chapter 4 alluded to the fact that there are no purely concrete essences, nor purely abstract ones in thinking, but that the two poles go together always. Modern philosophy has tried to place these two poles in different realms in one way or another since Descartes and Galileo, and Kant especially permanently demoted the realm of the imagination to the subjective. But the claim here is simply that, despite seeming to be two different things, there seems to be no concept into which they can reduce; they are undeniably experienced together. If consciousness were straightforward, such questions would not defy philosophers' attempt to clarify them for thousands of years.

These examples show that there are things about consciousness that are experienced as indubitably real but that defy conceptualization or representation. They are, to borrow Kant's phrasing, "Simply impossible to explain, even though it is an undoubted fact." More specifically, when trying to conceive of the experience of consciousness, one is compelled to reach for mutually implicative contraries—whether those contraries turn out to be abstract concepts or concrete metaphors. In the world of objects outside of us, there are certain contraries that are mutually exclusive and cannot logically coexist—being a square and being a circle, for example. But in the experience of consciousness, some contraries seem to demand each other's presence, such as the same thing being both subject and object at the same time; the *is* and the *ought* (and the *can*) always going together; the inseparability of the concrete and the abstract. The notion of "mutually implicative contraries" is a way of demarcating a genuine paradox from mere contradiction or irrationality.

Consider the well-worn allegory of Flatland, an entire realm that exists in what to us would be a single plane with no thickness.[8] For the beings in that two-dimensional world the two halves of any circle can be seen only one at a time. According to the universal experience of Flatlanders, to see the right half of the circle is to necessarily *not* see the left half, and vice versa. In Flatland the universal experience of the left or right halves one at a time might be characterized by a kind of either-or logical law that everyone would be obliged to accept as self-evident.

But Spacelanders observing the circle from beyond that two-dimensional plane, within three spatial dimensions of Spaceland, which also includes the entire plane-realm of Flatland, not only *can* see both halves of the circle at the same time, but *must* see the whole circle anytime one can see any part of it (with the exception of being in the plane of the circle, of course). Such a circle is always entirely in view to them. That means that what is logically impossible in Flatland (seeing the left and right halves of a circle at the same time) is logically necessary in Spaceland. For beings in the two-dimensional world, the notion of "seeing the right half and left half at once" would be a paradoxical utterance, violating the rules of that reality, and would be truly not conceivable in the minds of the denizens of that realm, even though it is *undeniable* from the vantage point of the Spacelanders. Seeing both halves at once is thus either logically *impossible* or logically *necessary*, depending on whether one is in the plane of the circle or outside of it.

One's direct and unmediated experience of certain features of consciousness, such as the identity of self-as-object and self-as-subject, is akin to that of a Spacelander seeing a circle in a plane in three dimensions, and such experience is neither puzzling nor not-puzzling because one is simply living it. But one's ability to think *about* those features of consciousness is akin to that of a Flatlander stuck in two dimensions trying to say something about that same circle, and the puzzles and difficulties arise in trying to imagine or conceive or define an entity that keeps showing up but which one lacks the tools to even think about.

Even if someone wishes to deny that the puzzling features of consciousness mentioned above are genuinely paradoxical and mysterious—and the arguments in favor of that point cannot all be made here—one can still accept a weaker version of the argument, by acknowledging that these aspects of consciousness lack convergent analytical solutions one way or another as a historical matter. The nature of subjectivity, the is-ought problem, and the relationship of the concrete and abstract (and other examples exist) continue to generate ever renewed attempts to properly conceptualize them. Even if one wants to avoid the stronger label "paradox" or "mystery," one can accept a weaker assumption that these features are stubbornly perplexing or defy definition, and the overall thrust of the argument of this chapter still holds, namely, that (1) human thinking is very hard (or indeed impossible) to clearly conceptualize, (2) that human beings thinking *together* is unlikely to be easier, and (3) that the difficulties in the former have a direct relationship with the difficulties in the latter.

Either way, at the level of individual consciousness there is no possibility of a "solution" or convergent account of consciousness, but one will always run into mutually implicative contraries in order to attain anything like a comprehensive or meaningful description. Moreover, these paradoxical features are not marginal but central and profoundly important questions pertaining to knowledge, understanding, morality, and rationality. For our purposes here, it is also important that that which is most paradoxical in consciousness is also most important in the conceptualization of institutions. After all, what is a culture or a religion if it is not concerned with ultimate questions of what is real, what is possible, what is worthwhile, and how these realities are related to each other?

Figures of Speech

These reminders about the paradoxicalness of consciousness are necessary in order to understand fully the significance of the conceptualization of institutions from chapter 2. Let us therefore make a few remarks about how the terms "civilization," "culture," "tradition," and "religion" usually are used ambiguously as *figures of speech*.

As chapters 1 and 2 made clear, one of the weaknesses of existing conceptualizations of our tetrad of metaphysical institutions is that there is no conceptual glue to hold together the disparate elements of which they consist other than *I know it when I see it*. That is, the definitions that aim toward comprehensiveness and complexity tend to be composed not only of several things but of more than one category of thing—for example, rules, norms, artifacts, systems, people, states of affairs, technologies, ideas, and behaviors. Part of the reason for this hodgepodge approach is that those who wrestle with such conceptualizations do not account for the fact that institutions are constituted by shared thinking, and that thinking itself is not a thing that can be conceptualized like a complex physical system. Rather than taking stock of the conceptual difficulties that are always going to be attached to consciousness, those who theorize large institutions treat them as if they were complex machines rather than (at least partially) paradoxical and mysterious entities.

The conceptualization of institutions offered in chapter 2 attempts to mitigate these difficulties by making the elements of the definition conform to the principles of mutual irreducibility, mutual implication, and mutual distinctness, which are meant to shield the conceptualization from certain forms of ambiguity. (Chapter 4 was then meant to outline the metaphysics that makes that conceptualization possible.) These principles are important because the interactions of ordinary objects become more complex very differently from the way paradoxical objects become more complex. It is not more difficult to conceptualize a jar of a million marbles than it is a jar of one hundred marbles. Conceptualizing a windmill and conceptualizing a helicopter is just a matter of a certain *amount* of complexity. A powerful-enough human imagination can scale up from one to the other. Or take the example of musical performance: There are people who can play a melody on a piano with one hand, but they cannot make their left hand play something different in order to play in counterpoint. But one can then overcome that inability and play with two hands doing different things as part of a greater whole. Then there are people who can not only play with two hands but can also improvise in real time with two hands. Some musicians can play a pipe organ in which their two feet are doing something different from their two hands as part of a whole imagined act of musical creation, a feat most pianists would struggle with at first. And then there are rare figures such as J. S. Bach, whose musical imagination was so powerful that he could *improvise* a performance using two hands and two feet. The same faculty of human imagination can become capacious enough to do things unbelievably complex in the eyes of others, but what Bach could do did not breach the very category of playing a musical instrument. His was the same human imagination, albeit a massively developed and refined one. Playing with two hands and two feet is complex but still, for certain people, a fully imaginable whole. A master of a complex craft does not take it step by step but is able to "see" or "hear" or "feel" the whole as a whole. Such feats of imagination might be out of reach for most human beings, but not all of them.

But a paradoxical object, like consciousness/thinking, *begins* by being unimaginable as a whole. Everyone experiences consciousness, but there is no one who is able to think *about* the mutually implicative contraries of consciousness all together at once while the rest of us have to struggle to train our imagination. That is the very nature of paradox as defined here, namely that something can be thought of only by successive or opposing concepts brought together. In order to talk about it with some sense of fullness, *multiple* contrary concepts will always be necessary. (This irreducible complexity means that if one speaks about the reality in question the reality will always be ambiguous in relation to the concepts used to explain it.)

It follows that, by scaling up what is already not fully imaginable as whole, one is going to end up with something that is *still* unimaginable as a whole, and in fact even harder to imagine because of the added complexity. One is dealing with an aggregate of realities that are *already* not fully comprehensible in nonparadoxical terms, so why should millions of such realities be any less paradoxical? Scaled up to that level, the rejection or abandonment of mystery and paradox leads to kitchen-sink collections of seemingly discrete entities that somehow all fit under a single label such as "culture" but that have no clear relationship with each other aside from the fact that one *knows* that they belong together.

It may seem that the ambition of the conceptualization from chapter 2 is overcome this problem and somehow capture the whole reality all at once. But really what the model does—and all it can do—is offer an analytical procedure or heuristic, just like the definition of a circle would function for a Flatlander. In Flatland, for example, to say "circular" is necessarily a kind of figure of speech in the minds of two-dimensional beings who can imagine only semicircles and who can think only of a whole circle by means of a heuristic or procedure—*first* by thinking of a left semicircle (let's say), and *then* thinking of a right semicircle, and then labeling those two acts of imagination as a single thing called a "circle" but without being able to capture it in thought as a whole thing. They cannot actually see or think of a circle but can only aggregate two separate acts of thinking and give that aggregation a name. A whole circle is, to Flatlanders, a theorized (and paradoxical) entity, not an experienced one, and "left-semicircle" and "right-semicircle" are irreducibly complex concepts. For them there is no way to resolve the two into a unifying image, and yet they know that the two concepts go together. By analogy, for many scholars, to call something "religious" or "cultural" is like a Flatlander calling something "circular," which is to say it serves as a kind of mnemonic or heuristic for a certain procedure of steps to get one's imagination around something that one cannot properly imagine as a whole all at once. What this means practically is that when one thinks "culture" or speaks about "cultural" (or religious, etc.) one is really thinking about one aspect of an irreducible whole, and our model provides a way of examining what aspect that might be at any given time.

So, the four concepts of our tetrad turn out to be figures of speech of a certain kind, but it is not immediately obvious what category they fit into. The two best candidates are *synecdoche* and *metonym*. A synecdoche is typically defined as an expression in which a larger whole is used to refer to only a part of that whole, as when one says, "Brazil won the world cup," and it can also mean the reverse, where a part is used to signify a whole, as when one calls a worker a "hired hand." A metonym is usually defined as something concrete that is associated with a more abstract concept, such as calling the monarchy "the Crown" or calling the American administration "the White House." The way that our tetrad of concepts relates to the entities within them resembles synecdoche in the sense that when one says something like "a religious practice" one has in mind only *some* of what is signified by religion, and so it might be thought of as a whole signifying a part. But calling something religious also seems to be something like the reverse of a metonym as conventionally defined, whereby an abstract concept is used to designate particular things instead of particular things signifying a larger abstraction. In any case, there is no reason to demand too much precision of definition here, since "synecdoche" and "metonym" are just conventions for naming certain kinds of naturally occurring figurative language. It is not crucially important whether they are classified as metonym, synecdoche, or something else. It is necessary only to accept that in their conventional usage, civilization, culture, religion, and tradition are always and necessarily figurative instances of folk language. There is nothing wrong with such figures of speech, and it would be impossible to have much language without them, but part of our concern in this book is whether these concepts have not only meaning but also certain kinds of *analytical* or *theoretical power*.

One uses simple names for complex realities all the time. But it is one thing to use rich concepts to bundle lots of things together, and it is quite another to use that bundle as if it were a prism by which to differentiate and analyze *other* things. There is nothing wrong with using capacious ideas such as culture and civilization, so long as one understands their limitations and does not call upon them to do explanatory work they cannot accomplish. The level of theorization necessary to assert "Islam is a world religion like Christianity" is far lower than the explanatory precision necessary to say, as part of a scholarly argument, "This is a cultural idea, not a religious one" or "Here is the line between Islamic and Islamicate." It is one thing to be able to point to the gibbous and crescent moon and say "These are lunar phases," and quite another to say of an object one finds in the desert, "This rock is a lunar meteorite." The term "lunar" in each instance is explanatory only within an appropriately developed theoretical framework. In the case of lunar phases ordinary folk knowledge is enough, but in the case of lunar meteorites a high level of specialized theory is necessary.

The concepts of religion, civilization, culture, and tradition denote realities so enormous and complex that, in order to say anything meaningful one must necessarily be speaking about some aspect or other of the reality in question, to the exclusion of other aspects. Such a claim seems intuitive enough, but the point being made here goes farther than that. The ambiguity of concepts such as religion and civilization is not only contingent owing to the quantity of individual elements (as in the case of a helicopter) that one cannot think about all at once, but rather is necessary and inescapable because the most unambiguous possible conceptualization is going to begin from mutually implicative contraries, and no powerful enough imagination will ever be able to overcome it.

It follows logically, when one can only refer to a reality using irreducibly complex concepts, that one will use one concept at a time to think about that reality. Thus, in any given instance one will inevitably (and understandably) use one aspect to refer to the whole, and disambiguating will always be necessary. The disambiguation necessary for qualifiers like religious, cultural, civilizational, and traditional is quite consequential, since this family of terms can refer to not only many things but also to things that are different in kind and in ontology. This ambiguity is even more consequential in light of the fact that the underlying terms have no consensus definition.

Therefore, whenever one invokes that reality by name for the sake of being *explanatory* in relation to something else, such as calling something a *religious* idea or a *cultural* norm, one is necessarily invoking some aspect and excluding the other aspects even if those aspects are all coming in rapid succession or are in close proximity in one's mind. It is impossible to actually use the term "cultural" (especially when it is being used analytically to further specify something else) to refer to all aspects of what is designated by "culture" at any one time. Rather, one is denoting *one* aspect of it while *presupposing* the others. Which one?

Our model also shows that, after one disambiguates and makes clear which aspect is meant, the remaining aspects are necessarily presupposed in that which is named or included. To recall an earlier analogy, one cannot *simultaneously* identify or even think about the altitude, latitude, and longitude of a helicopter, but when you identify one you are inescapably presupposing the presence of the other two. Unlike a part of a machine, one cannot exist except in the presence of the other two.

The principles of mutual irreducibility, mutual implication, and mutual distinctness of the various dimensions of shared thinking are regulative principles that help negotiate the puzzling nature of collective consciousness at scale. The proper understanding (or at least, acknowledgment) of the paradoxical nature of consciousness prevents the illusion that somehow one can *converge* on a certain kind of list-like definition of things such as culture or religion, and allows one to be realistic about the nature of its complexity. My claim is that by holding to the three logical principles, one can manage and regulate the ambiguities and difficulties involved without sacrificing complexity and flexibility, allowing one to scale from individual consciousness all the way out to large institutions. If one is beginning from something paradoxical and then one wants to conceptualize not only *it* but many such things interacting, it makes sense to use the same logical principles. Modern philosophy is at least open to the paradoxes of consciousness at the individual level, and still struggles to make sense of them, but when it comes to the social realm the social sciences seem to want to treat collective consciousness as an ordinary object.

When the disciplining effects of these three principles are not present, the individual concepts needed for any complex conception of institutions become fragmented from each other and then each one loses its intrinsic connection with related concepts and their boundaries become arbitrary. One loses any conceptual glue and instead has to resort to I-know-it-when-I-see-it and use kitchen-sink definitions (see the end of chapter 1). Moreover, when one relies upon nonparadoxical mechanical metaphors such as structure and system, one is left without any way of seeing (or at least conceptualizing) the cohesion, wholeness, and bounds of these things we call cultures and religions and traditions.

The Model of Physical Science

One reason why the social sciences have tended to fail to properly deal with the mysteries of conceptualizing consciousness is that they have tended to model their own activity on a very particular mode of physical science. Since the nineteenth century the effort to make the social sciences (and, to a lesser degree, the humanities) "scientific" has usually meant striving toward (but rarely reaching) a certain narrow mode of mathematical formalism and employing imaginative metaphors largely borrowed (often recklessly and with great distortion) from the physical sciences, especially "structure."[9] Many scholars in international relations, economics, history, and sociology have long lamented the adoption of methodologies and techniques that originated in the physical sciences that can send research and theorizing in unhelpful directions and produce results that are often deeply flawed. (No doubt the replication crisis is partly due to this.) "Physics envy" has led many in the social sciences and even in the humanities to adopt many poorly adapted metaphors and models and apply them to human affairs. This is not the place to get into the methods,[10] but general points related to the conceptualization of institutions are very relevant. Our concern here will be to explore the more basic philosophical questions of how prediction differs from understanding and how physical science and social science each leverage direct experience to discover hidden properties or entities.

In physical science there has long been an acceptance that one can predict what one does not fully grasp. This gap in modern science began with Newton, who lamented that he could not say what gravity *is* ("I frame no hypotheses"),[11] even though his theory of gravitation could predict the motion of bodies subject to it. It was a departure from the standards of early modern science to which Newton himself subscribed, which demanded that the workings of bodies be fully intelligible and imaginable in the sense of resembling a machine that an artisan could make. Over time, modern science eventually grew to accept that this gap between predictive theories and descriptive understanding was inevitable. In physics it is now taken as a given that the entities extrapolated from experience (hidden or theorized entities like electrons) are so unlike ordinary objects as to be unimaginable. Physicists today have an incredible power of prediction and manipulation of certain hidden properties of things, but they have accepted a lack of understanding about *what* they are predicting. Whatever electrons are, for example, their behavior can be predicted with incredible accuracy under experimental conditions, but no one claims to *grasp* what an electron is.

There are many phenomena in science that can be predicted and put to use, but understanding and intelligibility are not always a part of it. Basic notions such as "force" and "field" are used with great flexibility and functionality, but they are not things that anyone can imagine and are really just metaphors meant to capture certain patterns of behavior. As physicist Alan Lightman notes, "At least Copernicus understood that the Earth was a ball and had seen other balls move. The objects of physics today, by contrast, are principally known as runes in equations or blips from our instruments . . . [and] are far removed from human sensory experience."[12] The social sciences, for their part, really ought to be the inverse of the physical sciences, in that they should aim to understand what one cannot usually predict, but increasingly this is not the case.

Consider, for example, how one conceives of the relationship of individuals and aggregates. A typical assumption in the physical sciences is that with enough data points and with the right framework for interpreting that data, the behavior of large aggregates of individually unpredictable entities can be made predictable; in fact, the larger the data set, the more predictable its overall nature and trajectory will become. For example, one cannot predict the outcome of a single fair coin flip, but one can predict the statistical distribution of thousands of such flips. One can never predict where an electron will strike a photographic plate, but given many thousands of runs one can paint the exact shape of their distribution. One cannot predict the behavior of any particular cell as it travels in a blood vessel, but one can predict the amount and pressure of the blood that will flow through it. The rule of thumb is that the predictability and intelligibility of a system, taken as a whole, increases with the number of entities involved. The unpredictable or even indeterminate behavior of the individual elements cancel each other out at sufficient scale.

This statistical relationship between parts and wholes is also relevant to the behavior of everyday objects. Someone who can accurately calculate the trajectory of a baseball succeeds in *predicting* where it will land, but not by virtue of *understanding* all the forces at play such as the gravitational pull of the trees, or time dilation, or how its particles are entangled with other particles in the universe. The calculation of a parabolic arc is strongly predictive in one respect, but is weakly descriptive in a total sense. If one runs a double-slit electron experiment ten thousand times, one will be able to *predict* the distribution of the next ten thousand runs with very high accuracy, but that will still not tell you what an electron is.

Many social scientists will approach human aggregates as if they were analogous to such physical systems, by treating them as if they were made up of individually unpredictable or incomprehensible individuals (human beings) whose idiosyncrasies will tend to cancel each other out at large enough aggregates and that can therefore be intelligible the way that human-scale objects function in the world. The strange or unpredictable properties can thus be ignored at the right scale.

But this heuristic is misleading. One can poll ten thousand people in a population of millions in order to predict with reasonable accuracy the distribution of views of that entire population on that question, but that is not the same as understanding what human beings are and what accounts for the fact that some people hold one view as opposed to another. "In situation x, most people will do y" provides little understanding on its own outside of a descriptive understanding of what human beings are and hence what their potentialities are in some narrow domain. Predicting aggregates of decisions is not the same as understanding them, although such predictions can have their utility.

The intuition that strange properties or unpredictable behaviors can be cancelled out at the right scale originates in a process from modern science (physics especially): one begins from ordinary-scale objects and zooms in microscopically or zooms out macroscopically and discovers hidden properties that are not immediately apparent and appear only under carefully contrived experiment. The unstated and unconsidered assumption is that large aggregates of human beings can be studied or theorized without any regard to the difficulties of properly conceiving of what makes human beings what they are.

One might study human decisions with the same statistical methods used to study dice rolls, but that tells you only how human decisions result in a pattern akin to dice rolls. Moreover, statistical analysis of human behavior is often not the result of careful experiment but results from subjective choices about how to analyze a preexisting data set, where questions asked are reverse engineered from interesting results, a major problem in social science research.

There is also the question of paradox in physical science. As the example of quantum mechanics shows, when modern science predicts without needing to understand, this acceptance often takes the form of embracing a certain level of paradox. Indeed, in the modern world there is nothing inherently disreputable about paradox so long as the paradoxical entities are somehow predictable or can be put to use by scientists. Modern physics offers quite famous examples of paradoxes that fit the definition offered earlier, and physicists affirm that certain basic features of physical reality are paradoxical and even unpredictable. They accept mutually implicative contraries (e.g., wave-particle duality) and then find ways of working with them without erasing that paradoxical nature. Paradox, for the last century anyway, has not been treated as a barrier to understanding in quantum mechanics and relativity, and in fact has gone from a troubling failure of intelligibility to become something of a hallmark of cutting-edge science. In practice, physicists will accept the full implications of paradox *first* and then theorize and pursue science on the basis of that.

Physicists, remember, start with nonparadoxical ordinary objects (lab equipment and falling stones), study their behavior, use complex mathematics and experiment to infer strange and mysterious properties, and then conclude that seemingly nonparadoxical objects in fact have paradoxical and mysterious properties that are hidden from direct experience. In the classic double-slit experiment, one theorizes entities called electrons behaving alternately as tiny particles and also as extended waves, but it is important to remember that is that one using the concepts of "particle" and "wave" to analyze a non-wave/non-particle phenomenon that is neither wave nor particle in the sense of ordinary objects such as water waves and tiny grains of sand. Electrons are neither of those. But in the aggregate many electrons leave traces in our ordinary world as a certain pattern making them wave-*like* or particle-*like*.

Here is one place where conceptualizers of *social* reality often go wrong: In contrast to modern physicists, who take everyday objects and infer paradoxical properties, social scientists take *already* paradoxical objects (human beings interacting in large collectivities), recast them as nonparadoxical objects (deterministic or random systems), and then infer from that conception certain properties of institutions that conform to the properties of deterministic or random systems. But there is a key difference between the two—a veritable inversion. At ordinary scales, one can treat a baseball like a Newtonian object. A baseball is still subject to quantum and relativistic effects, but at its size and at earthbound velocities these effects are either too small relative to other forces or they cancel each other out for most purposes. Physicists are justified in treating baseballs as nonparadoxical entities (which are revealed to have paradoxical properties under experiment) because they actually *directly* interact with and experience baseballs as such.

Unlike the case with a physical system, when it comes to human beings what is first known to us is not the aggregate pattern but the paradoxical reality itself—the mystery is experienced first and then one tries to discover how its aggregates behave. With subatomic particles, one knows how the aggregates behave first and then one tries to discover the nature of the paradox of its constituents.

But there is no reason to suppose that anything like the cancellation of paradoxical properties at a certain scale happens with human collectivities. The way particles scale up to baseballs is *not* the way human beings scale up to civilizations. Philosophers have no business treating institutions as nonparadoxical systems made up of paradoxical entities (human beings' thinking), for the simple reason that no philosopher directly experiences institutions at all. Philosophers cannot even agree on what they are, never mind treat them as commonsense objects such as baseballs that behave like Newtonian systems. No one has any right to treat cultures or civilizations or religions or traditions as if they were objects in the hand like baseballs or lab equipment. If they were, generations of scholars would not need to argue over their nature. Physicists do not say things like "There are many definitions of photographic plates (used to detect electrons), and no consensus in the field as to which is right." There is no conceptual confusion about pointer readings or baseballs. Metaphysical institutions are not directly experienced in the way social scientists need them to be for the analogy to physical science methods to work.

In fact, philosophers theorizing social reality should be even more attuned to paradox and mystery than physicists are, since the very building blocks of their discipline (human beings) are shot through with paradox, unlike physicists, who are in a sense obligated to treat their lab equipment as if quantum mechanics and relativity didn't affect them. Indeed, the only way to get to anything remotely coherent when it comes to social reality is to accept the paradoxes of conceptualizing consciousness and try to take sensible steps to manage the challenges of scaling up to the level of institutions. The *I* is already mysterious. Why wouldn't the *we* be so as well?

These features of consciousness are why the metaphors of "structure" and "system," when applied to social reality, can be so misleading. To call something a "system" or a "structure" implies a level of understanding of its constituent parts that the social sciences do not possess and are in denial about, owing to their inability to step outside of the antidualist dogma. It leads toward a conception of social science that is little more than the physics of many brains.

To restate it: The structures and systems scientists deal with in the world of bodies are treated as being either deterministic or random in their workings, such that paradox and mystery arise only upon careful contrived experiment, observation, and theorizing. No one intuitively apprehends the wave-particle duality, time dilation, or quantum superposition. But the paradox and mystery of human consciousness are not theorized or extrapolated from elsewhere but instead are directly and inescapably experienced. Human consciousness is neither deterministic nor random, as argued above, but must be something else. That means that the intuition that paradoxical or unpredictable entities like those theorized in physics add up to the nonparadoxical and predictable experience of everyday objects cannot and should not be extended to human beings interacting in institutions. In physics one looks at structures and systems and discovers non-structure-like properties (e.g., quantum entanglement) that are mysterious and paradoxical. But the social sciences seem to assume that one can start from mysterious and paradoxical entities (human beings) who somehow organize themselves into structures and systems that are nonparadoxical and nonmysterious without any concern for the "hard problems" that persist in conceptualizing the components of that supposed "structure." Anthropologists and sociologists, for example, leverage their direct experience of entities that are partly paradoxical and mysterious (individual human beings' consciousness) in order to conceptualize theorized entities (cultures) whose attributes are treated as though they were straightforward and were not mysterious or paradoxical at all, using metaphors such as "structure" and "system" and statistical methods that originate in the other sciences. But large aggregates like cultures, civilizations, religions, and traditions are and always have been incredibly difficult to predict and treat functionally, especially since no one can even agree on defining what they are (see chapter 1). In fact, everyone, including scholars, has a much better intuitive sense of what makes individual human beings tick, despite their mysterious nature, as opposed to large collections of them—the exact inverse of subatomic particles and baseballs.[13]

Synopsis

- Consciousness is intrinsically puzzling and difficult to conceptualize, and accounts of it inevitably resort to paradox and mystery. Many well-known paradoxes related to consciousness continue to occupy philosophers in the modern world.

- Most accounts of the soul and its analogues in different traditions have focused on what this reality can *do* as opposed to what it *is*, but antidualism claims to have closed this gap and treats its own conceptualization of consciousness as filling in details.

- Despite its optimism, even the totalizing conception of antidualism recognizes difficulties such as the "hard problem of consciousness." In the social realm, however, such philosophical difficulties are treated as unimportant or nonexistent.

- The paradoxes or difficulties that are recognized in serious conceptualizations of consciousness do not disappear at the social level but become even more consequential and intractable as one introduces the fact of human beings thinking together.

- One purpose of the logical principles of the model of institutions—mutual irreducibility, mutual distinctness, mutual implication—is to mitigate the logical hurdles of conceptualizing consciousness both at an individual and at a collective level.

- Against the background of an antidualist stance toward understanding social reality, terms such as "religion," "culture," "civilization," and "tradition" turn out to be figures of speech that mask certain irreducible ambiguities.

- Our model of institutions is thus a heuristic for disambiguating such figures of speech, since in actual use they necessarily refer to irreducible individual elements that can never be conceived of simultaneously.

- One reason that large institutions have been so difficult to conceptualize is that they remain modeled after outdated notions from physical science, especially the heuristic that large aggregates are more intelligible and predictable than their constituent unpredictable elements.

- Social sciences invert the practice of physical science by treating theorized entities such as metaphysical institutions as if they were directly experienced deterministic systems that provide empirical data from which extrapolations are made.

- The social sciences should begin from the fact that they deal first and foremost with mysterious entities (human beings) and build paradox and mystery into their conceptualizations of large collectivities. The "structure" metaphor should be abandoned.

Part III

Islam and the Modern Project

Part III

Islam and the Muslim Peoples

Chapter 6

The Language Analogy

Having addressed the concept of institutions as a general matter, let us now turn to the encounter between the Modern Project and Islam so as to analyze them as two prominent examples of metaphysical institutions. One can view this encounter in terms of

the Modern Project conceptualizing the Islamic tradition

the Modern Project conceptualizing itself

the Islamic tradition conceptualizing itself

the Islamic tradition conceptualizing the Modern Project.

Natural languages like English and German, as mentioned in chapter 1, are important examples institutions as defined in this book, and the relationship within and between different natural languages is particularly helpful as an analogy or template for studying certain salient features of the encounter between the Modern Project and Islam. This chapter will be structured around just such an analogy, and following the list above one can view the relationship between two languages like English and German in terms of

English speakers conceptualizing German

English speakers conceptualizing English

German speakers conceptualizing German

German speakers conceptualizing English.

In simple terms, this chapter will approach the question "Is some x Islam/Islamic?" (x standing in for any particular practice, idea, belief, artifact, people, ritual, etc.) by exploring how or when some utterance is *English*. On the basis of the universal familiarity with how a language works internally and also how it relates to other languages, one can make useful analogies to some of the most important features and problems of how the Islamic tradition and the Modern Project relate to each other as metaphysical institutions. The premise here is *not* that the Islamic tradition or the Modern Project is "like a language" or "is a language." Rather, they are realities that can be studied as major institutions of great scope and complexity, and languages are also institutions, but of lesser scope and complexity and of easier access. The universal category here is "institution," not "language." Language as analyzed here is not the ideal or abstract reality of which different forms of human consciousness are all manifestations and permutations, as one finds often in modern philosophy, which has turned language into a kind of universal that goes far beyond what idiomatically is considered natural language. Language is simply a convenient example of an institution drawn from everyday experience to illuminate a difficult and complex topic. They are parallel examples; one does not derive from the other.

Let us first apply the model of institutions developed in chapter 2 to the reality of language.

Beginning from the triad community-practice-legacy, one can say that what makes an English speaker is that person's possession of a certain legacy and the practice that is based on that legacy. What makes the practice of speaking English is native speakers using their legacy to speak their language. What makes the English legacy is the fact that English speakers practice it the way one is supposed to practice it.

When to this first triad one adds the second triad of stability-dynamism-purpose, one can then analyze English in terms of memory, mastery, moral authority; being communicative, creative, and corrective; and being accessible, intelligible, valuable.

The community of English speakers' memory consists in their possession of the language (its vocabulary, its grammar, its corpus); its mastery consists in the ability to generate new uses in novel situations not determined by circumstances; and its moral authority consists in the fact that it is English speakers who serve as the ultimate arbiter of what counts as English. In other words, English speakers have a knowledge of the utterances in English (including utterances about utterances), which they have heard, read, and remember or otherwise have access to. They also must understand the rules, patterns, regularities, and possibilities of the language such that they are able to use it in the novel situations of life and understand both old and new uses when they encounter them. And finally, they are obligated to know the right ways and wrong ways, better and worse ways, correct and incorrect ways, to use that language.

The practice of English—the actual speaking and writing of it—is communicative in that the speaking of English is never an isolated affair but exists across space and across time by a group. It is creative in that it must be repeated but also modified because no language can be spoken the same way twice and must always be adapted. And it is corrective in that it always implies a right way and a wrong way to use the language, that there are principles involved and norms to be followed, and that certain uses will be kept and others discarded.

The legacy of English is all the instances of English usage to which speakers have access regardless of the mode of access, and which they likewise bequeath. English is accessible in that it must be called upon and cannot be hidden away from its users. It is intelligible and adaptable in that its forms are understood as something meant, such that those who receive it know what they are receiving as it was meant in new situations. And it is valuable in that the very existence of an inheritance presupposes a process of inclusion and exclusion, whereby something is deemed worthy of being kept viable while other things are not. Not every utterance or type of utterance is remembered; much is kept and much is discarded. English is tended.

Finally, one comes to the triad of accounts, heuristics, and norms, and when combined with both triads above one can say the following.

A simple example of a language account would be "By cerulean, English speakers have meant the color of the clear daytime sky."

An account takes the general form (either shown or told): "By *this*, English speakers have meant *that*." It is the stock and store of one's language which registers that *this* is English and *that* is not—the canon of English utterances, whether kept in writing or in memories. In the case of natural language this body of knowledge is not usually formal and systematic but is threaded through life, and the formal and systematic accounts such as large dictionaries are the exception rather than the rule. The knowledge that "by *this* English speakers have meant *that*" is more often shown than told. This memory, this knowledge of the language, must remain stable in the memory of the community, be communicated between members of the community, and be accessible as well.

But the accounts also change over time. The knowledge English speakers have collectively of "by *this* English speakers have meant *that*" is not frozen but takes different forms as times change. For example, how English speakers define or describe "cerulean" changes over time even if the word is used to refer to the same color—new shades of blue are named, shades of neighboring colors change, and so forth. It might be that people used to describe blue in terms of a certain plant, and now that plant is no longer common but a new plant of that color is, so the account of "Cerulean is . . ." changes. In general, one may need new taxonomies, new groupings, or more or fewer groupings, to remember and keep around the memory of utterances. In other words, the account that takes the general form "By *cerulean* English speakers mean this" will itself be modified over time (for example, today it can be expressed using precise wavelengths), and this presupposes that there are community members that can creatively carry out this adaptation and keep it intelligible in its new contexts. How one accesses a memory or stock of utterances now is not the same as it was one hundred years ago or will be one hundred years from now, and that change has to be both stable and purposive. The *Oxford English Dictionary* is revised and comes out in new editions, for example.

There is a point to language that is determined by the community, and people care about it and tend to it and value it and, if anything, it has correctness. Along with the fact that these accounts of "By *this* English speakers have meant *that*" both remain stable over time and also get modified and proliferate, there has to be a tending and regulation of it that takes place. The community decides which accounts are kept and which are discarded (e.g., which ways of defining and describing "cerulean"), and by definition these community members (English speakers) are the ones with the authority to make those decisions, and they make those decisions by virtue of deeming those accounts to be worthwhile.

A simple example of a heuristic would be: "When a person is asked, 'How are you?' one should *always* say something, and one *can* respond 'Fine thank you' or 'Not too bad, how are you?' or 'Don't ask!' *or* 'Can't complain' but *never* 'None of your business.'"

Rather than "By *this* speakers have meant *that*" (an account), language heuristics take the general form "In case of *this* English speakers can say *that*." There are recipes, as it were, that people carry around for speaking English in the sense of the general if-then dimension of things: "In case of situation *x*, in order to mean *y* one says *a, b,* or *c,* but *a* is most common." They consist in readymade possibilities of expression from which one can draw in novel situations, helping one to navigate new linguistic situations. As a simple example think of small talk and common courtesy. Heuristics consist of all the ways one can use language in novel iterations, almost always shown by example but sometimes as the result of instruction. As an example of instruction, think of an essay about poetics or a class on how to write an essay or teaching English as a second language, but these linguistic heuristics are almost always shown by example rather than received through explicit instruction. One mostly acquires heuristics by being in the presence of people using language creatively in an ordinary way, and has access to many forms of the general heuristic "In case of x one can say y." Think of something as simple as having a stock of a handful of phrases at hand that one knows can be used in a certain class of situation such as an informal conversation in which one has only the slightest interest, such as "I hear you" or "How about that?" or "Oh wow" or "Is that right . . . ?"

Like accounts, within the community of English speakers these heuristics are remembered, transmitted, and accessible. They are modified creatively and remain intelligible over time. And they are tended to, maintained and discarded, and deemed valuable.

A heuristic would be something like knowing that colors can be used to describe emotions, how to conjugate verbs, subject-verb agreement, possession—all the versions of "if x, then y" and in particular with language: in situation x one must say/could say/should never say y.

A simple example of a linguistic norm would be: "When it comes to 'that' and 'which,' 'that' should introduce a restrictive clause, and 'which' should introduce a nonrestrictive clause."

Norms are forms of thinking about how English ought to be spoken: all the ways one determines that *this* is the right way, or best way, to use the language. As a formal matter, norms of language can be found in the form of lexicons and grammars, but most of the time such norms are communicated informally in the very fact of community members choosing such and such utterance out of other possibilities in everyday speech. Through the very use of language one is making judgments about correct and incorrect use. This is shared knowledge about what makes for good or beautiful or simply the best use of English. A linguistic norm facilitates choice and preference and judgment of good language.

Norms are not a question of what people have meant in English, or of navigating the possibilities of English, but of choosing those uses that are the best and most correct. The understanding of whether "that" or "which" is more correct takes some form that has to be remembered by the commu-

Table 6.1. Language as an instance of shared thinking in a relationship of community, practice, and legacy; characterized by stability, dynamism, and purpose; and consisting of accounts, heuristics, and norms

	Stability	*Dynamism*	*Purpose*
Community	Human beings who keep a memory of: • accounts of how English has been spoken • heuristics for how English can be spoken • norms about how English ought to be spoken	Human beings who can extrapolate and create and iterate: • accounts of how English has been spoken • heuristics for how English can be spoken • norms about how English ought to be spoken	Human beings who judge, care for, and are the arbiters of: • accounts of how English has been spoken • heuristics for how English can be spoken • norms about how English ought to be spoken
Practice	Transmission and communication of: • accounts of how English has been spoken • heuristics for how English can be spoken • norms about how English ought to be spoken	Creation/ modification/ ramification of: • accounts of how English has been spoken • heuristics for how English can be spoken • norms about how English ought to be spoken	Keeping/discarding, regulating, refinement of: • accounts of how English has been spoken • heuristics for how English can be spoken • norms about how English ought to be spoken
Legacy	Availability across time and space of: • accounts of how English has been spoken • heuristics for how English can be spoken • norms about how English ought to be spoken	Adaptation and application of, intelligibility of new forms of: • accounts of how English has been spoken • heuristics for how English can be spoken • norms about how English ought to be spoken	Valuing of: • accounts of how English has been spoken • heuristics for how English can be spoken • norms about how English ought to be spoken

nity, transmitted and communicated between people, and remain accessible. But such linguistic norms also have to be adapted, modified, and remain intelligible in new contexts, because the way one teaches people how to use "that" and "which" correctly or most elegantly changes over time. And those norms have to be tended in order to keep the correct use of those words the same. The form that such norms take is regulated by a community that keeps and discards them because such linguistic norms are important to the life of the language (see table 6.1). Take any of these twenty-seven elements away (see chapter 2), and it ceases to be a language—either immediately or over time.

ﻩ

Now, having related the general model of institutions to the example of natural language, let us see how questions of the form "What is Islamic?" or "Is this Islamic?" can be made more clear by exploring the question "Is this English?"

Conceptualizations "within" Languages: English as a Normative Attribute

Suppose someone who encounters the phrase "The sunlit sky is cerulean" does not know what "cerulean" is and looks it up. A thorough dictionary definition will typically do two main things. Firstly, it will say how the word "cerulean" *has been* used by the relevant community of speakers—constituting a snapshot account and heuristic for understanding that word. Secondly, it will say how that word *ought* to be used. That is, each definition implies both a theory of how a word has been used and also an imperative backed by authority about the correct or best use of that word.

To look up a word like "cerulean" in this way is to ask the question "Is this utterance English?" in order to determine whether the utterance in question is *correct* English or *incorrect* English. A dictionary definition of a word is really a kind of conceptualization or theorization that is self-consciously geared toward establishing right and wrong linguistic practice.

A large dictionary will consist of tens of thousands of such micro-conceptualizations (theory-judgments, rules) of words and phrases meant to enable the reader to navigate correctness and incorrectness. An important feature of these conceptualizations is that they are *irreducibly complex,* which means that there is no single rule or algorithm from which the various definitions can be systematically derived. In other words, there can be no single formula or procedure for arriving at the definition of the thousands of words in any language. There are no least common denominators allowing various definitions to be synthesized. Each word must always be theorized on its own, making any dictionary a *bundle* of conceptualizations describing how authoritative speakers use their own language. Any time one is interested in correctness or rightness in language, one has ruled out any possibility of a single rule and instead must accept a large and irreducible multiplicity of conceptualizations.

The aggregate of these numerous intellectual procedures called "definitions" cannot amount to a conceptualization of English as a whole thing—a language as such—any more than the collected theories in physics, chemistry, and biology constitute a single conceptualization of what physical science is. To the degree that the many theories in the physical sciences are connected, it is not through a theory but through a general explanatory picture, which is by definition not theoretical. And besides, any such a conceptualization of physical science is hardly necessary to be a good physicist, chemist, or biologist.

It is the same with language. It is never the case that one first conceptualizes "English" as some unified entity before moving on to determine whether some utterance is correct or incorrect English. The act of looking up "cerulean" is never preceded by "Well first we have to establish what English really *is* before we can check this word." One already knows what language one is dealing with, and that one is not going to check a dictionary of German. "English" does not need first to be conceptualized or defined for one to look up "cerulean," since English is presupposed in the very endeavor of looking up an utterance in an English dictionary in the first place. To know how to look up "cerulean" does not (indeed, cannot) require or presuppose any conceptualization of "English," but simply an awareness that one is *in English.* A conceptualization of the language in which a dictionary is written would add nothing to the definitions in the dictionary. Once one is inside that English-speaking situation, a dictionary essentially constitutes an extended collection of communications from a particular speaker (the lexicographer) to a particular audience (the researcher) about how the relevant language community (fluent English speakers) correctly uses its language, consisting in multiple theorizations (definitions) of the individual elements of that language (words and phrases). Ultimately, it arbitrates correct and incorrect usage.

But to inquire about the correctness or incorrectness of some utterance like "cerulean" presupposes that one is asking the right questions. Put simply: if dictionaries provide a way of checking correctness and incorrectness, how does one know that one is checking the correct dictionary?

Conceptualization "between" Languages: English as a Thing

What about those situations in which one does in fact need some conceptualization of English, not to establish correctness or incorrectness but rather to establish whether one is dealing with English at all? Beyond the matter of correctness and incorrectness there is another way of asking "Is this utterance English?" namely, "Is this utterance English or some other language?" To answer this question, one needs a different kind of procedure from the consulting of a lexicon, because rather than determining correctness *within* English, one would be demarcating *between* English and its counterpart languages, an endeavor that requires getting to a unified sense of English as constituting such and such language as distinguished from some other language. This unifying notion would be something entirely different from the sum total of definitions one would find in an English dictionary (or rules of grammar). While a dictionary can differentiate the correct use of "crimson" from the correct use of "cerulean," it would not be able to tell us what English is in relation to German, Dutch, or Frisian. (That is, is it correct to say *cerulean* or *himmelblau*?)

Consider the two utterances *Karl refudiated me* and *Karl hat mich widerlegt*. An English dictionary can tell us that there is no such word as "refudiate" and therefore the sentence *Karl refudiated me* is not English; and since the words "mich" and "widerlegt" are not words in English, it can also tell us that the sentence *Karl hat mich widerlegt* is not English. However, the dictionary cannot tell us that *Karl hat mich widerlegt* is actually German. *Karl refudiated me* is un-English in one sense (incorrect usage owing to a jumbling of "refute" and "repudiate"), while *Karl hat mich widerlegt* is un-English in another sense (correct usage but in another language). Because of the limitations inherent in any dictionary, any researcher would first have to know what to be interested in. Is one attempting to separate separating correct from incorrect English, or is one considering whether another language might be involved? Differentiating living languages from each other and determining the correct way to use a single living language are two different procedures.

How, then, would one know whether one was in the world of English or the world of German or some other language? How would one choose, in the case of some new utterance, whether to consult an English dictionary or a German one? The dictionary itself could not tell you, since the dictionary could tell you only that you were using English incorrectly (or, in the case of the German dictionary, that you were using German incorrectly), and it would not be able to differentiate between bad English and non-English (or again, in the case of the German dictionary, between bad German and non-German).

Suppose an English speaker runs across the word *himmelblau* in an online photo and wants to know what the word means. What does that person do? One could have a very simple heuristic for guessing whether some utterance was German (e.g., seeing a series of words in a Roman alphabet with many capitalized words midsentence and a prevalence of the "ch" combination), or a very complex heuristic resulting from years-long study giving one a detailed map that can specify down to the city block what language is spoken depending on the street in Europe where someone grew up. However, even the most sophisticated and complex such heuristics for determining whether some utterance was English or German would not be able to determine correct and incorrect usage of either language, because the purpose of such methods is to find demarcations *between* languages, not *within* them.

More importantly, no such heuristic or procedure for locating English or German on a linguistic map could ever amount to a true theory or conceptualization.[1] Regardless of the simplicity or complexity of language identification, there is no systematic (i.e., theoretically unified) technique that enables one to locate an utterance on the linguistic map. Rather, one identifies a language through context, intuition, hints, finding clues to its origin, or through trial and error—never through an algorithmic theory or conceptualization. One simply makes one's way.

There are rudimentary or quasi- "conceptualizations" or "definitions" that are adequate for certain purposes; these really amount to rules of thumb. For example, *The New Oxford American Dictionary* defines English as "the language of England, widely used in many varieties throughout the world," and German as "a West Germanic language used in Germany, Austria, and parts of Switzerland, and by communities in the US and elsewhere." This description might help you to purchase the correct bilingual dictionary or download the right app for traveling, but not much more than that. As we shall see, all such formulations offer is a way to consult *authorities*, and to leverage existing knowledge to identify those authorities who are the real source of determining what a language is.

In fact, the procedure of determining whether some utterance is correct or incorrect in some language, as well as the procedure to differentiate between languages, both depend inescapably on *authority* and *trust*.

The Role of a Community's Authority

In the case of the sentence "The sunlit sky is cerulean," the authority to decide correctness resides with the authors of the dictionary entry for "cerulean," since the person who is looking it up knows that he is already, as it were, in the world of English, and by his very act presupposes trust in the authority—the *moral* authority—of the dictionary author.

An English speaker interested in determining whether some particular utterance (e.g., *himmelblau*) was German would not first set out to discover and articulate conceptualizations for every potentially German utterance; that is, he or she would not start by writing a German dictionary. Rather, one would find out if the utterance was in a German situation through some other procedure (such as those rules of thumb described above) and *then* find an authoritative speaker (in the form of a dictionary or a competent native speaker) to consult about the (potentially correct/incorrect) German utterance. In all instances, demarcating *between* languages presupposes the identification of such authoritative speakers of the languages in question; any procedure for placing certain utterances into the category of "English" and others into "German" would rely on actually existing speakers of those languages.

We can know that *Karl hat mich widerlegt* is not English because a German speaker would be able to tell us it is German. That means that any procedure for assigning an utterance into English or German would have as a necessary (though not sufficient) condition that we already know who the English speakers are and who the German speakers are, because it is on the authority of the relevant communities that one can determine what constitutes those languages.

Moreover, neither one of these two kinds of procedure (that is, establishing correct language and establishing which language one is dealing with) depends upon the other. They are analytically independent, meaning that neither procedure runs through the other or is analytically connected to the other. Instead, each one runs through a source of authority. Consider:

a master of a language does not rely on any demarcation between that language and others in order to speak it. Shakespeare did not need to know how to demarcate between English and linguistically adjacent languages. He simply wrote or spoke as a human being in his mother tongue. If he had had no such conceptualization of English, he could have still composed a comprehensive dictionary, that is, a catalog of theorizations of the many words in English. A method for demarcating between "English" and other languages would not be a precondition for his work because English was *his* language, although such a conceptualization might help him to refine his dictionary and make it more useful to many different kinds of people and purposes. At the same time, formulating a useful demarcation between English and German does not make one a speaker of either language. A monolingual Chinese researcher could manage a workable technique for distinguishing English from German, one potentially more sophisticated than that of native speakers, without thereby being able to authoritatively differentiate between correct and incorrect uses within English or within German. One does not establish linguistic boundaries through consulting dictionaries, nor dictionaries through observing linguistic boundaries.

Crucially, both kinds of procedures (differentiating between correct and incorrect use in a language, and demarcating between languages) require the identification of a group of *standard language users*—the language's community. It is the living speakers of languages who sustain those languages and give them their respective scope and their limits. Any conceptualization within or between languages depends on its speakers, not the other way around. There can be no conceptualization within or between human languages that does not involve identifying who the speakers of that language actually are.

That is, one cannot determine membership in that community of language speakers by applying an if-then procedure or rule that itself requires that community's own speech as that procedure's first input. Rather, the community's membership is determined extra-theoretically, or pretheoretically. The presence of authority in any possible conceptualization within languages or between them means that one is dealing not with purely theoretical (procedural, methodological, analytical) questions but with an activity that necessarily has a *normative* dimension to it: who does one trust or assume to be authoritative or to be the standard? Such presuppositions about trust and authority can never be reduced to an impersonal and objective method, a set of analytical steps, or an algorithmic process. One has to trust or simply assume, at some ultimate point, that one knows who speaks English and who speaks German, which is a judgment about who *ought* to be trusted or taken as standard, and that judgment or assumption cannot be theoretical (an if-then formalism). It is an assumption or belief that is necessarily brought *into* the method and does not come *from* it. In short, any conceptualization of English (within it, or between it and other languages) presupposes trust in some authority that does not itself rely on such a conceptualization.

Of course, the identification of such native speakers (or authoritative community members) is far from sufficient for theorizing or defining the various individual elements of a language, but it is always a necessary condition. Writing a dictionary is not just as easy as knowing who speaks English well but also requires major *theoretical* work (information gathering, classification, pattern recognition, etc.) once one identifies the standard English speakers. However, that theoretical work exists only in the intellectual space opened up by knowing who the authoritative or standard community is.

Living and Dead Languages

Some further nuances should be made explicit when the question of "authority" is raised. Let us look at a distinction in this language analogy that has not yet been addressed but that is extremely relevant to the discussion at hand, namely, the difference between *living and dead languages*. For example, the question "Is this utterance English?" differs from the question "Is this utterance Sumerian?" in two crucial ways.

First, English is a living language whose correct use cannot be judged simply by identifying patterns in utterances that have already taken place (a fixed data set). Rather, to correctly judge English one must also account for the fact that in order to speak English one must be able to extend past usage to novel situations in a way that is appropriate to but not determined by those situations (meaning that the data set of utterances to be theorized is constantly changing). In a "dead" language such as Sumerian all utterances have already taken place, being neither added to nor subtracted from. There is no extension of past use to novel situations in dead languages. One does not theorize a Sumerian word by also thinking about what some word might also be used for; all the uses of that word exist already. But theorizing a word in English—a living language—presupposes a future use of that word in a way that is not precisely the same as all prior uses. What will be meant by that word in the future will be the same (stability) and also different (dynamism) and also correct (purpose).

Second, if the investigator who is asking the question "Is some utterance English?" is a native speaker of English, then the investigator is a part of the very behavior he or she is investigating, namely, the correct production of English. Dictionaries of English are, after all, documents *in* English; the English-speaking lexicographer both records how English has been spoken and also decides how it *ought* to be spoken. English is not only a data set of past utterances to be classified in a repository of definitions, but is a living language that speakers use to extend past use to novel situations, and that ability to creatively link the past to the present *correctly* must be part of any answer to the question "Is this utterance English?," whereas that dimension of creative adaptation could not be a part of the answer to the question "Is this utterance Sumerian?" How Sumerian *ought* to be spoken, or what counts as "correct" Sumerian, cannot arise for anyone. The English speaker investigating Sumerian (a dead language) simply registers patterns of utterances and develops a theory of how those utterances relate to each other. Such a speaker neither deals with novel situations nor has any sway over how Sumerian ought to be used in such situations.

What this means is that, in the case of a living language like English or German, *communication, creativity,* and *correctness* are inseparable and mutually implicative. Any dictionary definition (registering and establishing correct use) is itself a creative act of extending the language in the context of a novel situation arising between human beings, since any definition is an *act* of a particular speaker communicating with a particular audience for a particular purpose at a particular point in time and in a particular place. That very act of communication has to be creative, because it is appropriate to but not determined by the novel situation between the lexicographer and the audience. Establishing correctness implies and presupposes an act of creativity that is not the result of deterministic rule following; there is no algorithm for writing a dictionary. Of course, one cannot depart from the rules or patterns on a whim, and the boundaries and strictures are real, but they are not mechanically deterministic. If the rules were everything, language would not be able to be used in new situations. If rules were nothing, language would have no content or stability.

Most language, of course, is not oriented toward dictating correctness; it consists mostly of instances of ordinary creative use. Yet every genuine attempt to communicate amounts to an implicit judgment about the correct way to use the language, since a speaker is always free to choose any combination of words for a new situation. To say "The cerulean crown rests upon the horizons" is an implicit affirmation that there are correct ways to use the various words in that sentence and that one is using them in one of those correct ways. To speak one's mother tongue is to presuppose that one is using it the *right* way. Being creative in a language necessarily determines what is correct by the very fact of being a contribution to that language. This correctness cannot result *solely* from a preexisting set of explicit or even implicit rules. Every human utterance has novelty in it, since no two situations are ever identical. No theorization of the past uses of a language can *fully* account for novel situations, so the speaker can speak correctly only by using reason and imagination and not simply by imitation. Whatever someone utters is, at some level, the *right* (appropriate, fitting) thing to say from that person's point of view, and also, necessarily, something that has not been said before in exactly the same way (since it relates to a new situation).

Hierarchy and Hierarchies in Moral Authority

The ongoing determination of correctness through creativity, and of creatively determining correctness, is part of how living languages stay living. In any living language, to establish what is correct and to creatively extend are always present together, and every native speaker is always, in every utterance, both creating and correcting, excluding wrong uses by the very act of creating new ones. But just how much creativity and how much correctness any particular native speaker is responsible for will vary. Even though all speakers of living languages determine the correct use of their language, they determine correctness *unequally*.

One might think that dictionary authors or some similar authority determines all of correct English as members of a certain privileged and influential group of English speakers, but the matter is more complicated. In the case of words such as "science" or "art," the moral authority to determine correct use is concentrated in a small percentage of the language community, and the freedom to extend use creatively is also limited to a relative few—national academies of science, for example. But for many other words, such as "water" or "sky," the authority to determine the right and wrong way to use a word is more universally distributed, and so too is the ability to creatively extend past uses to new utterances, and no dictionary author has the power to change the use of such words without massive coercion on the part of a state. But a relatively small group of people can change the correct use of "science" and "art" for the whole population by deciding to change their definitions in textbooks, dictionaries, and in the elite intellectual culture. Even so, while authority over what counts as English is widely distributed for some utterances and highly concentrated for others, it is always native speakers of English *as a whole* who ultimately determine the answer to the question "Is this utterance English?"

All native speakers taken together determine what counts as correct English, but they do so *unequally* such that different words' correct uses are determined by different subsets of the native speaking population. That means that the general question "What is the correct way to use the word *x*?" is actually a *multiplicity* of closely related questions that range over a spectrum because *the procedure for determining the answer will be somewhat different for each word*. Sometimes authority over correctness is widely distributed, as is the freedom to use these words in novel situations, while in other cases a small elite has greater authority over a word's correct use. Asking "Is this utterance English?" for a given use of "sky" is, therefore, is a somewhat different procedure from the analogous question for a given use of "science." In the case of "sky" no elite group could overturn the judgment of a majority regarding correct use except through massive coercion, but in the case of "science" it is often a tiny elite to which the majority defers.

Therefore, when we ask of some utterance merely "Is it correct English?" we have to remember that the actual steps we take to answer the question are going to be somewhat different each time—because the crucial first step (often implicit but always present) in answering the question "Is it correct English?" is to first determine *whose opinion matters*. Who sets the relevant standard (who governs or has moral authority over it)? The people whose opinion matters—standard English speakers—will never be the *exact* same group of people for each word. In the case of "sky" the standard group will be just about everyone, but in the case of "science" the standard group will be a relatively select few.

This spectrum or range of authority implies an intrinsic *hierarchy* among users of a language. English speakers as a whole acknowledge that some English speakers are better at English than others in different realms of language, and the latter group earns this recognition not by coercion but by mastery. It is often widely recognized by the majority that this minority possesses this authority by right and that they ought to be the arbiter of correct use in that language. This mastery—this *authority*—will also crystallize into a relationship of prescription, where the masters determine for the amateurs what correct usage will be through moral authority, not necessarily coercive authority. Determining correctness within a community of language users need not be arbitrary or authoritarian (although it certainly can be, as in the case of Turkish under Ataturk, Chinese under Mao, and to a much milder degree in modern French and German). Do English speakers not recognize that scientists *ought* to determine the correct way to use the word "scientist," and not the general public? An accountant does not really have a say over how "ontology" ought to be used in the English language, and one typically accepts that one ought to defer to those who know it and understand it.[2]

But there is not only *one* hierarchy. If one were to place the authority to determine the meaning of words on a scale from concentrated to distributed, two words that are equally distributed in the percentage of speakers who determine their meaning are not determined by the *same* people. The people who get to draw the line between "art" and "craft," for example, are just as influential as those who draw the line between "philosophy" and "theology," but they are different (and perhaps partially overlapping) elites sitting atop somewhat different hierarchies within the same broad institution (a language). There are different kinds of clout.

Thus a language (and by analogy metaphysical institutions that are much larger and more complex) consists of multiple interrelated and interdependent hierarchies that "govern" different aspects of the institution. The utterance "water" cannot be isolated from all the other utterances that it works together with to make a language, but at the same time those who determine the correct use of "water" are a slightly different group from those who determine the correct use of other utterances upon which it depends to be intelligible.

One could thus ask of an institution, like a language, how far apart are the people at the bottom and top of the hierarchy in terms of authority (what is the height of the institution?), but one could also ask how many different overlapping hierarchies there are (what is the breadth of the institution?). There is no single dictator in a natural language; even in the most authoritarian cases the majority of the language cannot be budged.

۞

With this discussion of language in hand, let us now turn to Islam and see if these salient features of the institution of language—correctness, creativity, and hierarchy—can illuminate some aspects of Islam as a metaphysical institution.

First, as a matter of idiomatic usage, let us recall that the words "Islamic" and "Islam" both can denote an *attribute* the way "English" can. For example, the *ṣalāh* is an Islamic ritual, but one can also say of the *ṣalāh*

"This is Islam," by which one means "This ritual is properly Islamic." But also, both "Islamic" and "Islam" can also denote Islam as a *thing* in itself (like "English"), as in the case of "the Islamic religion," which really means "the religion, Islam," as when one says "the English language" or "that language, English"). Since both "Islam" and "Islamic" can be used to denote either a subject or a predicate of some subject, one must disambiguate which sense is being used in any given instance.

Even with this clarification in mind, the question "Is some *x* Islamic?" is already highly ambiguous, because correctness and incorrectness is almost never framed in the Islamic tradition in terms of "Islamic" versus "un-Islamic." The Arabic terms *islāmī* or *ghayr islāmī* are not technical terms in any traditional Islamic discipline to denote right or wrong, and appear among modern Muslims only as interpretations of ideas or modes of thinking from outside of the Islamic world, consciously or not. Consider how "Arabic philosophy" appeared in Arabic as *al-falsafah al-ʿarabiyyah*, a concept unknown to the tradition itself but that made its way into the Arabic language because of the use of the term in Western languages to mirror Latin theology/philosophy, meaning Latin-language or Arabic-language thought. "Islamic" did exist in the sense of identifying the relevant subject matter, as in the title *Maqālāt al-Islāmīyīn* (The Views of Islamic Groups) of al-Ashʿarī (d. 936), a survey of views, including many considered to be heretical by the author but that nevertheless fit inside the conversation of Islam (as opposed to Christianity or Judaism). For al-Ashʿarī the groups he discussed were not *islāmī* in a normative sense but simply as a fact of self-identification. Therefore the use of "Islamic" as a normative designation is already problematic and smuggles in a presupposition of Islam as a kind of identity rather than a community with a practice and legacy.[3]

Indeed, when in everyday speech one calls something Islamic in the normative sense, it is really an ambiguous catchall term that stands in for a spectrum of terms that exist within and between the various institutions of Islamic life. In the transactions and ritual actions dealt with by the Sharīʿah (the Islamic legal tradition) one would not speak of "Islamic" versus "un-Islamic" but of obligatory (*wājib*) versus forbidden (*ḥarām*), or discouraged (*makrūh*) versus recommended (*sunnah, mustaḥabb*), and so forth, or one would describe transactions as being invalid (*bāṭil*) or not. In matters of creed, one might speak in terms of *shirk* (polytheism) or *kufr* (disbelief) or *zandaqah* (a difficult word to translate, close to "heretic"), not of an "un-Islamic belief." In the realm of ethics, the language in Islam used is especially rich, beginning from the Quranic and Prophetic vocabulary of virtues and also including ideas derived from other systems such as ancient

Greek ethics. Almost all of the various stations of the path of Sufism, for example, are virtues that name the right and wrong way to be. Sufis do not talk about the aspects of the path as being "Islamic" but instead describe the stations of the path such as repentance, trust, love, sincerity, and other concepts drawn from the Quran and Sunnah. In fact there can be no true sense of something being "Islamic" that is not some version or aggregation of the normative judgments made internal to the tradition itself. Anything else is just exegesis on the folk use of "Islam" or "Islamic" by one's authoritative community, be they Muslim or not.

Added to these terminological difficulties is the profusion of other terms used in the modern world that do not map very well onto traditional Islamic categories of rightness and wrongness, concepts such as "orthodox," "mainstream," "heretical," "antinomian," "heterodox," "canonical," "authoritative," "conservative," "sectarian," and so forth. All such terms presuppose a certain world and system of ideas within which they can be understood and used sensibly, and those presuppositions do not always match the presuppositions that make terms such as *ḥarām* and *kufr* intelligible in their own context. Even more problematic is when the adjectives "traditional," "cultural," "religious," and "civilizational" are used to designate rightness and wrongness when it comes to Islam, amounting to a compound equivocation in which a modern concept such as "religion" is projected onto Islam and then the many facets of that irreducibly complex idea are bundled into a single undifferentiated label like "religious" in order to function as a normative label—a subject that will be discussed further in chapter 7.

❦

With these terminological reservations in mind, let us move on. Suppose one comes across a practice or an idea and wants to know whether it is Islamic or not, or is Islam or not. Does something exist in Islam that is akin to a dictionary for a language? It does, in the form of the already-existing Islamic intellectual legacy that records the views of authoritative Muslims who have expressed their views through example or by offering explicit theorizations (whether these are written down or not). The list is long and includes books of law (*fiqh*), Quran commentaries (*tafsīr*), collections of *ḥadīth*, manuals of *taṣawwuf* (Sufism), ethics (*akhlāq*), creed (*'aqīdah*), works of *kalām*, and collections of *fatāwā* (legal opinions), not to mention the unwritten aspect of Islamic civilization as manifested in the exemplary lives of figures such as the *'ulamā'* (scholars) or the *awliyā'* ("friends [of God] or saints) or the Imams in Shiism. Each of these sources serves as a reference (either by example or by instruction) for the answer regarding correct and incorrect practice within the metaphysical institution of Islam.

As with verbal languages, there exist multiple references crafted for different purposes, and there can be no single source work or exemplar. Even for a natural language, a single truly comprehensive dictionary would be a physical impossibility because it would have to account for every possible utterance, and in fact dictionaries necessarily make a choice to stop their theorization of words at a certain level of detail, depending on their intended audience. Competing dictionaries can nevertheless be aggregated, as when a lexicographer records many different and even contested uses of words, ranking some as better than others or as equally correct, or calling some archaic or vulgar or slang. This is what encyclopedic *tafsirs* such as those of al-Rāzī (d. 1210) or al-Ṭabarī (d. 923) are meant to do in relation to the interpretation of the Quran. Such works contain many, often dissenting, views and also an implicit or explicit preference about which ought to be considered correct.

As with dictionary definitions in a language, each potentially Islamic reality whose correctness or incorrectness is being evaluated in the case of Islam must be theorized individually, and as with language there is an irreducible complexity such that no single formula (no matter how complex) could account for all instances of correctness or incorrectness. In a *tafsir*, for example, the commentator will typically explicate the correct understanding of the Quran verse by verse, and there is no possibility of a single procedure that, when applied to all the various commands, prohibitions, stories, arguments, and descriptions of the Quran, can give one the correct view of each one. Rather, each item is theorized individually, and thus a large *tafsir* constitutes numerous mutually irreducible arguments and assertions about what counts as a correct understanding of the Quran. The same could be said for any compendium of law, or commentaries on *ḥadīth*, or manuals of spiritual practice—and certainly the irreducible complexity remains when all of these are taken together.

Consider, as a simple example, the elements in the dictionary entry for "cerulean" and the entry about how to perform the *witr* prayer in a *fiqh* manual (see table 6.2). In both cases one will read about the correct way to use "cerulean" or perform *witr*, but one might also read how others have used "cerulean" or performed *witr* (e.g., technical or slang meanings of "cerulean," ways of praying *witr* from another legal school), common ways in which people incorrectly use "cerulean" or perform *witr*, and even mention of related words or prayers with which "cerulean" or *witr* ought not be confused (e.g., "cerulean" and "teal," or *witr* and *tahajjud*).

Table 6.2. Comparison of reference entries

Reference work:	Dictionary	Manual of *Fiqh*
Entry:	Cerulean	*Witr* Prayer
Correct use:	Such and such color	Such and such actions
History of use:	Used by different dialects in such and such ways	Practiced by different madhāhib in such and such a way
Related words:	Teal, turquoise, azure	*Tahajjud, qunūṭ, nawāfil, istisqā'*

Consulting a *tafsīr* or book of *fiqh* does not require any prior "conceptualization" of Islam, because one is already in an Islam situation, as it were, the same way a person consulting the dictionary entry for "cerulean" above is already in an English situation. One already knows what one is interested in and why.

Then there is the question of Islam as a thing as opposed to other things that are like it—other religions, civilizations, cultures, or traditions and in this book, more precisely, other metaphysical institutions. Consider the example of the idea that the Quran is "made." Whether this idea is incorrect Islam or simply non-Islam depends on the metaphysical institution in which the utterance "The Quran is made" is being explored. If one encounters this statement in the Quran commentator al-Zamakhsharī (d. 1144), then one already knows one is "in Islam," and when one checks the relevant dictionary (e.g., a Sunni creed if one is Sunni) one would find the assertion that God "made" (*ja'ala*) or "created" (*khalaqa*) the Quran to be incorrect. But if the speaker is a Catholic, then the assertion that the Quran is "made" would be correct Catholicism, because according to a relevant Catholic "dictionary" (e.g., a Catholic theological treatise discussing the nature of the *logos*) only the Son is "not made." Similarly, the statement "the Quran was made" could be uttered "correctly" as a member of the Modern Project—in the field of anthropology, for example—since religions and everything in them are made or constructed by human beings according to their metaphysical institution.

How, then, could one differentiate between "the Quran is made" as incorrect Islam and correct Catholicism or correct modernism in this example?

One would surely not first establish a "useful conceptualization" of Islam or of Catholicism or the Modern Project because one would already know what was at stake and who was involved when exploring the question. The situation of the researcher would already be clear enough. No "concept" of Islam would tell you who Zamakhsharī was, and no "concept" of Catholicism or the Modern Project could tell you who Thomas Aquinas was or who Julius Wellhausen was. By the time one is wondering about Zamakhsharī's notion that the Quran was made one has long since determined that one is dealing with Islam, and this judgment does not come about through some "concept" or procedure. One is already there, by virtue of some real-life experience that leads one to assume that the people one is dealing with are Muslims.

There are no doubt useful rules of thumb that can be deployed for certain purposes, as with natural languages. One can consult detailed history books that chronicle where Muslims have lived throughout the centuries, for example. But that would not amount to a "theory" of Islam. It would not provide a formula by which to differentiate Islam from non-Islam. And it certainly would not be able to serve as a way of determining whether some given practice or idea was *correct* Islam or *incorrect* Islam.

As in the case of determining correctness within languages and determining the line between languages, there can be no self-standing procedure that determines these questions apart from the question of identifying the relevant authority—native speakers in the case of English, standard Muslims in the case of Islam. "Is *x* Islamic?" is a question that can be answered only by knowing who the right Muslim is whose practice is taken as the standard. A Muslim does not need to have a conceptualization of "Islam" as such in order to practice Islam, nor does that correct practice depend on being able to theorize the lines between Islam and other religions. He or she simply *is* Muslim and *practices* Islam. A non-Muslim researcher trying to determine whether some practice is *correctly* Islamic or whether some practice is Islam or Buddhism takes as his ultimate rule the authority of Muslims and Buddhists. It is *their* lives and their choices that one relies upon and trusts, and having decided that they are the standard Muslims or Buddhists, one then theorizes and generalizes about them. Any conceptualization of Islam itself or of the line between it and other religions derives from the authority of a community. And the identity of that population cannot be derived from some concept, procedure, method, or rule that is formalized. One has to ultimately make a judgment about who has authority and who can be trusted.

Creativity and Correctness

A distinction was made between correctness and creativity in a living language such as English and a dead language such as Sumerian. Islam is a *living* metaphysical institution and therefore the proper conceptualization of what is correctly Islamic presupposes that in order to be *correctly* Islamic one will be extending past practice to novel situations in the future. Without such *new* realities, Islam cannot be a living metaphysical institution, just as English cannot be a living language if it cannot be used in novel situations.

If one were to conceive of Islam as if it were a "dead" metaphysical institution, one would imagine that all its expressions have already taken place and that all one can do is register patterns and relationships within that fixed set of expressions, and only the excavation of dead and buried expressions would change the conceptualizations. In this way of looking at Islam, all of the standard or normative practices have already taken place, and theorizing what is *correctly* Islamic need not take into account anything new. When Islam is treated as a dead institution, one assumes that Muslims are obliged either to repeat or fail to repeat what is given by a fixed set of teachings and exemplars.

But if Islam is correctly viewed as a living metaphysical institution, then one must, in one's conceptualization of it, account for its extension to novel situations. Indeed, Islam is not dead, and any conceptualization has to account not only for some fixed data set from the past but also the way the community practices its inheritance in the present and into the future of novel situations. Any possible conceptualization of Islam must include something about how the world is, the possibilities of navigating it, and how one ought to be in it. That is, any possible "Islam" will include answers to the questions of what is real, what is rational, and what is right.

Moreover, if one is oneself a Muslim, then the very act of conceptualizing something as correctly Islamic is itself an Islamic act, just as the definition of a word in English is something written *in* English. To judge that this or that thing is Islamic (or any of the other normative designations mentioned above) is to do something Islamic, and that judgment itself (and the expression of it) can be judged as either incorrect or correct.

To be correctly Islamic is necessarily to do something new, while to live one's Islam in new situations—whether at the level of doctrine or of living a virtuous life day to day—is precisely to also make an implicit claim about what is correct.

Let us discuss the question of creativity more concretely. It is undeniable that the Islamic disciplines such as *taṣawwuf* (Sufism), *fiqh* (jurisprudence), *kalām* (dialectical theology), *tafsīr* (Quran commentary), and *ḥadīth* have changed over time. The technical terminology and intellectual methods in any of these disciplines in the tenth or eleventh Islamic centuries would not be immediately comprehensible to an authority in these disciplines from the second or third Islamic centuries, although the practitioners in the later centuries would see themselves in continuity with those earlier authorities and as remaining faithful to them. In all intellectual fields of Islamic life new concepts came into being, existing concepts changed in their technical significance, and some concepts went out of common use. Ideas that were implicit became formalized and systematized, and existing ideas were refined, ramified, or combined. New schools of thought crystallized that were themselves institutions within the broader institutional matrix of Islamic life. At the same time there was crucial continuity and stability.

In the development of jurisprudence (*uṣūl al-fiqh*), for example, the terms *qiyās* (legal inference),[4] *istiḥsān* (moral adjudication of inferences), *ʿurf* (local norms), *maṣāliḥ mursalah* (considering public interest), and *sadd al-dharāʾiʿ* (preventing means of harm) were at one point in time *new*, but they are also taken to be *correct*. They were not correct *despite* being new but *by virtue of* being new in the right way. The newness was appropriate to circumstances, including the intellectual and cultural complexities of the society in which the law was (and continues to be) theorized. It is not only a fact that the expression of jurisprudence changed over time as observed from the outside, but the relationship between novelty and correctness is part of Islamic legal thinking itself in an explicit way. For example, one of the maxims of Islamic law is *al-ʿādah muḥakkamah* (roughly, long-standing local norms have legal authority). Each local society represents a novel situation that Islamic law must account for. Custom does not live in gaps created by areas of life in which Islamic law is not active, which might be something akin the modern line between religion and culture.[5] Rather, custom *constitutes* the law itself in certain respects. The *sharīʿah* dictates that a husband should provide materially for his wife, but it is custom (under the correct conditions) that determines what that is for a particular locale. It is not that Islamic law demands correctness *here* and allows creativity *there* but rather that it can be correct only by being creative in certain ways.

The discipline of *kalām* also remains correct through creativity, even in its very name, which, as al-Taftāzānī (d. 1390) neatly summarizes in the first pages of his commentary on the creed of al-Nasafī, began as a concern with faith and belief, then took on the name of *al-fiqh al-akbar* (the "greater understanding," as opposed to the *other* understanding, namely law), and then eventually took on other names such as "science of [Divine] oneness" (*'ilm al-tawḥīd*) and "science of discourse/dialectic" (*'ilm al-kalām*).[6] In the area of ontology, for example, early *mutakallimūn* spoke in terms of *ḥudūth* (coming to be in time) and *qidam* (eternality, uncreatedness) whose centrality gives way later to discussions of *wujūb* (ontological necessity) and *imkān* (contingency). Concepts had to be invented by various schools in order to formalize insights that had previously existed but that were not yet formalized. The doctrine of *kasb* is one of many examples, a word that occurs in the Quran (along with related terms such as *iktisāb*) in its idiomatic sense or earning or perpetrating but that takes on a technical sense of human beings "acquiring" actions they choose but that God creates and that therefore human beings remain answerable for. Within the Ashʿarite school, *kasb*—as an expression—was new but also right, and was deemed right partly by virtue of being new. Indeed, the self-image of the discipline of *kalām* is to be in dialogue and debate with ideas outside of Islam and questions that arise from within Islam, and the contingent and empirical variation of the outside and inward interlocutors creates novel situations that require creativity-and-correctness in order to be navigated.

Similar remarks can be made about the doctrinal and literary dimension of *taṣawwuf*, which has flowered in many different ways, including litanies, aphorisms, ethical literature, poetry, and systematic metaphysics such as the school of Ibn al-ʿArabī (d. 1240)—all forms of expression that did not exist in earlier centuries but that came into being at the hands of people who saw themselves as practitioners of a long-standing tradition that predated their own particular expressions and iterations of it.[7]

But the relationship between creativity and correctness in Islam is not restricted to such doctrinal or formalistic technical issues, significant though they are. Knowing how to be compassionate in new situations is both correct and creative, as is having patience, controlling one's anger, and overcoming fear in the face of new trials and tribulations. When the Quran talks about having a heart that can understand, it is called upon to understand *in the present*, which means it has to be able to understand that which is new. The Quran frequently calls for human beings to meditate upon the natural world, and the fruits of such meditation are ever changing in light of the expansion of Islam into new places and new knowledge about the world of nature. To have virtues of any kind is to presuppose principles that hold for new situations as well as old. Without principles—explicit or implicit—one is simply a stimulus response machine, a bundle of impulses. No Quranic virtue can be reduced to a formula or a series of examples, although those formulas and examples are essential parts of a tradition. The Names of God and the qualities of the believers the unbelievers mentioned in the Quran are the basis for an entire vocabulary of the virtues and vices in Islam, but they require not only imitation and repetition but also rationality and imagination. Moreover, the Quran and Sunnah are full not only of virtues and maxims but also of examples and exemplars that serve as concrete models of being a good human being, and without the capacity to adapt to novel situations one could never really enact such models in real life. There must be dynamism in order for there to be stability, because the world changes and the person in the world changes as well, and the purposes that gave rise to the exemplars cannot be fulfilled through mere repetition of what those exemplars did.

Now, if compassion, courage, patience, and understanding are not part of one's concept of Islam, or do not seem to fall under the category "correctness," then one may want to revisit what one deems "correct" Islam to be.

Closely related to and continuous with the realm of the ethical and the virtues is the aesthetic and the arts. Consider the example of Islamic calligraphy, which has changed over time and varied across geography. Traditional Islamic calligraphers consider themselves to be part of a living institution, and the relationship between creativity and correctness is especially clear in this form of artistic and sacred expression, which requires of learners a relentless imitation and repetition of existing forms acquired at the hands of a master, but also similarly demands of practitioners a spontaneous apprehension of what is appropriate and suitable in a given instance and that gives rise to the creation of new forms that are alive in their new context. Old and new presuppose each other. Calligraphing the Quran is often considered the ultimate form of visual art in Islam, universally present in Islamic cultures, and it is undeniable that its rootedness and orthodoxy have never ruled out the role of creativity and imagination.[8]

Or consider an even more universal creative practice: the recitation of the Quran itself. Across the Islamic world, on a daily basis, every observant Muslim improvises a melody while reciting the Quran. It is a particularly clear example of correctness *demanding* creativity. There is no set melody that one follows, and one is obligated to choose some kind of melody (if only two notes). Of course, there are strong elements of correctness in the recitation of the Quran, as the right pronunciation (*tajwīd*) of its consonants and vowels requires high levels of precision and discipline, not to mention the various rules of starting, pausing, and stopping that are codified in the various *qirā'āt* (canonical recitations based upon the ʿUthmānic codex). But woven together with these stringent demands one has the simple but universal experience of standing during the *maghrib* (evening) prayer and reciting the *Fātiḥah*: each worshipper delivers a melody that no one has recited before, and by doing so not only does something permitted but also—and most of all—fulfills the demands of the recitation.

Mere repetition in such matters is an impossibility, and would lead to ossification. The extrinsic conditions facing an institution such as Quranic calligraphy change across time and space (e.g., availability of raw materials, the color palette of the environment, the nature of the prevailing forms of aesthetic life, the corpus of available texts to be calligraphed), as does the intrinsic nature of the community, which grows and shrinks and has a turnover of different human beings refining themselves and their craft in different times and places. The same can be said for Quran recitation, whose melodic intervals and pacing change according to the tonal vocabulary of the population involved. For much of the Islamic world today the recitation of the Quran has been dominated by Arab, Persian, and Turkish *maqāms* (musical modes), but there are other examples, such as the pentatonic modes used by well-known African reciters. There is a legal debate about the legitimacy, from the point of view of Islam, of using a *maqām* to recite the Quran, but this is often a poorly framed question that is akin to asking whether it is permissible to use a dictionary or grammar when writing a commentary about the Quran. A person trying to recite the Quran beautifully, as one ought to do according to the Sunnah,[9] cannot avoid choosing *some* melody, and that choice is naturally informed by that person's experience with various tonal systems. Some people are *aware* of what a given melody is, while some people are unaware, but everyone is reciting according to a *maqām* just as everyone speaks according to certain grammatical rules whether they can formulate them explicitly or not.

It is tempting to classify such aesthetic matters as belonging to the "culture" side of things, as if imitation and rigidity belong naturally to religion while creativity goes with culture—a line sometimes expressed in terms of the Islamic and the Islamicate (see chapter 8). But such a demarcation is arbitrary and reflects the history of modernity more than anything else. What could be a more important question in the ethical life (and hence the Islamic life) than aesthetics and art? In Islamic ethics, making other human beings smile and making the hearts of other people feel lighter are central virtues, and therefore aesthetics and ethics are never truly separate if only for the simple fact that beauty makes people feel good and ugliness makes them feel bad, and thus making others feel good or bad through artistic forms is a straightforwardly ethical matter. In a traditional civilization like Islam it was scarcely necessary to point out that it is *wrong* to expose people needlessly to ugliness, and it is pleasing to God and therefore *right* to make the world beautiful to the degree that one has a choice in the matter. Making sure men and women occupy different rows in the mosque is one kind of moral question, while making sure the mosque stonework uses a good color balance is a different kind of moral question. Labeling one religious and the other cultural is a subjective choice. For a certain kind of Muslim, crafting a brick correctly is very much a matter that involves remembering God, being self-effaced, and recalling the Prophet's saying that God has prescribed *iḥsān* (virtue, excellence, beauty) for all actions.[10] It makes no sense at all to artificially sever ethical questions from aesthetic ones, and hence it is mistaken to automatically assume that being correctly Islamic and being aesthetically refined are separate realms of life. This does not even touch upon the question of metaphysics and symbolism in art, which is not going to be taken up here.

In general, it is easy to assume that the choice for Muslims is between ossification (mere repetition and imitation) and plasticity (a limitless free-for-all of self-creation). But that it is a false choice.

Hierarchy and Hierarchies

These different kinds of creativity (spiritual, legal, doctrinal, ethical, aesthetic) also require an understanding that there are in fact different community hierarchies that must be considered in conceptualizing what is Islamic.

Recall that in languages each word's correct use is determined by a slightly different hierarchy of authority within the overall community of language users. The same holds for a metaphysical institution such as Islam. The nature of authority over what is *correctly* Islamic—what is real, what is rational, what is right—has changed over time. As the Islamic community grew in size and over a wide geographic expanse and came into many different kinds of cultural and political situations, the Islamic disciplines and specializations came gradually into being—the *fuqahāʾ* (jurists), the *mutakallimūn* (theologians), the *mufassirūn* (Quran commentators), the *ṣūfiyyah* (the Sufi masters), the *muḥaddithūn* (*ḥadīth* scholars), and so forth. That has meant that, rather than a single hierarchy of authority over what counts as right and wrong, there have always been multiple overlapping hierarchies such that asking the question "Is *x* Islamic?" amounts to asking, in each case, what the views or practices are of slightly different groups of people whose opinion counts for that question. There is no single person or group of people who remains static at the top. There may be one group for certain kinds of questions, but never *all* questions. Within Islam the relationships of guidance and reliance exist not only top-down but also across and between.

In conceptualizing authority we are not forced to choose either one person or group determining everything for everyone else, or of everyone determining everything for himself or herself. It does not work that way in language, for example, which is one reason why that example was chosen as a template. A speaker of a language knows that he or she cannot make any word in that language mean anything, but that speaker will have varying degrees of authority depending on their role in the language community. The fact that this multiplicity of hierarchies exists does not imply that meaning is not being communicated. Even if one agrees that conceptualizing Islam requires that one identifies who the standard Muslims are (which many will find hard to accept), is not a simple question of delineating a single group of authorities and a single group of followers. That has not been how Islam has existed.

The question "Is *x* Islamic?" is therefore actually a large multiplicity of closely related intellectual procedures that take as their input the practice of the relevant populations of Muslims, and that group does not remain static across all cases. The Muslims with the authority to declare that the Quran is not made but rather is uncreated is a relatively small subset. But the Muslims with the authority to determine what counts as adequate material care by a husband for a wife is much more widely distributed as it depends upon local custom. In Sunni law, those whose views count toward a binding unanimous consensus (*ijmā'*) are a relatively select group of qualified people (the *fuqahā'*), but those whose views count toward establishing customary practice (*'urf*), which is also constitutive of the law, is simply taken to be people of sound character in a particular locale and is thus broader. Therefore, the question "Is it correctly Islamic?" when it comes to whether there might be four or six daily prayers is answered with a different procedure from the question of what counts as a reasonable *mahr* (the amount of money designated by a husband to a wife as part of the marriage contract). The questions differ by virtue of the fact that *those whose opinion matters* (the holders of moral authority) is a different subset of Muslims in each case; authority is more concentrated in the case of the form of the prayers and more widely distributed in the case of the *mahr*. Just a few major scholars can prevent a consensus (at least in Sunni theory, since unanimity is the standard), while a few people in a given locale cannot change a legally binding custom such as how much financial maintenance is expected from a husband. There is no one invariant group of fixed membership that one can call "standard Muslims" for the purposes of answering different iterations of the question "Is *x* Islamic?" The set of people one considers to be standard Muslims will vary depending on the topic being explored, but there must always be *some* such group of standard Muslims anytime one inquires whether something is Islamic or not.

Typically, in modern academia, one is presented with a false dichotomy in which Islam is a matter of an elite group telling everyone else what to do (framed as power and resistance), or else it is a question of each person determining what Islam means for them. But the choice is not between saying Islam is either authoritarian or anarchical (a choice that really presents itself only if one first conceives of Islam as an identity not conditioned by intellectual or moral principles, a topic that will be taken up again in chapter 8). The language analogy is particularly useful in bringing out that there are multiple hierarchies arranged not only top-down and not only peer-to-peer but also existing as complex relationships of guidance and reliance that overlap and reinforce each other in multifarious ways.

The correctness, orthodoxy, fidelity, virtue, piety, and in general the "Islamic-ness" of some particular act or idea is always determined by authority, but in each case the shape of the hierarchy of authority will be different. This hierarchy or lack thereof might be explicitly codified or it might be implicit. These community members overlap and interact, and they are neither competing nor exclusive. It is difficult to find a metaphor to represent this, and the "structure" metaphor tends to make such subtle relationships difficult to portray.

One can compare the question of what breaks one's state of purity requiring a renewal of lustration or ablution (*wuḍū'*) versus what makes one a good spouse. The former is a highly technical question, and it could be that a single person in a city might determine the right *Islamic* answer for everyone else. But that very same person might be a bachelor and not at all possessed of the personal traits that would make a good husband and father, and it would be everyone else's duty—the same people who depended on him to know when to renew their *wuḍū'*—to guide him to get married and teach him how to be a good family man. Performing lustration with impure water is un-Islamic, and poor grooming and grumpiness by a husband is also un-Islamic, but there is a difference in the nature of each case as well as in the community of authority that determines whether that thing is Islamic or not, but they are not exclusive of each other and indeed are aspects of a single tradition.[11] The fact that these two examples are so far apart on the scale of different kinds of hierarchies is meant to illustrate the general point.

Or consider: what does it mean to venerate the old and to be kind to the young, as dictated by the famous *ḥadīth*,[12] and which is a common proverb in languages such as Turkish (so much so that many are not aware of its origin)? The *Islamic* position is determined by a widely distributed hierarchy. Does the maternal grandmother inherit property? The Islamic position is determined by a relatively small and concentrated hierarchy. Neither can do without the other, meaning that there is no Islam without both filial piety and inheritance laws.

Conceptualization as Input-Output Procedure

The foregoing discussion emphasized how conceptualization relies upon authority in order to function. One can reframe the question of conceptualizing Islam more formally, as an input-output procedure whose input consists of the activity of human beings who are considered to be Muslim, and whose output consists of a sought-after taxonomy into "Islamic" and "not-Islamic." Take the simplest form of such an input-output machine:

"Islam is whatever Muslims do."

To make the steps more explicit one could say:

"If a Muslim does it, it is Islamic;
and if a Muslim doesn't, it isn't."

In this case we are setting up a simple if-then procedure of the form:

If y, then z.
If not-y, then not-z.

There are two things that no input-output procedure can do. It cannot tell you what the inputs will be (the y), and it cannot decide what kind of outputs it is designed to deliver (the procedure is designed by someone already interested in the distinction between z and *not-z*). That is, no conceptual procedure can (1) provide its own premises, or (2) determine the purpose it is designed for. In the case of "Islam is what Muslims do," the procedure cannot tell us where to find the inputs: how do we find these Muslims? Neither can the procedure tell us why the formulator of the procedure is interested in two values (e.g., Islamic or not-Islamic) instead of five (e.g., obligatory, recommended, neutral, discouraged, or forbidden). Identifying Muslims (which is needed as input for the conceptual process) requires yet another procedure to answer the question "Who are the Muslims?" if the procedure is not to be arbitrary. One therefore needs to say something like

"Anyone who does x is a Muslim."

or, more explicitly,

"If one does x, then one is a Muslim;
if one does not-x, then one is not-Muslim."

One has, then, a second procedure of the form:

If x, then y.
If *not-x*, then *not-y*.

So now there is a process to determine who a Muslim is, which then enables one to determine whether something is Islamic. One takes the output of the procedure "If one does x, one is a Muslim" and plugs it into the procedure "If a Muslim does it, it is Islamic." But then this procedure raises the question: how did one determine x in the first place? The procedure that outputs Muslim/not-Muslim depends on the input x, so that procedure cannot decide what x will be.

One could then add another procedure: "If a behavior is based on Muhammad's message, it is a Muslim behavior, and if it is not based on Muhammad's message, it is not a Muslim behavior." This procedure can be represented in the form:

If w, then x.
If *not-w*, then *not-x*.

One can add up these input-output procedures and arrive at a single more complex procedure:

> If *w*, then *x*, and if *x*, then *y*, and if *y*, then *z*;
> but if *not-w*, or if *not-x*, or if *not-y*, then *not-z*.

Whether one is dealing with a single if-then statement, or a thousand if-then statements, when taken together these if-thens constitute a single algorithm, and they are ultimately suspended between a certain set of inputs oriented toward a certain set of outputs. A complex algorithm of if-thens can be seen as consisting of a single complex "if" oriented toward a single complex "then." The number of steps does not change the underlying logical structure. In this simplified case, the initial input is *w* or *not-w*, and the output is *z* or *not-z*.

"If *w*, then *x*; if *x*, then *y*; if *y*, then *z*," can be restated in plain language: "If a person who has carried out certain Muslim-making behaviors that are based upon following Muhammad's message does something, then that thing is Islamic; otherwise, it is not Islamic." Each step in the process is determined algorithmically by the previous step. One could program a powerful enough computer with the correct data and produce the right outcome. But the computer could not get the first input on its own—namely, a relevant group of people whose opinion or behavior matters. Once it had that initial data set, it could then simply run the program.

How does one get that first input, the *w*? What is included in and excluded from Muhammad's message? It seems one needs yet another procedure to find the *w* in order to keep the affair completely theoretical—that is, in the realm of if-then, method, or procedure. One could say that Muhammad's message is contained in some body of texts, while others would say it is some slightly different body of texts, or some other corpus. But then whose view is to be accepted? Some other parameter would be needed to decide between the groups, and then another one to find a way to decide on *that* parameter. To provide the input for the "If *w*, then *x*" procedure we would need some kind of "If *v*, then *x*" procedure, which would need some kind of "If *u*, then *v*" procedure—and the chain would seem to be destined for regress.

In real life, however, such endless regresses do not actually happen. Inputs cannot be supplied by the outputs of prior conceptual procedures ad infinitum. At some point the chain has to begin. When one goes back far enough one is going to find the boundary at which the inputs are determined in the real world (by presupposed beliefs) and not by any procedure. Moreover, it will always be the case that the outputs (the desired values of z and *not-z* that reflect one's interests in crafting the procedure) are logically prior to the procedure; the procedure is designed with those outputs *already in mind*.

All dictionaries, to use the analogous case, are necessarily circular *in a sense* because each word is defined in terms of the other words that are defined in terms of the other words, and so on. But the dictionary is not *viciously* circular because it presupposes a source of authority: the living speakers of the language who are the ultimate arbiters of the dictionary's content and correctness, of which the dictionary author is one example. The lexicographer both identifies the standard language community and also decides what the definitions are going to be useful for.

The conceptualizer of Islam will have a role is akin to the lexicographer's role in the virtuously circular system of a dictionary, by identifying the standard community of Muslims and by establishing the output values (e.g., Islamic vs. un-Islamic, or orthodox vs. heterodox, or religious vs. cultural). That conceptualizer's purposes will determine the character of the outputs, since one can get answers only to the questions one decides to ask.

The matter at hand for conceptualizing Islam, therefore, is the identification of that ultimate arbiter who decides or assumes the initial input. Who determines the standard Muslim?

Synopsis

- Language is a particularly helpful example of an institution that can be used as a template for understanding certain key features of larger, more complex institutions such as religions.

- One can think of the "What is Islam" or "Is it Islamic?" question in light of two ways of exploring the question "Is some utterance English?" namely, judging something's correctness within an institution (is it good English?) versus identifying which institution it belongs to (is it English or German?).

- The definitions of words in any single language are irreducibly complex conceptualizations that cannot be reformulated as a single concept, and neither can one formulate a concept for sorting utterances into different languages.

- Choosing which language in which to locate an utterance is a completely different procedure from establishing its correctness in its language. Is an utterance bad English or is it German?

- Whether one is establishing Englishness as an attribute of correct utterances or as the fact of being an English utterance, one always relies upon the legitimizing moral authority of English speakers themselves (or those of another language).

- In living languages, the conceptualization of correct use is itself an instance of correct use, unlike the case with a dead language. Using language correctly implies using it creatively, and being creative in language use presupposes one is being correct.

- A language like English is characterized not by a single hierarchy of authority or a single elite but by multiple overlapping hierarchies such that "whose authority matters?" when determining correct use changes depending on the nature of the expression.

- By analogy to language, a metaphysical institution like the Islamic tradition can be examined such that "Islamic" refers both to correctness and to the fact of something being Islam as opposed to some other thing such as Christianity or the Modern Project.

- "Islamic" as an attribute is a highly ambiguous term that functions as a catchall for a large spectrum of highly sophisticated evaluative categories that exist in Islamic law, theology, ethics, and spirituality.

- "Islamic" is also used interchangeably with certain modern terms such as "orthodox," "mainstream," "heretical," "antinomian," "heterodox," "canonical," "authoritative," "conservative," and "sectarian" that do not map well onto Islam's own normative measures in various disciplines.

- All potentially Islamic things judged on their correctness must always be theorized individually, and thus their conceptualizations are irreducibly complex and fit into no single analytical definition.

- Both identifying the correctness of a potentially "Islamic" thing as well as identifying its place in Islam as opposed to in another institution presupposes the role of reliable authority, namely, the population designated as standard Muslims.

- To be correct in Islam requires being creative, and being creative is conditioned by being correct. Islamic intellectual, artistic, social, and spiritual life offers many examples of creativity disciplined by correctness and correctness sustained by creativity.

- Rather than being constituted by a single rigid hierarchy or an absence of hierarchy, the tradition has always had multiple overlapping hierarchies each of which is relevant to the various dimensions of the tradition.

- The conceptualization of "What is Islam?" can be thought of as an input-output procedure whose first input is the behavior of the population of standard Muslims and whose output is a concept such as "Islamic" or "un-Islamic."

- The identification of the standard Muslim is at the root of any attempt to conceptualize Islam, regardless of whether the conceptualizer realizes this fact or not.

Chapter 7

Project and Tradition

The condition that the conceptualizer must have *some* standard Muslim as a first input and already have in mind a certain desired output (Islam versus non-Islamic) complicates the goal of a theory of Islam as a pure method or procedure separate from reliance on a normative human authority—a persistent goal of modern scholarship about Islam.

Indeed, getting to a "concept" of Islam as a purely analytical or theoretical conceptualization capable of dealing with all the specific relevant cases is precisely what one can never achieve—neither practically, nor even logically. Recall that one cannot churn out a dictionary of a language by plugging individual utterances into a brief and streamlined conceptualization of it—the way one can input different numerical constants into the variables of an algebraic formula. In fact, the better the theorization of actual language usage, the larger and more complex the bundle of theories must become. Gigantic dictionaries are more useful than small ones, but gigantic dictionaries never constitute a "useful concept" of English, for example. They can only be reference catalogs for how English speakers think their language should be spoken and has been spoken, amounting to *bundles* of rules explained by trusted authorities.

The analyst seeking after a useful or adequate concept of Islam is obviously not interested in building an immense compendium of rules akin to a catalog of dictionary definitions. Rather, the analyst is necessarily presupposing reliance upon someone, which is a nontheoretical and necessarily *normative* choice. It is nontheoretical because it cannot be framed any theoretical procedure without the assumption of an input—namely, a first given.

That first input of the procedure is not *self-evident*, since the standard Muslims and their behaviors do not present themselves to us like consciousness itself or the three dimensions of space. It is, rather, a contingent and empirical question to identify who they are. The identity of the standard cannot be determined by any method either, because knowing who the standard Muslims are does not result from any impersonal and invariant input-output procedure. The identifying of the standard Muslims must incorporate a normative or standard-seeking element, an act of trust. Otherwise, the first input would be arbitrary—a random selection. Therefore, the first input, since it is neither self-evident nor deductively necessary, has to be a product of some normative judgment on the part of the conceptualizer about who *ought* to be taken to be the standard Muslim and who *ought* to be trusted to make that determination.

Moreover, the nature of the output—the concept's very purpose for existing—cannot be determined by any procedure or method either, because any procedure or rule or algorithm by its nature cannot provide its own inputs and neither can it provide the motivation for the question that its output is meant to address. In other words, no procedure for conceptualizing "Islam" can tell you why you should be interested in the question "What is Islam?" as opposed to some other question.

There can therefore be no "useful" concept of Islam, from the point of view of an analyst, that does not include a way of consulting trusted sources of authority (a standard population) as determined by one's already existing purposes, which are determined somehow by someone (see "apex communities" below), and thereafter formulating generalizations about that standard population's behavior or views. It is fine to do that (indeed, inescapable), but it can never be a sheer conceptualization or any kind of purely theoretical endeavor detached from trust and prior assumptions.

Recall that a language dictionary is not useful because it provides a concept or theory of English. The entry for "English" in a dictionary is useful for some tasks, but that entry can never determine what counts as correct English in any individual instance. An analogous compendium of rules or theories adequate to covering all things Islamic would be useful in its way but it would fill rooms of shelves, and would lead us right back to the core of the problem: who writes that compendium and whose views are taken as standard for it? A relatively brief conceptualization of "Islam" that is similar in scope to the entry for "English" in a dictionary might be useful for some things, but it could never be used to determine what is correctly Islamic (or orthodox, true, real, mainstream, etc.) in any particular case.

There is no way out of these constraints. The only way to make some notion of "Islam" *useful* in the way some Euro-American academics hope—namely as an idea or rule that can be applied to many examples—is to make it relatively lightweight, streamlined, and unified in relation to the "phenomenon at stake" (to borrow Shahab Ahmed's phrase). Any concept or procedure being *used* to interpret phenomena has to be simple *relative to* the scope and variety of those phenomena. A rule that is nearly as complex as the system it is trying to describe is not much of a rule. One way to achieve the desired simplicity is by narrowing one's focus to a very small area of concern, but that defeats the purpose of conceptualizing *Islam* and not only some smaller phenomenon. Take the three examples of wine drinking, ecstatic poetry, or *waḥdat al-wujūd* ("the oneness of being"). Each of these topics could find an "entry" in an Islamic "dictionary" and each could be theorized as correct or incorrect, but those theories or entries would be irreducibly complex in relation to each other. No rule of greater generality and universality could account for them. Now, if no single theory could account for just these three items, what possible concept (useful or adequate) could meaningfully encompass "Islam" as a whole? In English, would it be possible to establish some rule for the correct usage of "crimson," "monkey," and "dignity" that was not merely a bundle of rules whose only common feature was the authority of the author of those rules?

If taken to be a question in search of some manageable concept, "Is it Islamic?" is necessarily a question about identifying authority, and not about theorization or analysis. The "phenomenon at stake" is too gigantic. The only way to use the word "Islamic" in any manageable way is precisely to pin its use on the identification of a standard. When one translates a text from a foreign language, one wants to consult a dictionary, not write one. If "Islamic" is to be a helpful concept, it can be so only in the form, as it were, of a lexicon, which leads us to the question: who gets to write the dictionary we are using?

When "Is it Islamic?" is posed as a question of identifying an authority, it becomes a relatively simple question with a relatively simple answer—as straightforward as identifying a dictionary author. Ultimately, the academic analyst must ask himself whether he is making *thousands* of decisions about how "Islamic" various things are (laws, rituals, poems, beliefs, jokes, buildings) or if he is making *one* decision about which human beings get to say how "Islamic" those things are. There is a decisive difference between writing a dictionary (an endeavor of laying out tens of thousands of rules for word usage) and identifying the best existing dictionary (a quest of identifying the people who have mastered correct use).

There is no third option.

Therefore, what one can actually achieve in "conceptualizing" Islam is precisely what is achieved in the authoritative reference work we call a dictionary: to detect and describe patterns in the practices of a standard community. *First* have an idea of who the standard Muslims are, *then* theorize what *they* do. To make an analogy to physical science: one cannot construct a theory without knowing what counts as data.

A Muslim Is a Kind of Human Being

Let us now turn to deeper presuppositions related to description, prediction, and understanding.

To theorize a thing is not merely to chronicle but also to predict, which means that if one has a good "theory" of Islam one would know what the standard Muslim *would* do in a new situation, an extrapolation or inference based upon an understanding of what Muslims actually are. If a reference work on Islam cannot inform the reader that a Muslim who is performing the *ṣalāh* (the five daily prayers) with his arms at his sides is probably Mālikī or Twelver Shīʿī, then in that respect it does not provide much of a theory, rule, or concept. A useful theory or set of theories about what Mālikīs do (for example) should allow for some kind of generalization about not only past practices but novel ones as well, and should also offer retroactive prediction. Otherwise, there is no theory at all but only storytelling and ad hoc taxonomy. One cannot possibly have a theory regarding that which is correctly Islamic unless one has an idea of how *standard* Muslims *would* behave or believe in a novel situation, which one could not know unless one knew what Muslims are. It would be absurd to say "I don't know what standard Muslims believe about this thing, and I have no conception of what a Muslim is, but I do know the correct Islamic view about it." For an analyst to define Islamic correctness (orthodoxy, mainstream-ness, etc.) is just for that analyst to know what the right Muslims *would* do or think, and what they are.

Think of what it means to define correct use in another language. For an English speaker to define or conceptualize *Himmel* by saying "The meaning of *Himmel* is . . ." is really to say, more fundamentally, "By *Himmel* a standard German speaker means . . . ," or, to make it even more logically explicit, "In such and such situation, a standard German speaker would say *Himmel*." To say that a certain kind of person *means* this or that, or that in such and such situation this person would say such and such thing is to presuppose some kind of knowledge about that person—before anything was said. One cannot define a word as if describing the shape of a coastline; words do not sit around *having* meaning. They are a special kind of conscious act carried out by a special kind of being. At root, a dictionary is a set of generalizations answering to thousands of iterations of the same question: "What is it like to be a speaker of this language with respect to the utterance _____?" That question has embedded within it the question "What is it like to be a speaker at all?," which itself presupposes the question "What is it like to be a human being?" Put another way: a particular mode of speech (a language) presupposes a general category of speech (languages as such), which presupposes beings capable of speech (human beings). The dictionary declares implicitly in every entry, "This is what a standard English speaker would say," which is, necessarily and inescapably, a claim to know something about what a *language-using-being* would do.

The connection between "what x does" and "what x would do" is crucial because it is not enough to point to patterns in behavior only to then refrain from claiming *understanding*, as if human behavior simply presented itself for description. A theory requires a sense of prediction and of insight. One cannot have a theory that detects patterns in existing and past practice and that also anticipates new practice without some sense of what the practitioner is. There are no practices without practitioners, just as in language there is no speech without speakers. Words are not substances that exist abstractly out there "having" meanings. Words "have" meanings because, and only because, human beings *mean* this or that *by* those words. Practices, similarly, are not simply things that happen but have as a necessary condition the reality of the practitioner who enacts them. Any practice is ultimately something human beings *do*, and something that *human beings* do.

For the purposes of conceptualizing Islam one does not have to proclaim one's presuppositions about human nature everywhere, but one cannot permanently evade or deny them either. One's basic presuppositions about human nature will dictate or at least influence which subset of Muslims are taken to be the primary inputs into one's conceptual apparatus, which in turn will help determine the output of one's theoretical procedures. One is always exploring a version the question "What would the right or standard Muslim believe, do, or want?," or, to make it more explicit, "What is it like to be a standard Muslim with respect to some particular thing?" That question presupposes the question "What is it like to be a Muslim?," and *that* question has as its more explicit form "What is it like for a *human*

being to be Muslim?" This latter question, in turn, presupposes a reasonable answer to the more universal question "What is it like to be a human
being?," which restated means "What would a human being do?"

One can express the nested presuppositions the following way, in order
of what question must be presupposed first before being able to answer the
subsequent ones:

What do human beings do, and what *would* they do?

What do Muslim human beings do, and what *would* they do?

What do standard Muslim human beings do, and what *would*
they do?

What would a standard Muslim human being do with respect
to this particular thing?

These questions constitute the implicit analytical structure of the questions
"What is Islam?" or "Is it Islamic?" One *must* pay a certain minimal attention to the question "What is a human being?"

The conceptualizer of Islam has to be able to account, if pressed, for
the question "What is it like to be the kind of being (a Muslim) who can
presuppose what is, what can be, and what ought to be, and in fact does
so in this particular mode of dealing with what is, what can be, and what
ought to be (Islam)—all while keeping in mind that I (the conceptualizer)
am just such a being who presupposes what is, what can be, and what ought
to be (from within the framework of my own metaphysical institution)?"
Any conceptualizer of Islam (Muslim or not) is always a human being. A
human being always has ultimate presuppositions about what is, what can
be, and what ought to be, and those presuppositions always exist in *some*
configuration or other. Indeed, any conceptualization of Islam necessarily
presupposes an answer to the question at the start of this paragraph—because
the heart of conceptualizing Islam is answering the question "What does the
right kind of Muslim human being believe, do, and want?" It is a situation
in which one human being (the conceptualizer) is trying to conceptualize
another human being (the concrete or imagined standard Muslim).

The tools at the disposal of the conceptualizers to answer this question—tools they cannot do without—are dependent upon their own metaphysical presuppositions about what is, what can be, and what ought to
be, including and especially their vision of what it means to be a human

being, and these tools and presuppositions depend necessarily upon their own metaphysical institution.

One can know what human beings are—what they do, and what they would do—only as a member of a metaphysical institution—that is, through trust, deference, reliance, dogma, and imitation. No one can do it alone. Consequently, it is impossible to explore or conceptualize a metaphysical institution such as Islam—which must presuppose a certain understanding of these entities called human beings—without being a member of a metaphysical institution oneself (relying on its authority, imitating its practice, accepting its dogmas), just as one can explore a natural language only from within a natural language—whether one's own or another. Despite its universalist self-image, the Modern Project studying Islam is not some special case but instead is one example of a general category of interactions in which members of one metaphysical institution studies another.

One might dismiss such metaphysical questions about human nature as having no bearing on actual historical or anthropological theorizing about Islam. Researchers may seem to get along just fine without thinking about metaphysics in the humanities and social science subproject. But this is ultimately an illusion. Methods and procedures for conceptualizing Islam, which appear to have nothing to do with metaphysics, have already presupposed their first input, namely the standard Muslims and what they do, and that first input is heavily dependent upon one's ultimate presuppositions about human beings. It is in choosing the standard Muslims where deep assumptions matter most. The procedures for conceptualizing the Islamic may not seem, at first glance, to be sensitive to the metaphysics of the scholar, but one's selection of the first input into that procedure is as metaphysical as any question can be. Those ultimate presuppositions are always there, and are always operative because the conceptualizer always belongs to some metaphysical institution himself, and they are far from trivial: What are a human being's potentialities? What type of metaphysical institution most effectively nurtures the realization of that human potential? Are the potentialities of what it means to be a human being able to be fulfilled in some particular institution or not? Which institutions—or which kinds of them—allow human beings to truly *be* human beings?

People typically presuppose answers to such questions, and they are different for different people. What one believes a human being to be will determine what one believes is possible for human beings, and it is on the basis of what is possible that one judges what is best for them. Crucially, however, in order to have a metaphysics refined enough to be able to meaningfully explore another metaphysical institution, one must be in a metaphysical institution. By this I mean that in order to be a religious studies scholar, or an anthropologist, or a historian, one has to have a set of ultimate presuppositions even to function, and those presuppositions do not come completely from oneself but from one's own metaphysical institution—whether one calls it a culture, a civilization, a tradition, or a religion.

For example, one necessarily believes that certain modalities of community are *better* in light of what human beings are and what the world is, that certain kinds of practices are *better* in light of what human beings are and what the world is, that certain forms of legacy are *better* in light of what human beings are and what the world is. They are deemed better because they are better *for* human beings given what human beings are and can be, and this judgment cannot take place in a conceptual vacuum. It is on the basis of one's ultimate presuppositions, which people may or may not even be aware of consciously, that one judges as better or worse the various complex realities that come to be called variously religions, traditions, cultures, civilizations, systems, and the like. The various configurations of metaphysical institution are judged *normatively* and cannot fail to be judged so. Put simply, in the eyes of some people, being civilized or cultured is good, while being religious or traditional is bad (see below). For others it is the reverse, and for many others there is a complex interplay of these attributes. But in all cases, one is dealing with questions of what is deemed to be good or bad in light of what human beings are and what they can be. A basic problem, as discussed in the early chapters of this book, is that often one is not thinking clearly about the real parameters by which these judgments take place. Because of the long-standing self-image of the Modern Project, it becomes difficult to recognize that when one makes judgments about things being "cultural," "civilizational," "religious," or "traditional," one is in fact judging *different configurations of the same parameters in the same conceptual space.*

The Modern Trifurcation of Metaphysics

To understand how this is so, we must briefly consider the historically contingent situation of the modern culture of ultimate questions. What does this encounter between one metaphysical institution (the Modern Project) and another (the Islamic tradition) look like?

Let us first look at the communities in question and especially the contours of their respective hierarchies. It was argued above that those whose opinion matters when one is conceptualizing "Is some *x* Islamic?" will be a slightly different group depending on the thing one is interested in. But there are two degrees of difference to be considered. To say that there are different groups of people does not have mean they are *discrete* groups of people. The words "umlaut" and "autumn" have different letters, as do "autumn" and "chirpy," but in the first pair the sets of letters are overlapping while in the second pair they are nonoverlapping.

When it comes to the most ultimate questions in Islam, the apex communities that deal with these ultimate matters of what is true, what is possible, and what is good vary from question to question, but those differences are characterized by significant overlap in terms of community, practice, and legacy. One can point to four institutional areas where ultimate questions of what is real, what is rational, and what is right are dealt with: ʿ*ilm al-kalām* (theology), *uṣūl al-fiqh* (legal theory or jurisprudence), *taṣawwuf* (the spiritual path), and *falsafah/ḥikmah* (philosophy). If one analyzes these disciplines each as a community practicing a legacy, one notices first that the communities are frequently overlapping hierarchies. The same scholar can write authoritatively on *kalām*, *taṣawwuf*, *fiqh*, and *falsafah/ḥikmah* without any contradiction or objection. There can also be significant overlap in terms of the intellectual procedures and methods used in each discipline. For example, many metaphysical expositions from the school of Ibn al-ʿArabī, later Sunnī *kalām*, and Islamic philosophy will rely upon the same core set of metaphysical concepts such as *wujūd* (being, existence), *māhiyyah* (essence, quiddity), *wujūb* (necessity), and *imkān* (possibility, contingency) and will also make use of formal logic as developed in the general Islamic intellectual culture. And it goes without saying that these disciplines have an important overlap when it comes to legacy in the Quran and Sunnah, and a common intellectual heritage from which they draw.[1]

By contrast, in the Modern Project as it stands today, the deeper one goes into ultimate questions of what is real, rational, and right, the more *fragmented* each type of question becomes from the other, such that one can speak of a *trifurcation* when it comes to the modern culture of ultimate questions.[2] Not only are the apex communities that deal respectively with truth, rationality, and goodness separate, it is widely considered important and necessary that they remain separate. In the modern world the apex communities we call Science, Philosophy, and Art/Culture are essentially discrete silos. Not only that, but it is usually considered important in the eyes of the members of these communities that the procedures or methods by which science, philosophy, and art are carried out are also entirely separate and different from each other in their essential aspects. This is the self-image of the Modern Project's metaphysical communities as it stands today.

The philosopher and novelist Iris Murdoch, who is interesting in this context because she is one of the extremely rare exceptions of someone highly placed in two of the three communities, said, "[Philosophy] is not science and it's not art, and it's very important that it's not science. . . . As soon as you start doing science you're falling right out of philosophy. . . . Although the style may be scientific . . . what you're doing is certainly not science, it's a kind of reflection on concepts." She goes on to say, "As soon as philosophy gets into a novel it ceases to be philosophy." Speaking of her literary versus her philosophical books, she said, "I would be very pleased if it was impossible to tell it was the same person writing."[3] Theodor Adorno, also an exception in being a philosopher as well as composer (though not as prominent a musician as Murdoch was a novelist), delineated these boundaries quite strongly: "A philosophy that tried to imitate art, that would turn itself into a work of art, would be expunging itself."[4] Speaking of Edmund Husserl, he complained, "What can be held against his work is its contamination with science."[5] In speaking of the line between science and philosophy he says, "In philosophy the authentic question will somehow almost always include its answer. Unlike science, philosophy knows no fixed sequence of question and answer."[6] And when it comes to art and philosophy he argues, "Both keep faith with their own substance through their opposites: art by making itself resistant to its meanings; philosophy, by refusing to clutch at any immediate thing."[7] Making a similar point he says, "Philosophy is neither a science nor the 'cogitative poetry' to which positivists would degrade it in a stupid oxymoron."[8] The philosopher Robert Brandom recognized the trifurcation implicitly, noting, "To specify the distinctive sort of understanding that is the characteristic goal of philosophers' writing is to say what distinguishes philosophers from other sorts of constructive seekers of understanding, such as novelists and scientific theorists."[9]

This trifurcation, about which much more could be said, means that if something is science, it ought not to be philosophy or art/culture, and if it is philosophy, it ought not to be science or art/culture, and if it is art/culture, it ought not to be science or philosophy. Since the second half of the nineteenth century these boundaries have remained surprisingly strict—a deep fragmentation that has broad and deep ramifications for global intellectual culture. To do science in the Modern Project (to establish what is real) is to be a part of the scientific community on the one hand and to operate on the basis of certain received ideas on the other. To do philosophy in the Modern Project (to establish what is rational) is to be a part of a certain academic network and to take as canonical a certain genre of arguments. And to do art/culture in the Modern Project (to express what is valued and worthwhile) is to be accepted in the global art world or cultural sphere, and to acknowledge a certain repertoire of cultural artifacts and practices. There is little meaningful overlap in any of these dimensions, and in fact the boundaries are jealously maintained. In Islam, as noted above, there has never been a single apex metaphysical community in the sense of a single group of people who remain invariant across all metaphysical questions (truth, rationality, goodness), and instead there is a convergence and coherence that makes it neither a fragmented reality like the Modern Project, nor a rigid hierarchy that disallows a range of interpretations and approaches.

The modern metaphysical trifurcation creates in the Modern Project's collective mind a certain stance or habit wherein one treats the realm of the theoretical independently of the descriptive on the one hand, and the normative on the other. It cleaves one's sense of reality from one's ability to be rational and cleaves both from what it means to be good. Think about how often one hears that philosophy cannot declare what is real or what is good, but that it can ask the right questions about what is real or what is good. Indeed, in the modern academy (which is where Modern Project philosophy resides with few exceptions), to philosophize requires implicitly a stance that treats as *inviolable* the boundaries with science on the one hand (philosophers rely on descriptions of the world, but they can never produce such descriptions) and the boundaries with art/culture on the other (philosophers cannot create or declare value, but they can theorize about it). In the real world of human beings, of course, these territorial boundaries do not exist. Human beings do not *actually* fragment their sense of what is real, rational, and right. No one can theorize in a way that does not presuppose both the descriptive inputs and the values in light of which such theorizations take place. The objective, the subjective, and the rational are always copresent, coimplicative, and irreducible to each other in human consciousness. But as historically contingent intellectual hierarchies, the trifurcation of ultimate questions into the domains of science, philosophy, and art/culture is undeniable.

This metaphysical trifurcation is a vast and complex subject, but for our purposes here it is particularly significant on the question of universality.

The fragmentation into three apex communities results, in part, from the Modern Project's universalist self-image of having no constraints on one's autonomy, and especially its imperative to be free from the bonds of religion and tradition. But when it comes to ultimate questions of what is real, what is rational, and what is right, it is impossible to have *no* constraints, if for no other reason than that these three dimensions of thought *constrain each other* (never mind that any institution is characterized by modes of dogma, imitation, and reliance). The rational is the rational always in light of the real and the right; the real is the real in light of the right and the rational; and the right is the right in light of the real and the rational. One cannot have objectivity or subjectivity or rationality without each of the other two. The Modern Project overcomes the mutual stickiness of these three dimensions of thought in relation to each other (and the mutual constraints to which they give rise) using walls of separation between the authoritative communities who deal with these dimensions of thought. In the Modern Project's culture of ultimate questions scientists do not concern themselves *as scientists* with philosophical or artistic matters; philosophers *as philosophers* do not concern themselves with scientific or artistic matters; and artists *as artists* (or culture creators and heroes more broadly) do not concern themselves with scientific or philosophical matters. Each apex community is free and unconstrained in its own realm, thereby fulfilling—in a certain illusory way—the constraint of having no constraints. But this autonomy is indeed an illusion, the result of the demand to be free from all tradition and authority, and especially the authority of God. Only by maintaining these discrete hierarchies can the Modern Project avoid allowing truth, rationality, and goodness to fully inform each other and to converge on the Absolute. But that is a complex discussion for another day, and these brief allusions will have to suffice for now.

Islam and the Anonymous "We"

With respect to the study and conceptualization of Islam, the metaphysical trifurcation leads to, or goes along with, a tendency by the Modern Project, as a metaphysical institution, to view itself as an aggregate of pure procedures or methods—scientific methods here, philosophical modes of analysis and critique there, and cultural self-expression elsewhere, none of which is considered to be dogmatic or traditional or authoritarian. But practices unconnected from authority and purposes can exist only in the Modern Project's self-image about its own antitraditional universality. They cannot exist in the wild. Procedures (the way things are done, explored, or produced) are always suspended between premises (a certain inheritance or canon) and purposes (a set of goals that are articulated and directed by an authoritative community). Any method (scientific discovery, philosophical argumentation, cultural creation) presupposes the community of masters who know how to implement it and who determine its constituent steps; whatever is produced by those masters using that method becomes part of the inheritance acknowledged and maintained by those masters. Even though practices are not reducible to the communities who implement them or the legacies upon which they are based, they cannot be understood properly without reference to them.

The tension between the self-image of modern inquiry as a pure procedure as opposed to the reality of it as a community practicing a legacy is not hard to find if one is attentive to it. In Shahab Ahmed's *What Is Islam?*, for example, there is a constant duality between the "we" (or "us") on the one hand, and Islam ("the phenomenon at stake") on the other. *What Is Islam?* and many works like it in the Euro-American academy is clearly and consistently written for that "we." To take an example, for Ahmed the historical practice of "self-professed" Muslims

> poses severe difficulties for the coherence <u>our</u> ordering of the world in terms of Islam, and of Islam in terms of the world—and thus poses difficulties for <u>our</u> efforts at making Islam and the world meaningful and coherent for <u>ourselves</u> . . .[10]
>
> These Muslims are deeply conscious of the importance that their claim to constitute Islam be a *coherent* one. . . . <u>We</u> owe it, not only to the Muslims whose exertions and lives comprise the human and historical phenomenon at stake, but also to <u>our</u> own efforts of meaning-making for our own selves, to take seriously this claim of coherence . . .[11]

Ahmed notes that "<u>we</u> must call into question the coherence of <u>our</u> own assumptions," and restates his vision for his book as providing a new conceptualization of Islam, with the goal of "a more accurate and meaningful understanding of Islam in the human experience—and, thus, of the human experience at large."[12] "<u>Our</u> task as analysts, whether historians or anthropologists, is to conceptualize this post-formative Balkans-to-Bengal Islam *as Islam* despite—indeed, *because of*—the inconveniences this task poses <u>our</u> analytical habits."[13] Whose task, and whose habits? When Ahmed laments the "assumption of the legal-supremacist conceptualization of Islam/Islamic by *Western analysts and modern Muslims alike*" doing violence to "the phenomenon at stake,"[14] one wonders whether these two categories of "Western analyst" and "modern Muslim" have any overlap at all and how precisely they are supposed to relate to each other. Who are "we" and why do "we" owe it to Muslims to do anything? (Also note that there are no "self-professed" Western analysts, only self-professed Muslims.)

This "we" does not go entirely unidentified, as when Ahmed speaks about "the North American and European dominated international academy whose humanities and social sciences project it is to conceptualize, analyze and valorize people and phenomena of the world,"[15] and elsewhere about "the power of the discourse of the Euro-American academy," which, despite the use of the third person, most certainly constitutes the "we" and "us" (or part of it) who constitute the audience for *What Is Islam?*

Ahmed's book is, in one respect, a sustained plea aimed at "us" to change "our" intellectual ways, but in light of his lengthy and intricate discussions of authority, rationality, presuppositions, and normativity as concerns Islam, it is frustrating that the reader is never sure whether or precisely how Ahmed considers himself within or outside of that "we," or just what standards a reader could possibly use to determine the boundaries of that "we" in general except by simply knowing who constitutes it already. For example, one is left without any hints as to how Ahmed would have classified the present author, or any number of other living Muslim academics. Is yours truly part of the "we," a member of the community to whom *What Is Islam?* seems to be addressed, or instead part of "the phenomenon at stake"? One is baffled by phrasing such as "When we/Muslims think of human and historical Islam, it is incumbent upon us/Muslims . . ."[16] What is happening in a sentence like this? How much is being communicated by that forward slash? Just who stands on one side of it, and who on the other? And who gets to decide, and according to what principles? Clumsy language such as "we/Muslims" shows that at least in some respect the argument of *What Is Islam?* does not hold together and that the author was, at least in the moment he wrote that sentence, perhaps naggingly aware of it. This "we" is everywhere in *What Is Islam?*, and it is representative of much of the scholarship that attempts to "conceptualize" Islam or even parts of it, and it consists of those "analysts, whether historians or anthropologists" who deal with Islam, or, as Ahmed calls them, the "humanities and social sciences project" of the Euro-American academy.

Since "we" are presented with an object of study (the "phenomenon at stake") that consists of people called Muslims and this reality in which they operate that is called Islam, is there a label that one can give to "us" and the reality in which "we" operate that would corresponds to that thing, Islam, in which Muslims seem to operate? Muslims and Islam have proper names that can be affixed to them; what names do "we" then bear? Their metaphysical institution is called Islam. What is "ours" called? "We" are clearly not operating within Islam when undertaking this kind of scholarship, so what are "we" within? The passing mentions of the "Euro-American academy" only seem to hint at the ultimate presuppositions of what is real, rational, and right that are always going to be operative when "we" study or think about Islam.

In short: we *who*? What is "our" metaphysical institution?

❧

This asymmetry between the "we" and the object of study (Islam) is one reason why the term "Modern Project" is used throughout this book. One ought not refer to Muslims as Muslims but then to "us" as disembodied "analysts" or "scholars" or "academics" or the like. The implication of such usage is that "we" carry out a universal practice while the object of study is trapped in some particular behavior that is determined by peculiar factors by which "we" are not limited. If one can construct the phrase "Muslim intellectual" then one should be able to say "*x* intellectual" in a way that also identifies that person adequately. One might call him a "Project intellectual." Even "modern" or "Western" are simply too general, as both terms also connote a broad time period or geographic realm. The Modern Project is a provincial institution, not a global potentiality of the human condition. There is no reason why one metaphysical institution should remain unnamed and universal, like some kind of chimerical metalanguage (see below), while at the same time another metaphysical institution should be called Islam and its community called Muslims.

One must reject the assumption, not always consciously held, that when "we" think, we *think*, but when *they* think, they think *Islamically*. "We" reason and imagine as such, but Muslims reason and imagine *as Muslims*. They are always particular and constrained in their Islamic-ness. "We" do not deny them their reason and imagination entirely, but it is a *folk* rationality and a *folk* imagination.

Irritating as it can be, this idea that Muslims possess a folk rationality need not be framed as Euro-American bigotry or malice, although no doubt such factors have been significant.[17] One can explore it just as well as a question of a deeply held self-image, a hyperuniversalist self-conception at the heart of the Modern Project that the apex communities of the project are unconstrained in their explorations of ultimate questions. Starting from this universalist pretension, the claim that there is a "modern science" *and* an "Islamic science" is *logically* wrong or nearly unintelligible, because the "modern" in modern science quite simply *means* "universal and unconstrained," and therefore to speak about "the universal and unconstrained way of exploring nature" (which is how "modern science" is understood) alongside "a particular and constrained way of exploring nature" (which is how "Islamic science" is understood) is to make a category error, not an empirical or historical one. The same logical problem obtains for Islamic philosophy as well as Islamic art. One would not deny the possibility of *Islamic* philosophy or art because one claims they are of inferior quality but simply because it would be a confusion of concepts. Science is science, philosophy is philosophy, and art is art. In practice, one can allow an "Islamic philosophy" or "Islamic art" *in a manner of speaking*, as long as it was clear that one is dealing with a folk philosophy or folk art, or a protophilosophy or proto-art, the way one could have a "science class" or "art club" in a middle school. In such instances, there might be no objection to speaking about Islamic art, philosophy, or even science for that matter—so long as the implication of the discussion were clear.

Since within the Modern Project one is *already* universal and unconstrained (really: universal *because* unconstrained) by definition, then, *any other* competing claim or production about what is real, rational, or right is either immature and incorrect (by being limited) or simply gratuitous (by imitating or duplicating "us"). "We" have nothing to learn, but since the universal always encompasses the particular they necessarily have something to learn from "us." To admit that there might be *something* there to actually learn would be to repudiate one's freedom from constraint and one's universality—freedom and universality according to a very specific understanding, it has to be emphasized. That is, if some truth or rationality, or fruit of imagination, exists in Islam that can be found only in Islam, and was not already within the Modern Project actually or potentially, it would mean that the Modern Project was never universal in the first place and hence *was not the Modern Project at all*. To believe that truth, reason, and goodness can exist *as such* outside of the Modern Project in a way that does not already exist (actually or potentially) within the project is, according to this way universal self-image, a logical mistake.

In the real world, and not in the abstract realm of thought, the "we" of the Modern Project is a finite number of actually existing human beings.

The apex communities that are trusted to articulate for "us" who "we" are (and who any "other" is) at the ultimate level are a discrete population of living individuals. These communities have the intrinsic moral authority to steer the Modern Project and sustain its culture of ultimate questions. By determining the boundaries of what "we" believe to be real (through science), rational (through philosophy), and right (through art/culture), they directly determine the nature of the "we." If the science world, philosophy world, and culture world do not consider you part of their respective worlds, *you are not in the Modern Project.* It is not simply that "one does" science, philosophy, or art. "We" do it, and "we" know who "we" are.

These apex communities do not rely upon a procedure or theoretical framework to determine who the "we" is, because they *are* the ultimate arbiters of the "we" when it comes to ultimate questions and the contours of their metaphysical institution. Remember, any true community has *moral authority* that is intrinsic and cannot be bestowed or removed by others. Thus, the demarcation of the "we/Muslims" relationship between the Modern Project and Islam is not *discovered* through any kind of stepwise rational procedure. No research program establishes that boundary. Rather, the fact that there exists a "we" on the one hand and an "Islam" on the other is the presupposition, *the first input,* that is the very condition for any substantial conceptualization or definition of "Islam" and "Islamic. And the Islamic is simply not who "we" are for the apex communities of the Modern Project. However fuzzy the boundaries might be in some cases, it is taken to be axiomatic that "we" are not Islam. To the degree that you are of one metaphysical institution, you are not of the other.

Now, a very important problem is created by the fact that the deeper one goes in the Modern Project the more fragmented metaphysical questions become. The communities that deal with truth, rationality, and purpose are all severed from one another, but at the same time each of those is severed from the study of the Islamic tradition as a serious matter. It creates a situation in which the Modern Project cannot really study Islam *as a metaphysical institution interacting with another metaphysical institution.*

Two broad facts about the relationship of Islam to the Modern Project and its humanities and social science *subprojects* (to borrow again from Shahab Ahmed) must be kept in mind:

1. The ultimate nature and boundaries of the "we" (i.e., we the Modern Project), including the fact that "we" are *not* Islam, are firmly in place before any conceptualization of Islam or the Islamic is brought up as a serious theoretical or analytical question.

2. The apex communities with the authority to set the ultimate presuppositions of what it means to be "us" (that is, what are the boundaries of what one can believe to be real, to be rational, to be right) have nearly zero overlap with the subproject communities (academics in the humanities and social sciences) whose task it is to conceptualize Islam.

In other words, what it means to be "us" in the Modern Project is determined internally to the Modern Project by certain apex communities whose role it is to say what is real, rational, and right, but it is rarely (indeed, almost never) members of those same apex communities who deal with Islam as a scholarly question. On the one hand there are the scientists, philosophers, and artists/cultural figures, while on the other there are the communities whose task it is "to conceptualize, analyze and valorize people and phenomena of the world,"[18] namely, the various kinds of historians, religious studies scholars, anthropologists, art historians, sociologists, and political scientists who generally lack the authority of those apex communities to set the basic parameters of the "we." So, the people doing scholarship on Islamic science are generally not from the science world; the people studying Islamic theology and philosophy are generally not from the academic philosophy world; and the people doing scholarship on Islamic art/culture are generally not art/culture creators.

That means that the apex communities of "our" metaphysical institution (the science world, philosophy world, and art/culture world) do not study the metaphysical institution of Islam but rely upon an intellectual network of subcontractors to whom that task is delegated. Are the scholars who interpret Islamic philosophy accepted as trendsetting philosophers by academic philosophy departments? Are people who do the history of Islamic science themselves accepted by scientists to speak on other topics related to modern science? Do those who have dominated the field of Islamic law have any standing in interpreting the law in the West? Are those who study the ethical and spiritual traditions of Islam taken to be ethical and spiritual exemplars or heroes in the West? The answer is almost always no.

Thus, the communities who are authorized to actually steer or revise the Modern Project's ultimate inheritance, methods, and aims—always from within, never in light of an outside institution—are not generally part of the process of conceptualizing Islam in the various fields of academic Islamic studies. This means that any attempt at categorizing some x as Islamic or un-Islamic (that is, any conceptualization or description of Islam as Islam, whether it is stated in terms of being Islamic, orthodox, religious, or mainstream), when carried out from within the Modern Project (by the social science and humanities subproject), necessarily relies upon and is constrained by a supreme dogmatic fact or input whose overall nature remains invariant and fixed, like an anchor point, throughout all possible reconceptualizations.

That anchor—that input—is the determination of who "we" are and who "they" (the Muslims) are. Any conceptualization of the "Islamic" and related terms depends absolutely on first establishing who the Muslims are—this group of people who are not "us." Establishing that first input is part of any subsequent conceptualizing procedure carried out from within the Modern Project. "We" already know in a vague and general sense (incontrovertible though it may be) who they (Muslims) or it (Islam) is, if only that it is not "us." Without that already existing, pretheoretical demarcation between the Modern Project and Islam, no conceptual procedure geared toward "What is Islam?" is possible, because it is that demarcation that determines both the inputs of the procedure and the purpose for which it is designed.

The social scientists and humanities scholars whose function it is to conceptualize Islam thus operate under certain constraints. They must accept the boundary of the "we" and "Islam" as they find it and can do little to change it. They cannot theorize or conceptualize without inputs (the standard Muslims) and without sought-after outputs (that is, some sense of a worthwhile output such as "advancing our academic understanding of Islam"), but because of their place in the Modern Project's hierarchies they have very limited control over those inputs and those general aims. It is the "higher-ups" who are free to explore and answer those questions, but the higher-ups do not know much about the "phenomenon at stake" (Islam) except in rather general terms, and as a rough approximation they really only know that Islam is not "us." In fact, the higher-ups (the apex/metaphysical communities of scientists, philosophers, culture-creators/leaders) are typically ignorant of Islam and the Islamic to a startling degree. The anthropologists and historians who actually do know something about Islam—but who are a subproject within the Modern Project—cannot change that there is a "we" and an "Islam" and have little to say about what makes the "we" who "we" ultimately are.

Still, because of the sheer historical magnitude of Islam and the scope of modern intellectual culture, there is considerable latitude in the way that the humanities and social science subproject can conceptualize and do theoretical work within the general bounds set by the Modern Project's apex communities. Even though the academic subproject cannot alter the demarcation between "us" and Islam, they can nevertheless select or assume something about who the standard Muslim is—never crossing the line between "us" and Islam but by making choices among the subsets of Muslims. They cannot change the overall mission of the Modern Project, but they can select the output value that they are interested in (e.g., some object of study in the Islamic context is religious *or* cultural, orthodox or heterodox, normative or antinomian, Islamic or un-Islamic, and so forth). In order to get from those inputs (which are constrained but not deterministic) to the outputs (which are also constrained but not deterministic), the academic subproject theorizes, conceptualizes, defines, and so forth. It is in this realm of theoretical procedures and concept creation—linking inputs to outputs—where the humanities/social science subproject exercises freedom and creativity in terms of "conceptualizing" Islam.

So, one academic book dismisses the very possibility of an *Islamic* philosophy while another affirms it in a limited sense. One article balks at the notion of *Islamic* art while another presupposes the validity of that concept. One scholar argues that ISIS represents a genuine manifestation of Islamic norms, while another sees it as a marginal phenomenon. None of these variations disturb that basic dividing line between the Modern Project and Islam, and they certainly have no bearing on the self-conception of the Modern Project internally. The various academic theorizations and conceptualizations that take isolated topics and define the correctness, orthodoxy, and standardness of some practice or idea in terms of Islam do not even have to be coherent with each other, and in fact they rarely are. Most every scholar has his or her own idiosyncratic view on a large spectrum of different kinds of questions. Very few works of academic scholarship strive for a totalizing and comprehensive conception of what is correctly or normatively Islam anyway, so individual pieces of research that make theorizing claims to determine what (normative, orthodox) "Islam" or "Islamic" really are do not generally make waves that could disturb the overall incumbent relationship between the "we" and Islam. These variations exist within the general bounds articulated by the Modern Project's culture of ultimate questions—the metaphysical institution's legacy.

What are those general bounds as it concerns academic theorizing about Islam? In short, and here one must state the matter starkly, it is that the "we" will remain the "we," and "we" will remain always more right and more rational—or simply, the rightest kind of metaphysical institution. Islam will never be rational and right where "we" are irrational and wrong. Where Islam happens to be right, "we" were already right in that same way, and usually more so. "We" encompass and transcend "the phenomenon at stake" with our rationality, imagination, and maturity of purpose, and this imbalance and asymmetry will be a prevailing condition in every situation where the Modern Project comes up against Islam. When "we" study them, it is through reason and imagination (even for those who pretend to disavow rationality), but when they study "us," it is a reactive and derivative behavior or routine. "We" are always a step ahead. Such ideas are not typically said aloud or even formulated in the mental horizon of Euro-American academics, but it is rare to find instances of conceptualizing Islam or the Islamic that fail to conform to these implicit maxims. If scholars do not actively subscribe to them, neither do there seem to be many instances of the academic subproject violating them. The sincere eccentrics—of which there are many—that simply enjoy their subject matter tend to avoid the "conceptualizing" question altogether. These remarks are not directed at every last Euro-American academic but at a prevailing tendency and, some might say, structure.

Whatever it means to be modern (or postmodern), it means one can never admit to being actually *contingent* or *particular*. Above all it is supposed to mean that one operates without the constraints of religion and tradition. This spirit of unshackled autonomy shows up when subproject scholars turn their attention to Islam. They are not conceptualizing *modernistically* or *postmodernly* or *Westernly*. They are *simply* conceptualizing, analyzing, defining, classifying, and valorizing, but not *as* anything or anyone in particular. It is all the same to restate it in the passive voice, wherein Islam is conceptualized, analyzed, defined, classified, or valorized. Who is doing it? Naming them or their purposes seems to be unimportant. It is as though a situation arises in which these universal unconstrained intellectual practices simply *happen*; this is often what is meant by the word "academic." Is there a non–Modern Project academy? In reality, in the Modern Project, "academy" is a proper name. As members in good standing of the Modern Project, the academic subproject that deals with Islam intellectually will—passively or actively, consciously or indifferently—maintain and sustain the unconstrained nonparticular nature of the Modern Project in relation to the constrained and particular phenomenon at stake, Islam.

Maintaining the Universal/Particular Asymmetry

As discussed at length earlier, the right approach to "conceptualizing" Islam or the Islamic from outside of it, and sometimes from inside of it, is quite simple to understand. All one has to do is consult the right Muslims one has already presupposed to be right, the way one would consult an authoritative dictionary. But that stance would make the "conceptualizing" apparatus of the Modern Project dispensable and reduce their intellectuals (specifically, the social science and humanities subproject) to mere guests or tourists in the land of the Islamic, and the universal self-image of the Modern Project cannot easily allow for that. There *has* to be a way in which "we" navigate the "Is it Islamic?" question in a way that Muslims are not able to, because when "we" conceptualize we *conceptualize*, and when Muslims conceptualize they conceptualize *Islamically.* "We" are universal, while they are particular. "We" are rational, while they have folk rationality. "We" are sophisticated about the relationship of rightness to power, while they innocently believe in truth and morality. However one chooses to define or reframe the distinction, the Modern Project's self-image maintains that boundary.

Indeed, the purposes of the social science and humanities subproject within the Modern Project, despite surface variety, do not vary all that much at the deepest level. There is a basic impetus for "us" to study them, with a basic underlying presupposition that what "we" are doing—whether it is called analysis, critique, or research or the people doing it are called academics, scholars, or investigators—we are doing that thing *as such.* "We" are never, cannot be, provincial. Even "our" performative denial of a universal standpoint is somehow universal. Islam or the Islamic has nothing to *actually* teach "us"—not really, and certainly not about defining or characterizing themselves. Anything learned or developed is always *internal* to the Modern Project. Whatever "they" produce has to first pass through a process by which it is indigenized as "academic" or some similar honorific. Thus, the unique universal status of the Modern Project, and the corollary that Islam is *not* internal to the Modern Project, is a fixed point and unshakable first given—again, not necessarily as a malicious strategy but as a consequence of an unshakable self-image. "We" study *them* for our own purposes. Whatever those purposes of "ours" are, and they are many and varied, they exclude by definition treating the "phenomenon at stake" as an institution or community of equal status to the Modern Project. Implicit (and sometimes explicit) to the mission or self-image of the Modern Project (regardless of whether such a mission is consciously held) is the maintaining of that privileged status of the Modern Project as unique and special in its universality, whether that means scientific rationality, historical criticism, sophistication about power relationships, moral and aesthetic imagination, and so forth.

But what happens when this universal conceit that "we" possess rationality and all others remain in a state of "folk rationality" or some other form of basic naiveté comes face to face with the growing and abundant counterevidence of a robust imagination, rationality, and elevated moral and aesthetic aims in "the phenomenon at stake," all of which render it impossible to attribute folk rationality, naiveté, lack of imagination, or moral immaturity to the Islam and Muslims?[19] What happens when one also considers the mounting failures of the rationality, imagination, and ethical and aesthetic aims of the Modern Project, whose philosophy and culture have run into many catastrophic dead ends? Not only does Islam seem far less folksy than "we" once believed, but the Modern Project seems ever less convincing in its universal (or performatively antiuniversal) claims.

Many of the moves to redefine or conceptualize Islam function—intentionally or, what is more likely, unintentionally—to maintain that relationship of universal/particular, rational/folk-rational, sophisticated/naive, superior/inferior, and to sustain the basic presuppositions about who "we" are and what "we" ought to be doing. The conceptualization of Islam partly serves to protect those presuppositions (we are us, and we are right) by modulating how we classify and define "the phenomenon at stake," Islam.

One way of maintaining this asymmetry is to capitalize on the ambiguity of terms denoting metaphysical institutions—our tetrad from chapter 1. One foregrounds Islam as "religion" or "tradition" and then evacuates the concepts of religion and tradition of all those favorable attributes with which "we" identify, and deposits those desirable realities into favored categories such as culture and civilization, while taking what "we" consider inferior and shunting them into concepts such as religion and tradition. In this spirit one says that the works of Islamic philosophy of obviously the highest caliber (e.g., Avicenna) are not *Islamic* philosophy but rather philosophy "in the Islamic world." Sufism (of the kind "we" admire) is not Islamic or Quranic or Prophetic but a kind of cultural or ethnic movement imported into Islam or a rebellion within Islam that mirrors the spirit of the Modern Project in breaking free of the bonds of "men of religion." Rumi is a freethinking "poet of love" or a "Persian poet," but not an Islamic poet. Islamic science is really just protoscience or, if it is science, it is really an alien or metacultural presence among the Muslims. Whatever phenomenon one finds mirrored in the Modern Project is reflexively reclassified from the Islamic (or religious/theological) into the Islamicate (cultural, civilizational, ethnic). This gambit of using "religion" or "tradition" as the reject pile for aspects of metaphysical institutions that "we" do not like is why it is so important to have a model/theory that enables one to understand religion, culture, civilization, tradition, and society as various labels given to different configurations of objects in the same conceptual space. A flawed conceptualization of the Islamic functions as a way of adjusting the definition of "religion" and "tradition" to include the things "we" disfavor and to make sure that "culture" and "civilization" (which "we" are in the habit of identifying ourselves as) are able to designate the things that we like. It really is not a conceptualization of Islam at all, not at root, but a taxonomy of what we take to be good and bad about ultimate questions. When our tetrad of terms is agreeably conceptualized, "we" can safely categorize the evidence we do not like into the disfavored of categories of "religion" or "tradition."

This approach usually goes along with a certain confidence about the Modern Project's mission of civilization and culture. There is a sense that there is such a thing as truth, goodness, rationality, and that "we" uniquely have it, or at least "we" are closest to it. In this Enlightenment-aligned approach, "we" believe that there is an abundance of evidence of our truth, rationality, and goodness, while they lack such evidence, and any emergent counterevidence can be classified as mere "religion" or "tradition" and can thereby be neutralized. The threat to this approach from Islam would come in the form of truth, rationality, and goodness that actually compete with the universalist claims of the Modern Project.

There is, however, another approach to conceptualizing Islam that is broadly "postmodern" and performatively antinormative and antiuniversal. In this approach, one conceptualizes the Islamic not in light of objective standards of what is rational, true, and good with the assumption that "we" possess them but by first undermining the very concepts of truth, rationality, and goodness themselves, and then arguing (while often pretending not to argue for it) that Islam is "whatever Muslims do." In this approach, one obliterates the very concept of the normative in all realms, such that the potential challenge of the Islamic to the Modern Project is not some contingent body of evidence of Islam's rationality and goodness but the fact that Islam asserts any norms at all. What is to be eliminated in this antinormative approach is the very possibility of the objective good, the objectively rational, the objectively real. If Islam makes such claims to objective truth or goodness, it is a danger for those reasons. Islam is not a problem for "us" because it *might* be objectively true, good, or rational (a possibility the Enlightenment advocate wants to disprove at all costs) but instead because Islam stubbornly maintains that such naive and even tyrannical concepts as truth and morality mean anything at all, and in so doing provides a viable antithesis to the performative relativism favored by many Modern Project intellectuals. Instead of making Islam a mere religion or tradition, the (performative) antinormative approach conceptualizes Islam in such a way as to empty it of *any* real moral or rational content. What remains of Islam is an object of study that leaves the Modern Project intellectual in his proper place, grasping what the "phenomenon at stake" fails to grasp, and reducing a community-practice-legacy to an identity, a routine, and an heirloom that can now be studied safely far away from problematic ideas such as "truth," "rationality," or "goodness."

Logically speaking, the Enlightenment-aligned approach is ultimately *self-undermining* (or *self-falsifying*), in that it could have been true with the right evidence, but it turns out to be false by the accumulation of evidence that the Modern Project does not in fact possess a universal rationality and morality above and beyond that of the folk rationality and folk morality of Islam. The second approach is directly *self-refuting*, in that it begins from a logical fallacy, because no inquiry can coherently dispense with truth, rationality, or goodness, since to deny such claims is to make them.

The first approach avoids having the subproject defer to Muslim authority (and thus cancelling its own purpose) in part by using the demarcations between religion, tradition, culture, civilization, and society to camouflage certain basic choices about what is good and bad, true and false, rational and irrational. Muslims may be able to determine what is *Islamic* in a limited sense, but crucially they are not the ones who get to decide the boundary between Islamic and Islamicate, or between religion and culture, or between orthodoxy and heterodoxy. "We" do that, not them. And if "we" decide what counts as cultural or Islamicate first, then all we are doing is carving out a realm we call "religion" or "tradition" and allowing the Muslims to squabble over whatever we have already decided *might* count as religion or tradition. Muslims can argue over whether drinking alcohol is Islamic, but "we" decide whether Avicenna is Islamic or Islamicate. The second approach avoids deferring to Muslim authority because there is no such moral or intellectual authority even to be had—such perceived moral or intellectual content is really about power relationships or something else. There is nothing to defer to them about—nothing about which one has native mastery in the first place, and so one is not in danger of somehow knowing "true Islam."

In both approaches, which often appear together in varying combinations even in the same book, one retains the universalist self-image (and its performative counterpart) while retaining for oneself the exclusive (or at least, preeminent) authority to "conceptualize" Islam.[20] "We" cannot defer to an authority who is Muslim, since "we" would lose the (implicit or explicit) claim to universal rationality that encompasses their folk rationality. But "we" also cannot claim to have authority in things Islamic akin to Muslims themselves, since "we" would then run headfirst into having to justify somehow becoming, as it were, orthodox Muslims. "We" could avoid these problems by saying that Islam is not really a living metaphysical institution at all but something else—that is, if it ever was alive, it certainly no longer is, and instead Islam is essentially an identity, a set of routines, an heirloom, variously ossified, plastic, and interest-driven, and constituted by various kinds of collective assertions, reflexes, and demands. Conceptualizing such an incoherent amalgam would necessarily be done from outside of it. Indeed, how it could it do it for itself? There's nothing there that could do it.

The Modern Project as Metainstitution

In light of these considerations regarding universality and particularity let us return to the language analogy. The Modern Project does not see itself, when it conceptualizes Islam, as doing something analogous to the English-speaking world conceptualizing German. That is the whole problem. Its academic subproject does not view itself as part of one metaphysical institution studying another metaphysical institution. It does not accept that everyone has a set of ultimate presuppositions and that there is no view from nowhere where all such presuppositions can be explored, since those very explorations presuppose certain positions on what is real, rational, and right.

Let us recall that, for an English speaker conceptualizing German, the question "Is this utterance correct German?" means "Do the *relevant* people think it is correct German?" and this question can be unpacked logically to mean "What would a standard German speaker say in such and such situation?" and unpacked even further to mean "What is it like to be a German-speaking human being in such and such a situation?" An English speaker must presuppose the population of people who set the German-speaking standard. The English speaker himself is obviously not one of those relevant people, since he must in all cases defer to some kind of German-speaking authority in order to conceptualize standard German usage. An English speaker cannot tell a German carpenter how to use the word *Himmel* or a German physicist how to use *Wissenschaft*, unless he were to cite some *other* native speaker of German, and such an invocation of authority by the English speaker could not be made on the basis of a theoretical command of German rules but could be made only on the basis of some relationship of trust, of reliance upon guidance.

But let us imagine a world in which English speakers *did* believe that part of their work required a "useful conceptualization" or "adequate theory" of standard German, *and* that they assumed or asserted that German speakers had not carried out such a conceptualization adequately for themselves that the English speakers could take up readymade. The English-speaking conceptualizers might think that by refining and complicating their theory or conceptualization of German to a sufficient level of sophistication (that is, by stringing together enough concepts) they could somehow avoid being forced to choose which Germans were most authorized to say what *correct* German usage is. So, the English speakers might attempt to formulate some definition or conceptualization of German such that it would appear that these English speakers were not presuming to rank German users as standard and nonstandard. Yet in reality they would *have to* be ranking German users, by virtue of what is implied by their theorization of what counts as correct German. After all, there would be no other way to get the inputs for the conceptualization. Now, any such endeavor by English speakers is *necessarily* going to spill over into the normative dimension, because the identification of a standard (which is a *precondition* of identifying correct usage) is by definition a normative question. One cannot evade that normative question through any series theoretical moves, no matter how sophisticated. One always has to decide the inputs first.

But no conceptualization of German formulated by an English speaker would ever be able to determine whether *Vorhandenheit* is authentic German or not. An English speaker cannot say "My conceptualization of German has determined that *Vorhandenheit* is not standard German." Rather, the English speaker could only report the views of German speakers about the

Germanness of *Vorhandenheit.* The English speaker could, for example, point out that some utterance is incorrect German by opening the biggest German dictionary he could find and saying, "That word is nowhere in here!" That would be a reasonable procedure, but it would not be a "concept" of German.

Let us further suppose that, while this English speaker's "theory" or "conceptualization" of German disallows or treats as ungrammatical the word *Vorhandenheit* (a word coined by the twentieth-century philosopher Martin Heidegger, sometimes rendered "presence-at-hand"), that same speaker would accept as standard English the word "disquotational" (a coinage from twentieth-century Anglophone analytic philosophy) according to his conceptualization of his own language. One could ask, Why does "disquotational" pass muster but not *Vorhandenheit,* considering that both came into use at roughly the same period? Furthermore, one would ask, Just what interest would an English speaker have in the first place in adjudicating the Germanness of *Vorhandenheit?* And by what right would English speakers arrogate to themselves this particular task, when one would reasonably expect it to be carried out by German speakers themselves?

One might resort to some question of "usefulness" to justify such exercises in the conceptualization of another language, but an English speaker does not *need* a "theory" or "conceptualization" of German before studying Heidegger or any other German author. One just tries one's best to read them. One could reverse the languages and ask whether a German speaker would need a "conceptualization of English" before reading Quine (another twentieth-century philosopher). Again, the answer is no, and a German speaker would have no right to exclude the word "disquotational" based upon his own "conceptualization" of English unless that exclusion somehow relied upon some standard English speaker as the source of authority for doing so.

Indeed, no "theory" or "conceptualization" of German would actually help an English speaker to study Heidegger, but his presumption that one is necessary might betray something about his estimation of German culture. Imagine an English speaker asserting that no words that came into use after Goethe are "really" German (according to that English speaker's conceptualization of German). What is that English speaker saying about German speakers and their language today? Would that not imply something about the limitations of the creative capacity of the German language (or German speakers) in that English speaker's eyes?

Of course, English speakers do not have such debates about conceptualizing German because they assume—and why would they not?—that the Germans have conceptualized their own language just fine. If the right

English speakers think "disquotational" is English, it's English, and if the right German speakers think *Vorhandenheit* is German, it's German.

Why, then, is it so hard to say that if the right Muslims say something is Islamic (e.g., orthodox, mainstream, traditional, religious) then it is Islamic? It should not be hard to say—*some* Muslims have to be the right ones. But it seems that relying upon the answer to the question "Do the standard Muslims say it is Islamic?" is precisely what is studiously avoided when the Modern Project conceptualizes Islam. Such a question presupposes the existence of people who constitute the authoritative community of their own metaphysical institution and do not need it explained to them and are in the best position to explain it to others.[21]

Is the Modern Project a Metalanguage?

Take four axioms about natural language:

> Every human being speaks a language.
>
> Not everyone speaks the same language.
>
> There is no language hierarchically situated above other languages (that is, there is no such thing as a metalanguage).
>
> One can approach another language only from within one's own.

By analogy, one has the following axioms about metaphysical institutions:

> Every human being has a metaphysical institution.
>
> Not everyone has the same metaphysical institution.
>
> There is no metaphysical institution situated hierarchically above other metaphysical institutions (that is, there is no metaphysical metainstitution or meta-metaphysical institution)
>
> One can approach another metaphysical institution only from within one's own.

The language analogy employed in this book is a way to think more clearly about the Modern Project's stance of *exclusivist universality*—the idea that some human beings have found way of being human that is *uniquely* free and unhindered by authority or by prior beliefs while all other ways of being human are still in their chains or in their intellectual childhood. Almost no one believes that one's own mother tongue is *more of a language* than other languages. An English speaker believes that there are at least several other languages communities who can be just as creative, correct, and authoritative in their own languages as an English speaker can be in his. No English speaker defines English as *the* vehicle of creative correctness, or of corrective creativity, such that another language that *also* claimed to be creatively correct or correctly creative would, by that very claim of being a living language, be undermining the English speaker's exclusive claim. No one thinks an Australian studying German is different in some basic respect from an Austrian studying English.

Some philosophers in the analytic tradition devised the notion of a "metalanguage," a kind of logically ideal structure that could be used to analyze languages, but it was always a fallacy that one could create a kind of language beyond language in order to understand the true nature of language, since all one is doing is creating a special code within an already existing language and calling it "meta." Not only is that code not a metalanguage, but it is dependent upon and enclosed within a natural language (as it happens, usually German or English). One imagines a nonexistent possibility (the universal metalanguage) and then presumes all other languages have a particular status. By locating the universal content only in this metalanguage's *form* the notion of a metalanguage artificially and mistakenly separates the universal content from the particular forms of natural languages.[22] In this way of thinking, all languages are trapped in their particularity, and we must create a metalanguage to access and express what is universal. The mistake here thus is twofold. First, it is impossible to create such a metalanguage because it is always a subset of an existing language, and second it is not the case that languages are particular both in form and in content, because languages are universal through their particular forms by which human beings mean and understand.[23]

By analogy, the apex communities of the Modern Project see it as a kind of *meta–metaphysical institution* that stands in relation to other metaphysical institutions the way a metalanguage stands in relation to languages. But there can be no such thing as a meta–metaphysical institution, and to posit one in the name of the universal also mistakes the nature of metaphysical institutions as they already exist. Rather than being above and outside of other comparable realities, the so-called meta–metaphysical institution is nothing other—and can be nothing more than—a legacy that is practiced by a community, which comes out of a legacy-practice-community the same way that an instructional code (metalanguage) is always ultimately ensconced in a natural language. The "meta–metaphysical institution" is operating in the same multidimensional space, just with different coordinates.

The Modern Project cannot see itself as a metaphysical institution because it cannot properly cope with the reliance, authority, dogma, imitation, and particularity—its own traditionality—that status entails. Its self-image rules out such things even though the reality conflicts with this image. It cannot relate to other metaphysical institutions properly for the very same reasons. It considers itself more of a language than other languages, or as the one adult language in the face of other child languages.

Furthermore, the Modern Project's Islam-conceptualizing subproject fails to grasp and is not even aware of the problem that its own metaphysical presuppositions about what is real, what is rational, and what is right (its shared accounts, heuristics, and norms) are completely operative in any endeavor to conceptualize another metaphysical institution. How could they not be? Could an investigator's views of what constitutes the possibilities of grammar, vocabulary, and diction for his own language not have a massive influence on the way he studies another language? When one studies another language community's vocabulary, grammar, and preferences/uses/choices (history of uses, patterns of uses, authoritative uses), one is doing so from within one's own language community's already existing vocabulary, grammar, and preferences/uses/choices. One is looking at another language community to see how words *have been* used by them, how they *could be* used by them, and how they *should be* used by them. But there is no situation in which the study of another's uses of language is not carried out by a being who is using language himself, meaning that such study takes place from within and *through* one's *own* sense of how one's *own* words have been used, can be used, and ought to be used.

No human beings have ever reached the level of knowledge, rationality, and purpose necessary to properly conceptualize things like metaphysical institutions without being themselves *part of* some metaphysical institution that they have been guided by, whose beliefs are treated as true, and whose ideals are treated as worthy of emulation. It is not metaphysically or logically impossible for some angelic figure to arise who needs none of these things, but that has not happened yet. It would be akin to someone being able to just start speaking a language without learning it. Defining culture or civilization is itself an act of culture or civilization, just like defining language is itself an instance of language. Can a person who has no culture define culture?

Rather than chasing after an imaginary universal view from nowhere or from everywhere, one must push deeper into the particular to make it as explicit as possible. What one calls definitions, theorizations, conceptualizations, or demarcations are all different permutations of the same type of intellectual *act of consciousness*. This act always has several inescapable parameters, because each is

a *particular* communication or expression

from a *particular* speaker

to a *particular* audience

for a *particular* purpose

in a *particular* place

at a *particular* time.

Each such particular communication or expression verbally differentiates between different parts of human experience, answering to different versions of the question "What is it?" The resulting formulations can be short or long, simple or complicated, and they can take the form of describing a nature, a behavior, or an essence, but they all—definitions, conceptualizations, demarcations, theorizations—are intelligible in terms of the *particular* parameters listed above.

Indeed, a definition, in the technical sense of this book, is a heuristic in instructional mode—a form of thinking that makes sense within a given institution.

Thus any definition *of* a thing is always first a definition *by* someone *for* someone.

These particulars also hold for conceptualizing one metaphysical institution from within another. Unless one can make clear *what* the definition of "Islam" is, *who* is defining Islam, to *whom*, *why*, *where*, and *when*, one is leaving relevant information unspecified. Not every definition requires such explicit disambiguation to be useful, but it must be at least possible to specify these several "wh-" parameters if called upon to do so by a reasonable interlocutor. Consider again the word "cerulean." If one looks up its definition on a Mac one will find that cerulean is "a deep sky-blue color," and it is possible to specify who wrote that definition (*New Oxford American Dictionary*, edited by Angus Stevenson and Christine A. Lindberg), the audience the lexicographers had in mind (literate Americans), what kinds of purposes it might be used for (for a literate public who needs to know that cerulean is not turquoise, but not precise enough for help in making professional dyes), that it is used in both physical and virtual contexts in America (e.g., it ships with Macs), and that its most recent edition was published in 2010. Notice that specifying these parameters does nothing to undermine or relativize the definition; in fact, knowledge of these parameters only enhances the usefulness of a good definition for all parties involved. The definition or meaning does not float abstractly with the word but exists concretely by virtue of these parameters.

Therefore, the conceptualization of Islam always has to be:

> a *particular* communication (a book like *What Is Islam?* or *The Venture of Islam*, or an article like "The Idea of an Anthropology of Islam" or an argument embedded in another communication)

> from a *particular* speaker (Shahab Ahmed, Marshal Hodgson, or Talal Asad)

> to a *particular* audience (the humanities and social science subproject of the Modern Project)

> for a *particular* purpose

> in a *particular* place (Euro-American humanities and social sciences departments)

> at a *particular* time (late twentieth/early twenty-first century).

There are no conceptualizations of Islam *as such*; one must be able to specify these particulars. When the particulars of the intellectual act of defining Islam (the wh-'s) remain murky, that definition lacks clarity and usefulness to precisely that degree, and when it comes to the study of metaphysical institutions it is precisely these relevant particulars that are often obscured behind a passive voice or behind pretensions to a view from nowhere.

Purpose, the realm of "usefulness" left unspecified above, has different levels, some deeper and some more immediate. As for the deeper ones: What is the Modern Project interested in? What is the basic mission of its humanities and social science subproject? What counts as a goal that is truly important to it? What justifies this intellectual activity? What counts as human flourishing and what is the subproject's place in reaching it? The Euro-American academy does not simply *do* things; they do *worthwhile* things, even if it is something as general as "rational inquiry."

As for the more immediate purposes: What, exactly, is one supposed to *do* with a conceptualization of Islam? How does it make scholarship better, and *what* does it make better? If it is meant to be "useful," then useful for what? When one goes to the trouble of articulating and arguing for how one knows that art cannot be Islamic, or that philosophy cannot be Islamic, or that science cannot be Islamic, or that ISIS is very Islamic, or that mainstream Islam is legalistic while marginal Islam is spiritual—*some* purpose is being fulfilled, however narrow or general.

One side effect of the Modern Project's failure to understand itself properly as a particular metaphysical institution is that it treats its own ultimate purposes as so obvious and universal as to render discussion about them trivial when turns its attention to an entity outside of it such as Islam. It is as though knowledge of the particulars—a particular idea, speaker, audience, purpose, place, and time—is not crucially relevant to the Modern Project's conceptualization of Islam. Since what "we" as Modern Project intellectuals are doing is universal, mature, rational, and unconstrained, the particulars of who, why, where, and when constitute mere bibliographic details. But that attitude is wrong. Knowing who Shahab Ahmed is (for example), who he is writing for, what makes it worthwhile to him and his audience to write and publish, and where and when the book is written can only *enhance* one's understanding of Ahmed's conceptualization. To the degree that one thinks that focusing on such particular parameters of conceptualization is a distraction, or that it undermines or limits the value of the intellectual contribution, exposes one's pretension to a chimerical view from nowhere—or from everywhere.

To insist on making these particular conditions explicit is not an argument for the kind of linguistic or cultural determinism one finds in many strands of continental philosophy, which, despite its pretensions to being postmodern or against metanarratives, is merely an extension of the same basic universalist claims through a mode of performative self-contradiction. The goal, rather, is to point out that one knows where an author is coming from by knowing where that person is standing (not to mention where one is standing oneself), and that the notion that anyone can speak from nowhere/everywhere will only contribute to a cultural or social imbalance between the two parties involved, and worse, it will add nothing to analytical clarity. Knowing everything about how a dictionary came to be does not in any way detract from the information in it (as said earlier, it actually enhances the book's overall usefulness). A lexicon is not just a method: someone has to write it and do so for some reason.

And yet, as discussed above, there is a persistent habit of universalizing the Modern Project's humanities and social sciences (especially when it turns its attention outside of itself) by framing them into pure practices detached from their inputs (the world as it is) and outputs (the questions one is interested in). Notice how scholars in the academic social sciences and humanities speak about "theory," which they say with the same expansiveness Muslims use when they say *al-Kitāb* (the Book). There are many books, but when you say *al-Kitāb* it is understood to mean one special book in particular (the Quran). When one "studies theory" at Yale or Berkeley with no qualifier, it does not mean the general category of the theoretical or rational or philosophical. Rather, it is meant the way Sufis talk about "the way"—not just any way, but a very special and particular way. Or think of the word "genealogy," which when it appears without qualifier really means Foucault's project; or "hermeneutics," which when it appears without qualifier really means Heidegger and Gadamer; or "deconstruction," which really means Derrida; or "analytic" when one really means a certain movement of ideas and thinkers drawing from the lineage of Frege-Russel-Wittgenstein; or "critical," which once evoked Kant's major works and in the twentieth century became a way to speak about the ideas of the Frankfurt school and which now in the twenty-first reflects a certain "social justice" framework. All of these aforementioned labels are general, but they are used confidently within the Modern Project without qualifiers to refer to a very particular practice, a particular authoritative community who carries it out, and an intellectual inheritance that informs and is produced by that practice. In short, entities such as "theory," "genealogy," "hermeneutics," and "logical analysis," and "critical studies" are local *institutions*, not just ideas. It is quite common for scholars to make it through graduate school and their early careers without understanding just how provincial these projects really are.[24]

And it bears repeating that no postmodern gambit defeats the provinciality of the Modern Project either, but instead will entrench it even more deeply. The tendency for Modern Project intellectuals to take a human intellectual practice and to particularize it for *everyone else* except "us" is often carried out more fanatically by those who claim to militate against universalism.[25] The postmodernists commit the universalist fallacy through a performative contradiction of denying things like a naive universalism, rationality, or morality (things that they presuppose through the very act of denying them), but of course it is only these trailblazing individuals, located entirely within the Modern Project, who have realized that one must not fall into naive conceptions like objective truth or morality.

Synopsis

- The identification of the standard Muslim can never be accomplished by any purely analytical procedure, but requires a pretheoretical judgment of trust in the authority of certain human beings—namely standard Muslims themselves.

- The true logical form of all conceptualizations of a thing's Islamic-ness is: What would a standard Muslim human being do with respect to this particular thing?

- Because one is necessarily conceptualizing certain human possibilities when conceptualizing Islam, the enterprise of conceptualizing Islam is in part a metaphysical question whether the conceptualizer realizes it or not.

- The Modern Project fails to understand that it is one metaphysical institution studying another because of its own idiosyncratic approach to ultimate questions and the nature of its own apex communities who deal with them.

- In Islam the apex communities dealing with ultimate questions (in *kalām, uṣūl al-fiqh, taṣawwuf, ḥikmah/falsafah*) are overlapping hierarchies with significant overlap in their practices and legacy.

- In the Modern Project, the apex communities of Science, Philosophy, and Art/Culture are discrete hierarchies that insist on the importance of separate legacies and practices for each community as a part of the autonomy of each.

- The autonomy and freedom from constraints at the core of the self-image of the Modern Project comes at the cost of trifurcating its apex communities, practices, and legacy from each other.

- The self-image of the Modern Project sees its practice and legacy as uniquely universal. Modern thinkers *think*, while Muslims think *Islamically*.

- The Modern Project typically fails to see that its own allegedly universal practices and legacy are determined by provincial apex communities.

- When it comes to Islam, the Modern Project's apex communities take it as axiomatic that the Modern Project is not Islam, but these same communities (scientists, philosophers, culture creators) are never those who can or do "conceptualize" Islam.

- The academic subproject whose role in the Modern Project is to conceptualize Islam is constrained by their apex communities' prior designation of who "we" are and that "we" are not Muslims. They have no power to change this status.

- The humanities and social science subproject functions, intentionally or otherwise, to maintain the universal-particular and superior-inferior imbalance in relation to Islam that the Modern Project sees as a defining trait and consequence of its unique universality.

- Sometimes Islam is conceptualized as less rational, less ethical, less imaginative than what is modern, but in other cases Islam is conceptualized as naively or tyrannically upholding the ideas truth, rationality, and goodness against the postmodern sophistications of the Modern Project.

- In general, the Modern Project falsely sees itself as a meta-metaphysical institution in relation to other such realities like Islam, akin to a chimerical metalanguage (really only a special code within an existing language) with pretensions of being outside of natural language.

Chapter 8

One Islam, Many Islams, or No Islam?

Let us now consider some significant and representative contributions in the academic literature to the conceptualization of Islam and the Islamic, focusing on three books that deal extensively with the topic: *The Venture of Islam* by Marshall Hodgson,[1] a classic global history that deals with the "What is Islam?" question so extensively that the relevant sections could constitute a small monograph on its own; *What Is Islam? The Importance of Being Islamic* by Shahab Ahmed,[2] the most extensive treatment of the subject to date; and the recent *Lived Islam: Colloquial Religion in a Cosmopolitan Tradition* by A. Kevin Reinhart;[3] as well as the highly influential article "The Idea of an Anthropology of Islam" by Talal Asad.[4]

Marshall Hodgson and the Boundary between Islamic and Islamicate

Marshall Hodgson's demarcation between Islam and Islamdom, and the corresponding attributes of Islamic and Islamicate—that is, between the religion and its corresponding civilization—is one of the most sustained and influential attempts to disambiguate the concept of "Islam" in the history of Islamic studies. Regarding the fuzziness of the demarcation between religion and civilization Hodgson acknowledges, "When I speak of 'Islamic art' I imply some sort of distinction between the architecture of mosques on the one hand, and the miniatures illustrating a medical textbook on the other—*even though there is admittedly no sharp boundary between.*"[5] Drawing a conceptual line between mosque architecture and miniature painting is helpful at a certain level of approximation, but it is obviously limiting. Hodgson's example shows that one is dealing not with a dividing line but with the names given to two ends of a spectrum that remains poorly theorized. It can be thought of as akin to defining a spectrum of colors: if one had a thousand swatches of the colors arranged in sequence such that the first one was red and the last one was blue and the middle one was purple, it would make sense to speak of these colors as being laid out along a red-blue spectrum, but only as a first approximation, since red, blue, and purple themselves remain at the level of folk understanding. Hodgson sketches just such a gradual spectrum from religion to civilization: "One can speak of 'Islamic literature,' of 'Islamic art,' of 'Islamic philosophy,' even of 'Islamic despotism,' but in such a sequence one is speaking *less and less* of something that expresses Islam as a faith."[6] It is unclear in such a graduated list when one leaves the realm of the religious and enters the domain of the civilizational, but one can clarify the nature of that ambiguity. As one moves from Islamic religion to Islamic civilization, there must be some kind of parameters or variables whose change can account for the possibilities in between, which is the point of the model of institutions developed in earlier chapters.

Hodgson's overall framework does not depend merely on his coinage of terms such as Islamicate and Islamdom but also on elaborate discussions of the terms culture, tradition, society, religion, and civilization. In a far-reaching but dense passage he tries to clarify the relationship between all these terms, and in so doing demonstrates many of the problems created when one attempts to use such terms as theoretically illuminating ideas. When read with our model of metaphysical institutions in mind, the ambiguities and definitional problems in this paragraph will be readily apparent:

> Islamdom does not designate in itself a "civilization," a specific culture, but only the society that carries that culture. There has been, however, a *culture*, centred on a lettered tradition, which has been historically distinctive of Islamdom the *society*, and which has been naturally shared in by both Muslims and non-Muslims who participate at all fully in the society of Islamdom. For this, I have used the adjective "Islamicate." I thus restrict the term "Islam" to the *religion* of the Muslims, not using that term for the far more general phenomena, the society of Islamdom and its Islamicate cultural traditions.[7]

Here we see a proliferation of several key institution-concepts in one paragraph which, upon inspection, rely heavily upon each other but are not well delineated in terms of each other. What does it mean exactly for a society to carry a culture, or for a culture to be centered on a tradition? How does one distinguish between a *cultural* tradition and a *religious* tradition,[8] or understand what constitutes a society such that people of multiple religions can participate in it? Hodgson's argument would not be completely obscure to scholars in the relevant fields; they would get the point, but only because they have a familiarity with Hodgson's scholarly judgment and an educated person's grasp of the terms involved, but they could not rely on any kind of terminological precision. It might appear that in defining "Islamdom" Hodgson is making use of certain clarifying concepts such as religion and civilization, but if one looks deeply into these concepts one discovers that they are not very clear all. Elsewhere Hodgson shows himself to be only too aware of the ambiguities surrounding these terms. He devotes considerable attention to what he thinks a tradition is and ought to be,[9] and also what he understands by the term "religion," and has a great deal to say about the contingency of the concept of civilization and about his own preferences in that regard, but his substantial caveats do not ultimately clarify his terminology, and show only that his definitions and conceptualizations do not hold up well to scrutiny.

Take the example of "society." On more than one occasion Hodgson distinguishes both culture and civilization (the "Islamicate") from the society ("Islamdom") that gives rise to them or that carries them, meaning that culture and civilization are the things that the society in question makes and does and that it can leave behind. But the distinction between "a society" and "the culture it carries" is arbitrary. One cannot separate a society from what it produces since the very social connections that make up a society *are part of what society produces*. A society is not a mere given, like geography or climate. It has to be sustained and cultivated (hence, *culture*), and something must account for its cohesion over time. Society is the legacy of society. If one can say that a culture is carried by a society, one could just as easily say that a society is carried by its culture—or that a culture carries itself.

Consider also Hodgson's treatment of "tradition." He argues that human beings can be united by ideals, norms, and commitments, and that "group commitment" is a key part of what he calls a tradition: "Thus Islam could be defined as commitment to the venture to which Muḥammad's vision was leading; which meant, concretely, allegiance to Muḥammad and his Book and then to the continuing community of Muḥammad, or at least (later) to a supposed faithful remnant of that community."[10] (Notice that "community" makes an appearance to explain tradition. But is it not the tradition that makes a community a community in the first place?)

Islamdom, for Hodgson, consists mainly of this community of Muḥammad but of other communities as well—Christians, Jews, Hindus, Buddhists, and others who are part of Islamdom but not part of Islam. Nor are these the only communities he discusses. In his section on "tradition" he explicitly speaks of art, philosophy, political life, law, and economic order as areas of life that can be understood as traditions.[11] These realities, for Hodgson, can be understood through what he calls the three "moments" of a tradition: the initial creative act, group commitment, and cumulative interaction. Under this rubric he makes no distinction between Islam and things he elsewhere calls "culture" or "civilization," such as art or commerce. All these different kinds of communities, taken together, constitute Islamdom, each with their respective "group commitments": "This group commitment retains its vitality through cumulative interaction among those sharing the commitment; above all, through debate and dialogue, as people work out the implications and potentialities latent in the creative event to which they are bound."[12] Islam, but also law, philosophy, art, and commerce, form a texture of "group commitments" or allegiances all of which must maintain their vitality.

One can agree with Hodgson in some respects here. Yes, large populations consist of communities of various kinds; yes, these communities all have various kinds of commitments; yes, they interact and engage with their own "initial creative act"; and yes, "that interaction, that dialogue, itself is made up of a sequence of creative actions and of commitments stemming from them—secondary actions, secondary commitments, up to a point, but genuine actions, encounters and discoveries, all the same."[13] This is all true, and for Hodgson (in this section at least) it holds equally true whether one is speaking about the religious commitment of Muhammad's community or "Occidental artists vis-a-vis Italian Renaissance painting" or "liberal education built around an agreed-on core of classics" or "a tradition of law" or "philosophy and . . . science."

But one must ask: if there are "creative acts," "group commitments," and "cumulative interactions" on both sides of the religion/culture divide, why, then, is that precise divide into the Islamic and the Islamicate so important as to form a basic conceptual division in Hodgson's work? Hodgson himself may help one toward an answer with his concept of "precommitment": "Precommitment can lead the unwary—and often even the most cautious scholar—to biased judgment. Bias comes especially in the questions he poses and in the type of category he uses, where, indeed, bias is especially hard to track down because it is hard to suspect the very terms one uses, which seem so innocently neutral."[14] The relationship between the precommitment of cautious scholars and the biases they produce presents us an important moral question that cuts both ways. Such biases can be badly motivated, but in the case of a scholar such as Hodgson (and many more could be named), they clearly are not. It is enough to read his erudite caveats and qualifications to understand that his categories and analysis were the results of his best efforts to answer what he saw as valid questions and to be careful about precommitments.

But what *are* precommitments? Are they factual, methodological, moral, or all three? One purpose of the model of metaphysical institutions in this book is to neutralize the effects of such biases by creating a universal template by which to make such biases, if not absent, at least transparent.

Hodgson's own discussion of precommitments hinges on identifying five "major cultural traditions of ultimate overall commitment" (again, is this description actually clarifying and useful?) relevant to the study of Islam: the Christian tradition, Judaism, the Islamic tradition, Marxism, and Westernists, which latter he describes as "those whose highest allegiance is to what they call Western culture, as the unique or at least the most adequate embodiment of transcendent ideals of liberty and truth."[15] He states,

> Properly, we use the term "religious" for an ultimate orienta-
> tion (rather than "philosophical" or "ideological"), so far as
> the orientation is personally committing and is meaningful in
> terms of a cosmos, without further precision of what this may
> come to. . . . We may call "religious" (extending the term a
> bit) those cultural traditions that have focused on such com-
> mitments. . . . But in common usage the term is extended still
> further. A person's actual "religious" life does not necessarily
> consist in creative cosmic commitment; it consists in his par-
> ticipation in religious traditions given to him—in any aspect
> of them. . . . For historical purposes, it is not very feasible or
> even desirable to separate out these different extended usages.[16]

He further attempts to give a sense of what "religious" might mean: "For some purposes, one can apply the term 'religious' wherever an experience of the numinous or a notion of the transcendent (commonly linked thereto) becomes life-orientational. . . . For the purpose of classifying the traditions (if one must), a more general definition will help: one can apply the term 'religious' to any life-orientational experience or behavior in the degree to which it is relatively most focused on the role of a *person in an environment felt as cosmos.*"[17] Hodgson does not succeed in giving a theoretical basis for asserting that some "major cultural traditions of ultimate overall commitment" count as religions (Muslims, Christians, Jews) and some do not (Marxists, Westernists). Even the idea of the "transcendent," which shows up in his description of the religious, appears in his characterization of the Westernists' "transcendent" ideals. It is much more likely that there is a received cultural consensus in the West to call certain things religious, and that Hodgson is naturally and perhaps reflexively producing a rationale for it. Little here turns out to be theoretically helpful (i.e., applicable to other areas by virtue of some explanatory power), and these definitions of "religious" come across as impressionistic and ruminative more than anything else. After all, many atheists have strong beliefs about the nature of reality, and they conform their lives to that belief which includes a definite idea of a cosmos that begins with a Big Bang and evolves over billions of years. Sometimes this cosmos will take the form of a multiverse in which anything that can happen must happen, including the events of one's own life, sometimes coupled with a belief that one's own consciousness will someday become immortal in a cloud computing system. Would a transhumanist who freezes his brain in hopes of immortal consciousness in the multiverse not qualify as "religious" in his orientation under Hodgson's formulation?

The phrase "major cultural traditions of ultimate overall commitment" is Hodgson's attempt to offer a universal category into which the given realities he mentions can fit—not unlike the idea of "metaphysical institution" developed in this book. He does not, however, properly theorize it, and instead uses it to bundle various realities that he understands to belong together.

≈

Hodgson's use of the terms "religion," "civilization," "tradition," "society," and "culture" demands of the reader to first master what he means by these terms and then to trust that he has made the right choices from among different possibilities of use. He is aware of this, and admits that such entities as civilizations do not merely present themselves to scrutiny:

> The specification of such units [i.e., civilizations] is only partly given by the data itself. In part, it is a function of the inquirer's

purposes. . . . Social groupings have intergraded or overlapped almost indefinitely throughout the Eastern Hemisphere since long before Islamic times. If we arrange societies merely according to their stock of cultural notions, institutions, and techniques, then a great many dividing lines among pre-Modern civilized societies makes some sense, and no dividing line within the Eastern Hemisphere makes final sense.[18]

Drawing lines between civilizations, therefore, "requires adopting an explicit basis on which to set off one body of peoples from another as a civilization; but too often such groupings have been taken as given, on extraneous grounds, and characterizations have then been attempted without regard to the basis on which the grouping was made."[19] He goes on to say, "There are many ways of grouping into 'civilizations' what is in fact an endless chain of interrelated local cultural life. We must know why we make the selection we do. Often one may make alternative combinations according to what questions one is concerned with."[20] Hodgson's analysis of the demarcations between civilizations here is sound,[21] and it is easily transferred to the boundaries between one culture and another, one society and another, and one tradition and other—so long as these realities are not well theorized. Where one draws these lines, and how many lines one will draw, will depend upon the scholar's interests and indeed the scholar's most ultimate assumptions about human nature and the nature of the world.

Furthermore, that same contingency, that same subjective element, is operative in the conceptual boundaries not only *within* but also *between* the categories of society, religion, culture, and civilization. Demarcations such as that between "religion" and "culture" are just as sensitive to the purposes of the inquirer as are those between one civilization and another, and they are no more fixed, natural, or necessary. Whereas it is easy for most historians and anthropologists to visualize how the same *geographic* space can be divided up in different ways and that boundaries do not simply appear, they often fail to realize that the *conceptual* space (of metaphysical institutions) occupied by the categories of "civilization," "culture," "religion," "tradition," and "society" does not merely present readymade boundaries to the researcher.

᠀

At a more general level, Hodgson finds himself caught between two opposing claims regarding what makes Islam Islamic. The first he expresses in this way: "When we look at Islam historically, then, the integral unity of life it seemed to display when we looked at it as a working out of the act of islâm almost vanishes. In such ever-renewed dialogues, among settings formed apart from Islam at all, *is not anything possible provided only it possess a certain general human validity?* We can no longer say that Islam eternally teaches a given thing, or that another thing is necessarily a corruption of Islam."[22] This almost sounds like "Islam is whatever Muslims do," an idea that will be discussed further below. But there is a response, and Hodgson provides it himself: "What then is Islam? Can we study it as a meaningful whole? . . . Clearly, yes: but only in the way that any cultural tradition, whatever its internal contradictions, is a whole. However diversely it develops, or however rapidly, *a tradition does not lend itself indifferently to every possible opinion or practice. It imposes limits* which are none the less enduringly effective for being impossible to formulate in advance."[23] Regarding the "anything is possible" tendency he notes, "Not every scholar, and certainly not every Muslim, will be happy with so strong a limitation as I put on the existence of any eternal 'true' Islam. . . . Perhaps my usage [of Islam] should always tacitly presuppose some such adjective as 'historical,' as against 'ideal' or 'metaphysical.'" But regarding the global unity of that historical Islam across diverse cultures he says:

> Among Christian or Buddhist peoples, religion has indeed been very central also. But it has informed the culture of Christian Occidental and of Christian Abyssinians, for instance, almost entirely in isolation from each other, so that there is no single civilization associated with Christianity. Nor is there one civilization associated with Buddhism. But—despite the vaster areas covered—those who participated in the tradition of Islamic faith, so far as they developed any culture of their own at all, never lost contact with each other: their cultural dialogues were always intermeshed. The bonds of Islamic faith, indeed especially the irrepressible transcendent ideals implied in the root meaning of islâm, with their insistent demand for a godly transformation of all life, have been so telling in certain crucial aspects of the high culture of almost all Muslim peoples that we find ourselves grouping these peoples together across all their different regions, even apart from considering other facets of high culture. Islam offered creative impulses that ramified widely throughout the culture as a whole, even where it was least religious. It is largely around the central Islamic tradition that the concerned and the creative built and transmitted a common set of social and, above

all, literary traditions; these were carried in many languages but looked largely to the same great classics, not only religious but secular, and especially to the norms which they express, applicable to all aspects of life.[24]

It is perplexing to read Hodgson claim "When we look at Islam historically . . . the integral unity of life . . . almost vanishes" while at the same time have him describe a set of creative impulses, norms, traditions, and classics so coherent that they achieved a "decisive continuity" despite the "greatest diversity" of forms—greater than the diversity of Christian or Buddhist peoples, by Hodgson's own estimation. Within the bounds of the "historical" as against the "ideal," what Hodgson says about the continuity and global unity of Islam is about as close as one can get to saying that Islam "eternally teaches a given thing."

So, one reads in Hodgson that in terms of being Islamic, anything is possible—but also that anything is not possible. One must avoid affirmation of an "ideal" Islam—but Islamic civilization also has an unsurpassed unity because of its "irrepressible transcendent ideals." Islam as a historical reality has a vanishing unity—but also a decisive continuity. These contradictions are real.

Hodgson knows too much to say that Islam has no enduring content, but he also wants to maintain the intellectual distance of the historian and "circumscribe" such questions in order to leave them, to the degree possible, to the believer who is authorized to decide what counts as "ideal" or "metaphysical" Islam. He finds himself caught between his recognition both of the great diversity of Islam in history and also its great unity. He registers both insights honestly, but he is unable to successfully combine them into a coherent theory.

When we turn to other attempts to navigate the demarcations around Islam, this "ideal" or "metaphysical" thing that "imposes limits," which Hodgson is willing to wrestle with and whose presence he cannot bring himself to erase, will be theorized in such a way as to denature it until it becomes something else entirely.

Shahab Ahmed and Contradiction in Islam

Throughout *What Is Islam?* Shahab Ahmed is reluctant to make the transparently untenable claim that "Islam is whatever Muslims do," but his conceptualization of Islam, and the constructive arguments he offers to support it, amount logically to the same thing. He says:

> Islam as Muslim engagement with Revelation-as-Pre-Text, Text, and Con-Text contains already within its very structure and dimensionality the premise and promise of multiple spatially-differentiated truths. These contradictions are not merely *externally contingent*; rather, they are *structurally inherent*. Fundamental and outright contradictions of Truth and Meaning are thus structurally and logically and objectively internal and intrinsic to Islam. Contradiction hence emerges as not merely inherently Islamic, *but as coherently Islamic: contradiction inheres to and coheres with the spatial-structural dynamic of Revelation to Muḥammad.*[25]

There are insurmountable logical problems here that no amount of empirical examples marshaled from Muslim history can overcome. To declare that contradiction *as such* is inherent to some "structure" of practices or ideas is precisely to declare a free-for-all in which there can be no structure at all. Unrestricted contradiction means that there are no principles, no patterns, no limitations in the relevant structure. If something can mean anything, it means nothing. To declare contradiction to be inherent to the very essence of Islam is exactly tantamount to saying that no standard of exclusion from the category of Islam is even possible. It is a kind of liar's paradox or relativist fallacy.

Rules or principles are things that, by their very nature, are contradictable. There must exist examples that could violate them. If it cannot be broken, it is not a rule. If one asserts that contradiction is *inherent* to Islam, whatever contradicts any Islamic rule will be automatically included in Islam, and therefore there was never a rule in the first place. *What Is Islam?* opens with the example of a Muslim asserting, "My family have been Muslims for a thousand years . . . during which time we have *always* been drinking wine. . . . You see, we are *Muslim* wine-drinkers." The concept of Islam developed by Ahmed—with its internal contradiction—could not rule against such an assertion. Neither could it, for that matter, exclude assertions such as "We are *Muslim* pork-eaters" or "We are *Muslim* gamblers" or "We are *Muslim* pimps." Ahmed has a principle of inclusion, but no principle of exclusion, which means he offers no principle at all. He cannot answer the question "What is Islam?" because he cannot answer the question "What isn't Islam?"[26] To assert that Islam can be anything and to make it impossible to conceptualize something that is actually not Islamic is to say that Islam has no legacy, no principles, no values. It is a sophisticated way of asserting, "Islam is whatever Muslims think it is," and Ahmed's conceptualization of Islam provides absolutely no barrier to making such an assertion. It turns Islam into a phenomenon of endless creativity but without any sense of correctness or discipline, making of it an aggregation of reflexes and pointless hoarding.

It was not inevitable for Ahmed to commit this logical error. He gets many things right. To describe Islam—as *What Is Islam?* correctly does—as a "multi-dimensional phenomenon"[27] or to note that there exist "different registers of truth for different people" in society where there is "a hierarchy in which people are arranged according to their capacities to *know*"[28] does not at all require any talk of "inherent contradiction," yet Ahmed insists on making that unjustified leap. He fails to realize that to recognize that there are multiple *dimensions* of truth is precisely to *avoid* many problems of contradiction, because there is more than one dimension or parameter by which entities can be related to each other. Since he uses a dimensional metaphor, he could have mentioned that no value for height could contradict a value for width, for example. The moon is not either round or white; it can be both round and white because the dimension or parameter of each attribute is different. His metaphor of different *registers* is precisely a way of showing that what might be an apparent contradiction is not actually so—because the thing in question is at another register. An F# is discordant in the key of C major but not B major. Similarly, a *hierarchy* implies differences in level or priority, which again create a framework in which apparent contradictions are not contradictions at all because they are, as it were, located at different levels in the hierarchy. But Ahmed does not talk about *apparent* contradiction; he says that contradiction is *inherent* to Islam. It is contradiction all the way down. And no type of contradiction is ruled out.[29]

It is important, in order to understand just how badly Ahmed goes wrong here, that one distinguishes between contradictions of various kinds (e.g., contraries, opposites) as well as between contradiction on the one hand and mystery or paradox on the other. Not every differentiation or opposition is a contradiction properly speaking, depending on the parameter of differentiation in question. Here are some examples of different kinds of contradictory assertions.

Two statements can be contradictory in that they cannot both be true and they cannot both be false (e.g., "God is One" and "God is not One"), or they can be contradictory in that they cannot both be true but they might both be false ("Ghazālī was born in 1058" and "Ghazālī was born in 1059"). One could refer to these as *descriptive* contradictions.

There are also contradictions that are *theoretical* or predictive, such as "All people will die" and "All people will never die," which cannot both turn out to be true and cannot both turn out to be false, and also "Pregnancies average thirty-nine weeks" and "Pregnancies average forty-one weeks" cannot both turn out to be true, but they might both turn out to be false.

And there are also contradictions of a *normative* nature. For example, "Wine drinking is *ḥarām* (forbidden)" and "Wine drinking is not *ḥarām*" cannot both be true and cannot both be false," but "*Dhikr* (remembrance of God) is the best act" and "*Jihād* (struggle for God) is the best act" cannot both be true but they might both turn out to be false.

In other words, the contradiction between descriptive propositions such as "*x* is *y*" and "*x* isn't *y*" is different from the contradiction between theoretical propositions such as "if *x*, always *y*" and "if *x*, never *y*," which is likewise different from the contradiction between normative propositions such as "*x* is better than *y*" and "*y* is better than *x*." Using different terminology, one can have two contradictory axioms, or two contradictory theorems, or two contradictory maxims. Basically, something cannot be both a thing and not that thing (descriptive); something cannot be both probable and improbable (theoretical); something cannot be both good and bad (normative).

Describing these various kinds of contradiction—and there are surely other ways of classifying oppositions—is necessary here only to show that contradictions are never *simply* contradictions but are always contradictions according to some kind of parameter or in some respect. In other words, a contradiction has to be (and can only be) one of several types of contradiction. The assertion that Muslims are allowed to drink wine contradicts only the assertion that wine is forbidden; it cannot contradict an estimation of how long it takes to ferment grape juice.

Ahmed frequently speaks of different domains in which contradiction occurs, and he observes that in fact Islam has been characterized by hierarchy and by an inward/outward dynamic, which he sometimes refers to as spatial differentiation and multidimensionality. This is all entirely correct. But to observe the presence of hierarchy and an inward/outward dynamic and then to jump to "contradiction" is a total non sequitur. Ahmed is making his conceptualization of Islam consist of *outright contradiction,* but his recognition of hierarchy and inward/outward dynamic is the very thing that will *avoid* outright contradiction. To say that wine drinking is *ḥalāl* (permissible) even though wine drinking is *ḥarām* (forbidden) is an *outright* contradiction. To use wine as a symbol for the love of God in a poem and to also refrain from drinking fermented grapes is *not* a contradiction; rather, they are two realities at different levels (hierarchy), or it could be said that one pertains to the inward and the other to the outward. Ahmed seems to be arguing instead that hierarchy and dimensionality *entail* outright contradiction, which is a grievous logical error:

> To live with outright contradiction, as societies of Muslims have done, one must be able to conceive of contradiction in such a way that contradiction is coherent and meaningful in terms of one's paradigmatic values and truths. This is not possible unless a Muslim conceives of contradictory Truth as arising necessarily and directly from the structural and spatial dynamic of Revelation to Muhammad as Pre-Text, Text, and Context—that is, unless a Muslim conceives of contradictory Truth as coherent with and meaningful in terms of Revelation to Muhammad.[30]

In a strange reversal, Ahmed takes the *solution* to the analytical problem of contradiction in Islam (namely, the existence of hierarchy and dimensionality in Islam that helps us to make sense of apparent contradictions) and turns it into the very condition by which outright contradiction comes into being. For Ahmed, the very generation of "(Islamic) Truth and Meaning in two main spatially-differentiated the trajectories, namely, *hierarchy* and *interiority/exteriority*" is what enable Muslims "to conceptualize Islam in terms of contradictory meaning-making."[31]

Taken together, despite the frequent recognition that there are levels and dimensions to Islam, what we are presented with in *What Is Islam?* is a notion of "contradiction" that is purely arbitrary. "You see, we are *Muslim* wine-drinkers" is proclaimed without reason or reasoning. Do they drink wine because of something? It seems they just *do*. Others just don't. And since both are Muslims, there is a "contradiction." Ahmed argues, "Sufism *subjects the concept* of the Quran to the demands of a total Truth-matrix."[32] First, this is a wildly exaggerated claim that will not be explored here. Second, in allegedly interpreting the Quran this way, does what the Sufis do make sense? Do they justify it somehow? It seems, rather, to simply be something Sufis just *do*. Other Muslims just *don't*. There are no actual parameters of disagreement, and no way of situating the allegedly contradictory things in relation to other kinds of contradiction.

A closely related problem is that Ahmed seems to conflate contradiction with paradox, and he further implicates the notion of metaphor into that confusion: "There is a sense in which all metaphor is paradoxical, since all metaphor speaks of something in terms of that which it is not."[33] Ahmed argues that by saying that "Richard is a lion" instead of saying that he is "exceptionally brave" he is "creating a space for the generation, exploration, and production by communicative, experiential, and interpretive association, differentiation, and projection of the concept 'lion.' When I say 'Richard is a lion,' I am saying 'Richard is, at once, a lion and not a lion.'"[34] This is simply wrong. To say that Richard is a lion is to point to a discernible trait shared by Richard and the lion. The metaphor is based upon a partial resemblance, and the detection of such resemblance is the job of reason and imagination. One is not saying that Richard is *at once* a lion and not a lion, or even that Richard is not fully intelligible except through lionness, but rather he is *in one respect* like a lion but is not so in other respects. None of the "association, differentiation, and projection" that the use of such metaphors enables has anything to do with paradox or contradiction at all. It has to do with analogy, similarity, ambiguity, and polyvalence.

A paradox is not an outright contradiction (namely, a mere logical mistake) but rather is the failure of a reality to be conceivable or exhaustible in any single imaginable or conceivable idea. When Ibn al-'Arabī uses the phrase "He not-He"[35] to describe the self-disclosure (*tajallī*) of God, that joining of contraries is expressed at the logical level *at the service* of pointing to a reality outside of the verbal contradiction. The contradiction is not *inherent* to that reality but rather to the possible articulation of that reality in human conceptual categories. It is not merely a self-indulgent maneuver in order to say something playfully.

Paradox, unlike metaphor, arises when no possible concept can account for a reality that itself cannot be denied (see chapter 5). Take, for example, the experience of consciousness. Your own consciousness is characterized by change and identity. Your consciousness is always changing and yet you are always the same consciousness. It is not that we *happen* to lack a concept that can capture the nature of consciousness's change and sameness. We seem to be in principle *incapable* of thinking *about* consciousness except by using the two notions of change and sameness, and are compelled to express a reality we could not possibly deny in terms of that which is contradictory on the logical level but indubitable in the experience. Our experience of consciousness is not a core of unchangingness surrounded by that which is changing, like a body and different outfits of clothing. Rather, it seems impossible to conceive of one separate from the other when it comes to one's own consciousness. That makes it a mystery or a paradox; our concepts fail while the reality cannot be denied because we know it by direct experience—as was discussed extensively in chapter 5. That is the argument of Ibn al-ʿArabī for paradoxical formulations such as "He not-He" (*huwa lā huwa*). It is the rational and verbal equivalent to representing a three-dimensional object on a two-dimensional plane.

A metaphor is something quite different. Using the image of a lion to describe Richard's bravery is adequate for the purposes of the author employing the metaphor. There is no contradiction to sort out. Richard is simply lionlike in one respect but not in another. (A metaphor might be used to *represent* a paradox, but that is a different matter.) It is worth noting that the highly developed discourse on symbol and figurative language in Islam did not raise questions of contradiction or paradox as an inescapable aspect of metaphor.[36] One can have metaphor without paradox (Richard is a lion), and paradox without metaphor (He not-He), or a metaphor expressing a paradox (the story of Solomon's vizier and the angel of death expressing the paradox of *qadar* or the Divine "measuring out").[37]

It is unfortunate that throughout his discussion of paradox Ahmed brings in other related but separate concepts such as metaphor, ambiguity, and apophatic language, all of which are important and interesting aspects of how Muslims have expressed themselves but none of which necessarily involves contradiction or paradox. There are other problems: What is the difference between contradiction and contestation? Or between contradiction and juxtaposition? Or mere disagreement? These are not synonyms. And Ahmed's book provides little to distinguish between them. In general, there is no precision about or diving lines between contradiction, paradox, metaphor, ambiguity, apophatic language, ambivalence, polyvalence, and absurdity. Reading *What Is Islam?* one would conclude that they just all seem to be different versions of the same amorphous fact of nonexclusivity. It is as though any language that was not dryly mechanical or legalistic in nature belonged to a tragically suppressed and quasimagical realm of creativity and freedom. Considering just how much of Ahmed's conceptualization of Islam depends upon "contradiction," these problems undermine the entire constructive side of *What Is Islam?* even while it remains an impressive and useful history in many respects.

*

Yet another problem running throughout the book, related to the concept of contradiction, is Ahmed's constant invocation of "meaning." He often uses the notions of "meaning making" and "meaningful" to explain the different modes of "contradiction," as when he speaks about "meaning making in terms of Islam." Unfortunately, he translates the Islamic *ma'nā* as "meaning" (correct for certain uses of *ma'nā* but not others) but then continues the discussion about meaning in a way the clearly relies upon the idiomatic uses of "meaning" in English that do not correspond to the concept of *ma'nā* at all. There is no such thing as "*ma'nā* making" in Islamic intellectual life in the sense that the idiomatic English phrase "meaning making" is usually understood; nor does *ma'nā* correspond to the sense of meaning in the word "meaningful" as it is usually deployed. In short, Ahmed equivocates on the notion of "meaning" and "meaningful" as referring to that which is important or significant, possesses semantic content, or signifies an intelligible essence present in forms. There is a poetical resonance in his comments about meaning, but very little by way of precision and analytical clarity despite the richness of the examples he invokes. Is a thing meaningful because it is important? Because it conveys semantic content? Because it is intelligible? Is a meaning a result of hermeneutical engagement? All of them together?

The issue here is not that "meaning" is an ambiguous word, which it always is, but that Ahmed often uses it as a way of crowning an argument without ever disambiguating what sense of "meaning" he has in mind. Too often "meaning" in its various guises in *What Is Islam?* is an empty vessel or even cipher onto which the author loads his entire argument. Rather than explaining anything, "meaning" itself requires explanation or at least disambiguation, and yet it often occupies the role of ultimate clarifier. This deployment of "meaning" enables one of the fundamental logical errors plaguing *What Is Islam?* mentioned above, namely, the fact that Ahmed has no principle by which anything could possibly be excluded from being (potentially) *meaningful* in Islam. When anything can be meaningful in terms of Islam, then Islam is literally meaningless. To speak in terms of "meaning" is simply to put a name on all the ways in which Islam lacks content, principles, or values that might exclude or disavow something. Ahmed's argument, or the clear implication of it, is that if something is "meaningful" to a Muslim, it is Islam": "*Something is Islamic to the extent that it is made meaningful in terms of hermeneutical engagement with Revelation to*

Muhammad."[38] But what does it mean to *make* something meaningful? What is the nature of that "making"? What *wouldn't* or *couldn't* be meaningful? There seems to be no way to say.

Another major logical problem Ahmed recognizes, only to commit the same fallacy himself, is the notion that, rather than try to theorize a single thing called Islam, researchers should simply speak about many "Islams." Ahmed criticizes Bryan Turner's call—certainly not the first or the last (see below)—to "abandon all reified notions of 'Islam' as a universal essence in order to allow us to study many 'Islams' in all their complexity and difference" by saying, "What Turner does not tell us is how those 'Islams' are meaningfully to be conceptualized as the plurals of no singular."[39] On this point Ahmed is exactly right, which makes it all the more strange that some pages earlier he says, "A valid concept of 'Islam' must denote or connote all possible 'Islams,' whether abstract or 'real,' mental or social."[40] This sentence is a logical disaster. Valid to whom, and under what rules? Denote and connote in what language and for what purposes? And possible according to what constraints? What is "possibility" in this sense, and could it include *anyone* who says the words "I am a Muslim?" Could this rule be extended analogously to Western science, academic philosophy, or modern art? Does "possible" mean that one could make the claim, or are there objective criteria such as duration, population, cultural production, and so on that form the standard? And if there are such standards, who gets to determine what those standards are? None of these questions is actually answered in the book. How is Turner's call at all different from Ahmed's saying that a valid concept of Islam must denote or connote all possible Islams? Ahmed retains the notion of singular Islam of which there are plural Islams, but that singular is simply a dotted line drawn around all possible Islams with the proclamation that the contradictions are merely inherent to that concept of Islam.

These ambiguities and fallacies related to the concepts of contradiction and meaning are not tangential to Ahmed's project of conceptualizing Islam. They are central to it and thoroughly undermine it. The "valid concept of Islam" Ahmed is describing can only be meaningless, and the ideas he marshals to make his case about how many Islams can be conceptualized together—contradiction, metaphor, paradox, meaning—do not have anything resembling the kind of clarity or precision they would need to even begin to make such a case. He does not demonstrate that Islam coherently handles such contradictions. He simply proclaims the "coherent contradiction" of Islam as a historical fact.[41]

Talal Asad and Islam as a Discursive Tradition

Talal Asad's article "The Idea of an Anthropology of Islam" (1986) has become a touchstone for many scholars working on conceptualizing Islam.[42] As the title suggests, it was prompted by anthropologists' failure to provide a useful concept of "Islam" to use in their work, and much of Asad's attention is given to often valuable critiques of those efforts. When it comes to his own contribution, after having discussed the shortcomings of other views, he states, "Islam is neither a distinctive social structure nor a heterogenous collection of beliefs, artifacts, customs, and morals. It is a tradition." For Asad, a successful anthropology of Islam must use the right concepts, and for him the right concept for Islam is "discursive tradition."

But when it comes to defining "discursive" and "tradition" Asad's conceptualization immediately runs into logical trouble. He says,

> A tradition consists essentially of discourses that seek to instruct practitioners regarding the correct form and purpose of a given practice that, precisely because it is established, has a history. These discourses relate conceptually to a *past* (when the practice was instituted, and from which the knowledge of its point and proper performance has been transmitted) and a *future* (how the point of that practice can best be secured in the short or long term, or why it should be modified or abandoned), through a *present* (how it is linked to other practices, institutions, and social conditions). An Islamic discursive tradition is simply a tradition of Muslim discourse that addresses itself to conceptions of the Islamic past and future, with reference to a particular Islamic practice in the present.[43]

If Islam is a discursive tradition, and if a tradition "consists essentially of discourses," that makes Islam a discursive set of discourses. No new information is added by the modifier "discursive." To say "discursive tradition" in this way is like saying "unmarried bachelor." It is redundant, or circular. Moreover, if Islam is a discursive tradition, does this mean that there are *non*discursive traditions somewhere? If such nondiscursive traditions exist—that is, if some traditions do not consist essentially of discourses—then Asad's own definition of "tradition" is wrong or incomplete.

One might look for a way out of this impasse in the temporal aspects of tradition Asad mentions regarding the past, present, and future, but this will not help either. *Any* discourse will relate to a past, a present, and a future. How could it not? One could say that Islam is distinctive in being very old, being incredibly vast and variegated, and being likely to endure—that is, it has a long past, a massive present, and an open future—but these are merely differences in scope. One might say that Islam is a "long-standing discourse" or even a "megadiscourse." But discourses are discourses, whether small or large. If one were to reverse the phrase and say that Islam is a "traditional discourse" the maneuver would solve no problems, since utilizing Asad's own definition of "tradition" one would simply produce the same result that was produced by unpacking "discursive tradition," namely, "Islam is a discursive discourse."

It is crucial to note that when Asad speaks of "discourses" he is using the technical sense established and developed by Michel Foucault and his epigones. "Discourse" in this sense does *not* refer to an everyday notion of communication or debate. No one who reads the words "discursive" or "discourse" in the general neighborhood of Foucault should think of the idiomatic meaning of these words; one is dealing essentially with homonyms. "Discourse" in this technical sense refers to the assertion of power through language, to mechanisms of control that are disguised as—or appear in the form of—rational practices. Power is the cause; ideas are the effect. "Discursive" refers not to the exchange of ideas qua ideas but to the way in which power constructs ideas—constructing not only this or that idea but also constructing the very subject who is taken to be the originator of those ideas.

Some have characterized Asad's conception of "discursive tradition" as a combination of Foucault's "discourse" and Alasdair MacIntyre's "tradition,"[44] but such a combination is incoherent, not least because MacIntyre rejected the basis of Foucault's notion of "discourse," and MacIntyre's own definition of tradition rules out the basic presuppositions of Foucault's vision. For MacIntyre a tradition is "an argument extended through time" and an argument is *actually* an argument, or can be one potentially if the parties involved do it correctly. That is, there exists for MacIntyre the possibility for rational human beings to exchange ideas and to both agree and disagree about elements of their common tradition *freely*. MacIntyre, in *Three Rival Versions of Moral Enquiry: Encyclopaedia, Genealogy, and Tradition*, discussed at length the internal self-contradiction of Foucault: Foucault presupposes "standards of reason-giving, reason-accepting, and reason-rejecting"[45] but claims to reject them, asserting that language and ideas are ways in which power relationships construct the subject.

Reason and rationality, as aspects of the constructed-by-power subject, are therefore also constructed-by-power relationships. One cannot ascribe this notion of rationality to MacIntyre or imagine that it can somehow be reconciled with MacIntyre's own clearly stated vision of rationality and his clearly stated rejection of Foucault's basic premises.[46] Indeed, while the stated definition of tradition as a set of discourses makes "discursive tradition" redundant, attempting to use evoke MacIntyre's conception of tradition makes "discursive tradition" an oxymoron.

It is clear that this notion of discourse as constructed-by-power relationships is indeed what Asad has in mind. In critiquing previous attempts by anthropologists to situate "orthodoxy," Asad wants neither to deny the importance of orthodoxy nor to reduce orthodoxy to a set of doctrines, simplifications which he believes other anthropologists have fallen into. He says, "Orthodoxy is not a mere body of opinion but a distinctive relationship—a relationship of power to truth." But the kind of power he has in mind is not the power of the ideas qua ideas. Let us recall that doctrines, teachings, and communications are things that are potentially *right*, and therefore they can be persuasive or coherent or inspiring or satisfying, but Asad mentions none of these possibilities. Rather, orthodoxy is about the ability of "social, political, economic etc." *power* to "regulate, uphold, require, or adjust." Orthodoxy simply *is* that relationship of power.

Yet Asad also wants to emphasize that the arguments and ideas in Islam (whatever such things as ideas really are) are not lacking in nuance and complexity, and that traditional orthodoxy is not merely a set of simplistic commands established by a small group of rule makers. He notes that "reasons and arguments are intrinsic to traditional practice" (and here one must assume me means "practices proper to a set of discourses") and so an anthropologist ought to describe and analyze those reasons and arguments. He goes on, "It is here that the analyst may discover a central modality of power, and of the resistance it encounters—for the process of arguing, of using the force of reason, at once presupposes and responds to the fact of resistance. Power, and resistance, are thus intrinsic to the development and exercise of any traditional practice."[47] The primacy of power runs through Asad's overall construction of a concept of Islam, but it is not made clearly because it is marred by the initial redundancy and confusion around the concept of "tradition."

There are two ways to restate what I take to be the core of Asad's underlying argument (namely, what is left when the definitional confusions about tradition are removed). The minimalist version of the argument is that

Islam should be *studied as a discourse* (as Foucault understood that term) in which case one is arguing for anthropologists to be *methodologically* Foucauldian as concerns the conceptualization of Islam. The maximalist version of the argument is that Islam simply *is a discourse*, in which case one is being—for lack of a better term—*metaphysically* Foucauldian as concerns the conceptualization of Islam, meaning that one should accept Foucault's account of human nature and human relationships as well as his other basic presuppositions about knowledge, truth, and morality.

Again, Asad does not deny something he calls rationality in Islam, and he firmly rejects those who see Islam as "unchanging, repetitive, and non-rational,"[48] but the question is: What precisely does he mean by rationality? Let us recall the role of power. For Asad, the relevant power relationships are not unchanging, and they are not repetitive, neither in the modern West nor in the Islamic world. Therefore, one should expect that the subjects who are constructed by those evolving power relationships would not be unchanging or repetitive either—neither in the West nor in Islam. But change that comes randomly or deterministically is different from change that comes from the actual free choice of rational beings. Does "rationality" simply refer to the mere existence—the mere fact—of complex, nuanced, contentious arguments existing as things in the world? If so, that bare fact still would not tell us whether rationality was the product of random processes, or deterministic ones, or instead the product of actually free rational agents. One must specify which of those three options it is. Does "creativity" simply refer to the fact that there now exist ideas that did not exist before, or does it mean that a free being actually thought of something new in light of something old? In short, one must know and indeed always presuppose the answer to the question, What is a human being such that one can distinguish between a person being rational and a person being nonrational?

When Asad defends Muslims against accusations of rigidity, imitation, repetitiveness, and ossification, it seems inescapable, in light of his own conception of discourse and traditions, that his argument amounts to "Islam's constructed-by-power ideas are just as dynamic, varied, and sophisticated as the West's constructed-by-power ideas." One might agree with Asad about the comparability of the two civilizations' dynamism, variation, and sophistication, but that is quite separate from the question of what ideas and arguments themselves are made of. And this is no trivial matter, since no version of Islam could possibly accept the metaphysical presuppositions about human nature, knowledge, and morality embedded in Foucault's notion of "discourse," which certainly has nothing to do with Islam in any of its historical manifestations. Would any Muslim, at any time in history (before the twentieth century, at least), accept that his or her rational and moral commitments were the result of power relationships in society constructing subjects who then form those commitments as a function of that power matrix and that *that is all those commitments can be*?

Islam Cannot Simply Be Whatever Muslims Do

We have encountered in this chapter the tendency by some scholars to say or imply different versions of "Islam is whatever Muslims do," an idea whose implication, as we will see, is that Islam has no permanent moral or rational content, or really any content at all. Both Asad and Ahmed disavow the idea and appear to recognize its incoherence. As Asad notes,

> The idea [Michael Gilsenan] adopts from anthropologists—that Islam is simply what Muslims everywhere say it is—will not do, if only because there are everywhere Muslims who say that what *other* people take to be Islam is not really Islam at all. This paradox cannot be resolved simply by saying that the claim as to what is Islam will be admitted by the anthropologist only where it applies to the informant's *own* beliefs and practices, because it is generally impossible to define beliefs and practices in terms of an isolated subject. A Muslim's beliefs about the beliefs and practices of others *are* his own beliefs. (2–3)

Yet both Asad and Ahmed nevertheless salvage the fallacy's essential impact, however unwittingly, by creating frameworks that render the fallacy *not* a fallacy in the first place. Their conceptualizations of Islam have the effect of merely changing the rules of the game, such that the fallacy of "Islam is whatever Muslims do," namely, the unavoidable fact that Muslims knowingly contradict each other in what counts as being normatively Islamic, no longer has to be an obstacle to overcome.

Ahmed accomplishes this rule change by incorporating his expansive sense of "contradiction" into the very essence of Islam. The "inherent contradiction" of Islam means that the fact that different Muslims believe that other Muslims are wrong no longer matters, and indeed such mutual opposition between Muslims is what one would have to expect considering that contradiction is inherent to Islam as Ahmed sees it. "Islam is whatever

Muslims do" can be recast, as informed by Ahmed's conceptualization, as "Islam (with its dynamic of inherent contradiction" is whatever Muslims (who contradict each other about Islam) do." There is no logical problem in saying that a dynamic of contradiction (Islam) results from contradictory claims (whatever Muslims do). In fact, contradiction is exactly what one would expect, and therefore there is no reason to even consider coherence as a factor.

Asad, for his part, changes the rules and rescues "Islam is whatever Muslims do" by casting all points of agreement and disagreement (and hence contradiction) as functions of power relationships. If orthodoxy simply *is* these relationships of power, as he argues, then the apparent disagreements are not *really* contradictions at all. They should be seen, rather, as articulations and narratives that fulfill the needs of power and resistance. Power relationships are the province neither of agreement nor disagreement; power neither agrees nor disagrees. Rather, power is met with resistance in a push-and-pull struggle. One could call a certain collision of powers a "disagreement" but that would have to be understood through the lens of the concept of a "discourse." Defining Islam as a "long-standing struggle of power and resistance by means of ideas" (which is what "discursive tradition" amounts to) thus paves the way for Islam to be thought of as the aggregate outcome of those relationships of power and resistance between human beings. Asad's objection is not so much to a contradiction but to what he sees as an *oversimplification*, the failure of anthropologists of Islam to account for the full nature of the power relationships and how they are expressed multifariously as "discourses." For Asad, the manifestations of orthodoxy—which simply *are* those relationships of power—are complex and nuanced. When one set of power relationships collides with other sets of such power relationships, that encounter of power with resistance gives rise to formulations and narratives that themselves collide with each other, and this process often gives rise to articulations that are extremely sophisticated. We commonly see those collisions of power and resistance as objective "disagreements" about right and wrong in which conceptions of truth and the good can have content that is *not* fully determined by relationships of power, but the concept of a "discourse" shows this stance to be naive.

In short, Ahmed overcomes the fallacy of "Islam is whatever Muslims do" by baking contradiction into Islam, in essence arguing "Not only is it Islam *despite* being contradictory, it is Islam *because* it is contradictory." Asad overcomes the fallacy by dissolving the very concept of contradiction in a solvent made of power relationships; he transcends (really, subverts) the dichotomy between contradiction and coherence altogether. Asad's and Ahmed's conceptualizations are logically equivalent to the formula "Islam is what Muslims do" because they both make it impossible to exclude *anything* a Muslim does from the category of Islam. (It can be noted that "Nothing a Muslim does isn't Islam," which is logically equivalent to "Islam is what Muslims do," is also the necessary implication of these conceptualizations.)

This inability to exclude or set limits brings us to the absence of permanent moral and rational content in Islam. Rendering it impossible to exclude anything a Muslim does from Islam is an implicit declaration that no principles are involved. Islam can have no permanent moral or rational substance because not only is Islam whatever Muslims say it is (the essence of both Asad's and Ahmed's conceptualizations), Islam is whatever Muslims say it is *for any reason or for no reason at all*. Ahmed's "inherent contradiction" is tantamount to a disavowal of all rational or moral principles, since principles have to include *and* exclude and Ahmed's conception excludes nothing. For Asad, the reasons are not reasons but the mere push and pull of power and resistance. Power neither has nor lacks principles; it is simply the wrong concept, like asking whether algebra is hot or cold. There is nothing independent of power that could be permanent or constant.

Overlapping Hierarchies Again

The fallacy of "Islam is whatever Muslims do" is not only the failure to deal with the fact that Muslims' beliefs about other Muslims' mistake *are* their beliefs, which is not a problem at all if one selects the standard group correctly. In point of fact, "Islam is whatever Muslims do" is not problematic exclusively for the reason that Asad lays out. A deeper and far-reaching problem is, as we saw in the discussion above regarding the if-then chain, identifying the "Muslims" in such a formulation.

Coming back to the language analogy, if one were to say "English is whatever English speakers say it is," no one would offer the objection "That definition is problematic because part of being an English speaker is to correct other English speakers about their incorrect usage!" This is true, of course. After all, aren't style book authors, lexicographers, copy editors, and English professors English speakers too? Isn't their very act of correcting, revising, and adjusting the speech of *other* English speakers part of their speech? Nevertheless, one does not despair of knowing what "English" is because of these disagreements among English speakers.

As we saw earlier, to talk about that which is Islamic and un-Islamic *normatively* (as when one talks about that which is orthodox, or religious as opposed to cultural, or mainstream/core as opposed to marginal) is never to explore a single question at all but always to carry out an irreducibly complex multiplicity of judgments. In the case of a dictionary, we saw that the procedure whereby one determines the correct use of words is different for each word because the relevant population of standard speakers is somewhat different in each case. To write the definition for "epidemiology" would require theorizing the language use of a relatively elite group of people, yet no matter how differently that very same elite group used the word "elbow" it would not change the definition of "elbow" in the dictionary, because that small group—who had so much relative authority over the correct use of "epidemiology"—would share authority with almost the entire English-speaking population on the definition of "elbow."

Therefore, the deeper problem with the notion that "Islam is whatever Muslims do" is not only that it oversimplifies or that it entails contradiction but that is fails to disambiguate these basic parameters. The notion that "Islam is whatever Muslims do" takes what is actually a multiplicity of closely related theoretical procedures that range over a variable (i.e., which Muslims' views matter) and collapses them into a single procedure by treating that variable as a constant (simply "Muslims"). This range of procedures has the *general* form: (1) find out which Muslims' views count on a particular question, and (2) theorize those views. The first step includes a variable, namely the particular subset of Muslims whose views count for that particular question, which will always be a different group in each case. It is therefore a mistake to treat that group of standard Muslims as a fixed group or *as if it were* a fixed group across all potential cases to be researched and conceptualized.

The mistake of treating the input of standard Muslims as fixed takes two forms. The first form of this fallacy is to present the "Muslims" in "Islam is whatever Muslims do" as referring essentially to all Muslims everywhere. That way, the conceptualizer is (seemingly) not picking winners and losers, and is not answerable for choosing the *standard* Muslim; one would seem thereby to avoid the normative. The second form of the fallacy is to present the Muslims in "Islam is what Muslims do" as a relatively small elite who always count as the standard group, and who remain more or less constant over time; their views and practices are then taken to dominate those of other Muslims. This assumption requires the choice of a standard Muslim, but it is not really a choice of a moral or rational standard in the sense of someone who is somehow objectively *more* Islamic; rather, it is a form of the analysis of power relationships that answers the question of who exerts influence over whom. (Such a conception fails to acknowledge that hierarchy is not only a matter of coercion and power but also can result from relationships of earned and deserved trust.) In any event, it sets aside the question of right and wrong (correct and incorrect) in favor of describing a relationship of power.

Thus, the conceptualizations of Islam discussed here do not make allowance for this variability of the standard input and the reality of overlapping and interrelated hierarchies. There is only one output value toward which the conceptualization process is geared (Islamic vs. un-Islamic) and there is only one relevant population to serve as input (all Muslims, or an invariant subset of powerful Muslims). But as we have seen, there are several "output values" that are used to speak about how "Islamic" something is—orthodox, traditional, virtuous, just, mainstream, pious, and many other words that describe the normative, and there is the multiplicity of particular cases that one is interested in judging. And for each output value and particular case, there is necessarily the assumption of who counts—who is the right population to look at in order to determine how Islamic something is. Any acknowledgment of this range of possible input values and range of possible output values is absent in these conceptualizations.

In both cases of treating the standard Muslims as an invariant group, the conceptualizer seems to be absolved from having to take a stand about what the conceptualizer thinks true or correct or real Islam is. But that choice is not something anyone can avoid; it is in fact a precondition of the activity of conceptualizing Islam. Not only does the conceptualizer have to choose what true or real or correct Islam is (really, who the standard Muslims are), but if he believes there is anything in the world called Islam at all, he also has to make that choice pretheoretically, the same way an English speaker finds out who speaks German authoritatively not through some theoretical or analytical procedure but by managing it through hard-to-theorize procedures of trust. These are logical necessities, not empirical or moral contingencies. This situation can never change. All the conceptualizer can do is to enhance the theoretical sophistication of what he does with that first input. The selection of pretheoretical standards can never be driven out completely but at best can achieve a level of broad acceptance within a particular community (e.g., the Euro-American academy).

Since this stance of assuming a standard Muslim is unavoidable, it is a better practice to be reasonably transparent about who that standard is assumed to be, to accept that such an assumption can be revised in light of new evidence or new arguments, and to proceed to theorize what Islam is on that basis. For a given case to be theorized (e.g., a practice, a doctrine, a ritual) one would make a *reasonable* assumption that such and such Muslims are the ones whose views are relevant to theorize that particular case, and then rigorously theorize it, with an openness to revising one's initial assumption about which Muslims' views are relevant to the theorization of that particular case. For example, if one is studying how menstruation relates to purification and prayer, one might make a reasonable assumption that the Muslims whose views are relevant are the jurists or *fuqahāʿ*. Upon theorizing and conceptualizing the views of those jurists, however, the researcher may realize that the initial assumption was too simple, because the theoretical activity brought up other considerations that caused the researcher to reconsider the first input (the standard Muslims). Then, through trial and error, or intuition, or consultation, the conceptualizer would make *another* reasonable assumption about the standard population of Muslims whose views are relevant (perhaps including writings by physicians) and then theorize on that basis. That revision would never be purely theoretical, but it would be informed by the researcher's previous theoretical activity, which he would use as part of the recipe for making a revised *reasonable* assumption about which Muslims' views were relevant for that particular case. The relevant Muslims would never be *all* Muslims everywhere, and it would also never be the exact same subset of Muslims.

In any case, Asad and Ahmed are both writing as members of the broad "we" and thus are subject to its constraints, actively or passively. The "Islam is whatever Muslims do" formulation allows the subproject to, at will, choose the inputs (a group of Muslims) and the output values (orthodox vs. heterodox) and then, unconstrained by any corrective rational or moral principles from Islam itself, fashion a set of ideas that will link together those Muslims and those output values. Why is this a desirable situation?

With the inputs and outputs firmly under control, and the theoretical procedures unconstrained by moral or rational limitations, the scope for "conceptualization" is vast. A conceptualization of Islam offered up by the humanities and social science subproject does not have to make sense to any Muslim (who might be called faith-based or provincial for pointing out such an incoherence), and it can include beliefs and practices that are repugnant to Muslims, since there are no moral principles intrinsic to Islam that could be used to temper the theory. Islam can, in effect, be anything at all, and any conceptualization that does not violate the basic parameters of the "we"/Islam dynamic of the Modern Project will pass muster as long as it is *interesting* enough to the audience for whom it is intended—the "we." One thing this situation allows is an almost limitless supply of possible research projects, small and large, that fit into the general category of "the study of Islam." Scholars will always have something to write about.

Let us remember that in the real world, the input will never *actually* be all Muslims. Any scholar can claim interest and competence only in some particular time, place, and population.[49] Only rarely are totalizing theories about Islam attempted. Since the inputs are almost never all Muslims but only some population or practice of interest, the absence of moral and rational principles in Islam that could function as objective constraints means that the chosen phenomenon can be studied through whatever theory is fashionable in the academy at the time. Even if the conclusions conflict with other conclusions by other scholars somewhere else, does it really matter? Any problem of incoherence or immorality—that is, if Islam or Muslims come out looking irrational and/or bad—can be deferred indefinitely under the cover the prevailing tolerance for contradiction and contestation exemplified in Asad and Ahmed's conceptualizations.

There is yet another implication, intended or not, of the axiom that Islam has no permanent moral or rational content and that it is whatever Muslims everywhere say it is. If *I* am a Muslim, it also means that Islam is whatever *I* say it is. Ahmed's concept of Islam allows a Muslim to be "a Muslim who drinks wine" (to use his example) because that contradiction is the kind of thing that is inherent to Islam. In Asad's case, a Muslim can do the same because orthodoxy is a form of power, and drinking wine could be simply resistance to power. That is, since contradictions are not problematic, and since I, like you, am a Muslim engaging in Islam, then whatever I am doing (whatever that is, so long I do it "as a Muslim") is *just as Islamic* as what you are doing, and the fact that your and my views about Islam are contradictory is not only not a problem but stems from the very nature of Islam itself. Or, one could say that what I am doing is *just as Islamic* because this thing we call Islam is a discursive tradition, and what I am doing is part of that the push and pull of power, an act of resistance that is not outside of that discourse. One is neither a good Muslim or a bad Muslim—one simply is a Muslim for any reason or for no reason at all.

Kevin Reinhart and Anti-Essentialism

Whatever restraint or caution about the fallacy of "Islam is whatever Muslims do" that one finds in authors such as Asad and Ahmed is completely left behind when we come to Kevin Reinhart's *Lived Islam,* which takes the anti-essentialist approach to answering the question "What is Islam?" to its furthest extent. Not only is Islam not treated as the domain of the believer to decide its ideal or metaphysical form (Hodgson), and not only is it not a discourse (Asad), and not only is it not something to which contradiction is inherent (Ahmed), it simply *does not exist.* Reinhart's claim is that it is a mistake to believe that "this set of practices and even creedal commitments that we call Islam constitutes a real object in the world."[50] One is confronted with "the variety of Islamic practice that confounds any kind of essentialism."[51]

Reinhart presents his anti-essentialism about Islam through a tripartite division drawing from sociolinguistics, dividing Islam into what he calls Dialect Islam, Koiné Islam, and Cosmopolitan Islam. Unlike the language analogy in this book (see chapter 6), which is based upon the idea that natural languages are forms of institutions and that religions and cultures are also forms of institutions, Reinhart is instead making a direct analogy to a certain way of understanding language drawn from sociolinguistics, but he is careful to point out "that to say Islam is *like* a language is not to say that it *is* a language. These features of Islam that we isolate heuristically are not real; they have no ontology."[52]

Regardless of the nature of his analogy, however, the entire enterprise begins from the kind of arbitrary assumption discussed earlier. That is, the author presupposes the existence of some population of Muslims but provides absolutely no criteria by which people can be included or excluded from this population other than the fact that these people feel they belong together, or that Reinhart does. He allows no objective criterion outside of their own intuitions about who the Muslims are, saying things like "Muslims believe the term 'Islam' to be a profoundly meaningful one, and that the term 'Muslim' has an actual referent."[53] For him "Muslim" does not *have* such a referent, even though Muslims *believe* it does. Reinhart is not saying Muslims believe in a divinity that doesn't exist, but rather that they believe in a set of beliefs that doesn't really exist. They believe in a belief. Astonishingly, he even says that for Muslims "the *idea* of a *ritualized life* is more potent than the actual prescriptions of the normative Islamic life."[54] Muslims "imagine" themselves to be "religious kin," and Islam is "conceived of as a set of symbols, principles, and practices." Notice the distancing here: Islam is not a set of such things but at best it is *conceived of* as such a set. This argument is akin to saying that English speakers speak English by virtue of "conceiving of" English as a language they all speak, not by virtue of actually being able to communicate with each other as speakers of the same language. In short, for Reinhart, Islam has no content (indeed no ontology), and it is enough that Muslims *conceive* of it as having content in order for them to belong together under the name "Muslim." The only defining factor is that people should *feel* or *imagine* themselves to be a Muslim or believe that there is an Islam to which they all somehow belong. (They cannot even believe in some common thing. Rather, at most they all believe in the *idea* of a common thing.) What exactly is the procedure that Reinhart might use to determine that people "conceive of" Islam this way, or that they merely imagine themselves to be religious kin? What is the difference between "religious" kin and other kinds? It seems more likely that Reinhart simply makes an assumption about who Muslims are and imputes to them these subjective states as a way of justifying his intuitions. He collapses a community into a mere identity.

Anticipating the most obvious objection to this line of reasoning, he says, "To say, glibly, 'Islam is universal, because Muslims all believe in the Qur'ān,' is to miss the fact that the Qur'ān is variously understood and appropriated. It is affirmed by all Muslims and that affirmation unites Muslims, but it is also, like South Indian or South Alabaman English, locally inflected. It is perhaps the most important of the cognates shared by Muslims; it helps to constitute the Koiné of Islam."[55] To note that all Muslims believe in the Quran is a statement of fact that cannot be dismissed by calling it "glib." It is one thing to say that "the Quran is variously understood" and is "locally inflected," which Muslims know already, and which has been known for centuries by anyone with even a passing knowledge of *tafsīr* (systematic Quran commentary), but it is quite another matter to infer that this multivalence means the Quran fails to be universal for Muslims. Many passages of the Quran have been understood in a multitude of different ways, while other passages have been understood in only a limited number of ways, and still others have been understood in one way only.[56] This *range of ranges* of opinion—spanning unanimity and different degrees of disagreement—belies any assertion that the Quran can just be understood in any way whatsoever, which is a proposition that the anti-essentialist must commit himself to. If one believes that there are certain things the Quran cannot mean, then one has just espoused an essence. The Quran cannot mean simply *anything*, and even if some people wish to say it can, no one actually believes it can, including those who utter that claim. Reinhart himself essentializes the Quran when he speaks of its "austere God."[57] Can "austere" mean whatever anyone wishes it to mean?

Anti-essentialism fails on other grounds. Suppose there are two people, person A and person B, who claim to be Muslim, where person A accepts that both person A and person B are Muslim, but person B believes himself to be Muslim but rejects that person A is a Muslim because of A's stated beliefs. This happens all the time—recall Asad's important observation that including and excluding others from Islam is *part* of a Muslim's Islam. If the anti-essentialist scholar claims both A and B can be right, then anti-essentialism tells us nothing about who counts as a Muslim in the first place, and one cannot even begin theorizing about Islam, lived or otherwise, except on the basis of some intuitive starting assumption of who the Muslims are. And if he claims both A and B are wrong, then anti-essentialism fails again for the same reason. If the anti-essentialist scholar claims A is right but B is wrong, then he has taken a position on what limiting factors exist with respect to Islam and has corrected person B about his religion, and has become an essentialist about that specific factor at least. If the anti-essentialist scholar claims B is right and A is wrong, then he once again becomes an essentialist for affirming B's views about Islam's limiting factors.

To state the matter frankly: there are no anti-essentialists in the real world, just as there are no actual skeptics or moral relativists. There may be anti-essentialist claims, but essences are presupposed by their denial, and so all anti-essentialist claims are self-undermining. Such is the case in general, but it is also the case with respect to the example of theorizing Islam in this way, because some population of Muslims is presupposed before any theory about "What is Islam?" can be developed. In fact, most of what avowed anti-essentialists are cautioning against is really oversimplification or overidealization. To point out that there is no such thing as "blue" because really there is only turquoise, azure, royal, cobalt, sky, and cerulean (or the literally hundreds of discernible shades) is true in the sense that an overly simplistic notion of blue can be very misleading or limiting for certain purposes. But the anti-essentialists are not saying that the common view about "Islam" is simplistic, misleading, or lacking in nuance. Rather, they are saying Islam simply does not exist. This denial is exactly akin to saying that there is no "blue" since the hundreds of varieties of blue "confound any kind of essentialism" and therefore there is no reason why crimson could not be a blue as well. If one tries to point to any reason why crimson cannot be a blue, one has stumbled right into an essence.

The anti-essentialism breaks down in still other ways. Reinhart in fact points over and over to an essence—albeit a rather skimpy one in his view.

There are for him certain "core" Islamic practices and beliefs that "structurally give rise to, provoke, and create a space within which the rich dialect features of local Lived Islam can thrive."[58] How can something that *does not exist* give rise to or provoke anything? If it "gives rise to" something then it must precede, either temporally or logically, the thing to which it gives rise. Even so, Reinhart is mindful to emphasize how paltry "the Islam of texts" really is. He calls it a "religious Lean Cuisine" that is "really quite sparse." Its "ritual thinness" is so thin, in fact, that it results in a "featureless plain" around it which people can happily fill right in.[59] Textual Islam is "thin gruel,"[60] and a "lowest-common denominator."[61] Whether these evaluations of Cosmopolitan Islam's "thinness" and "sparseness" hold up to the slightest scrutiny is beside the point, because they show that the anti-essentialist assumes some stable core, however insubstantial it is imagined to be. That is all that is necessary to puncture anti-essentialism. "The core is very small" is decisively different from "The core does not exist."[62]

Finally, one must address what Reinhart means by the "Islam of texts," which for him is something other than the Lived Islam that is a real object in the world. "Lived Religion is an approach that studies the religiosity of those who don't write books, though it studies also the religiosity of clerics that isn't expressed in their books."[63] He goes on to say, "What we mean here by Lived Islam, then, is the Islam of ordinary Muslims, and of the 'ulamā' 'when they are at home.' 'Lived Islam' refers not so much to the Islam we see in books by Muslim scholars telling Muslims how to be Muslims (though, as we shall see, those too have a place in our study) as to what we learn of Islam when we observe Muslims, converse with them, live with them, and so on, whether in Iraq or North Carolina, whether among illiterate tribal folk or Azharī scholars."[64]

A lot of definitional work is being done here by certain presuppositions about the meaning of "ordinary." Who gets to say what counts as ordinary? Do ordinary people not read as part of their ordinariness? Are there no bookish Muslims? Must one step away from "texts" before one can be really Muslim? Reinhart is not saying that it is worthwhile to study those aspects of Muslim life that are not written in books. That would be inarguable, but it is not his argument. Lived Islam is "distinct from an Islam of texts,"[65] and Lived Islam is the *only* Islam that is real in the world.[66] Lived Islam is a rich tapestry of dialects, while the "Islam of texts" is *no one's* dialect;[67] it "has no ontology" and "is not an object in the world."[68]

This line of reasoning regarding the role of "texts" in all major Islamic cultures around the world from Mauritania to Indonesia through the centuries is truly baffling as a matter of empirical fact. To highlight just one dimension of this question, many Muslim bibliophiles (such as the present author) have a spirituality that is intimately tied to the reading of great books, to reading the Quran with *tafsīr*, and to a kind of spiritual and intellectual joy derived from reading even books of law or theology, and of course also the act of writing. Who is to say that this Islam is not truly "lived" until the books are closed and one goes and does *anything else* as long as it does not involve a "text"? Just as a question of human temperaments, why should a small minority of people who find joy and spiritual elevation through "texts" be somehow less authentic or less worthy of being called an example of "Lived Islam" than a comparably sized minority who cannot read classical Arabic and who talk to spirits in the mountains? Who gets to call one group genuine, while the other group is engaged only in a kind of myth-making performance?[69] Reinhart does not say that only a *small number* of Muslims have texts as part of their Lived Islam or native dialect, but rather claims *literally no one does*.[70] It is simply not true. It is perfectly arbitrary and presumptuous (and not a little patronizing) to claim that a scholar is not quite living when he has his nose in a "text" and then that he becomes suddenly alive once he walks away from it. Why this inability to see literate and learned Islam as *lived*? People everywhere get passionate and deeply spiritual about their books and, yes, their sacred texts. Even quite apart from the empirical fact that the Islamic world is full of such individuals, just who gets to decide what is "ordinary" in the first place?

Whatever the intention, such a demoting and scare-quoting of "texts" (which is becoming increasingly common among scholars of Islamic studies) has the effect of severing Islam from its immense literate and learned dimension and turning Muslims into a specific kind of anthropological object amenable to a narrow mode of study. To state it plainly: many prefer to do ethnography (which, after all, ultimately results in the writing of other "texts") about people who are not writing texts back, because such a situation would place the researcher and his subject on the same level of rationality, thus violating one of the unwritten maxims for many in the modern academic enterprise. Moreover, as a practical matter of research time and attention, just what is a sociologist or anthropologist supposed to do with someone sitting in a room writing a book and leading a life of the mind? Most of what is happening—the intellectual life—is hidden from him, and because the ethnographer cannot relate to or understand much of what is happening with the "texts" or because the learning curve is too steep to reward research time, he focuses on things he can see and hear instead, and accordingly gravitates toward a theory of Islam that makes his chosen object of study the only real or interesting one.

Synopsis

- Marshal Hodgson's demarcation in his *The Venture of Islam* between the Islamic and the Islamicate is a manifestation the intuitive folk boundary between religion/tradition on the one hand and civilization/culture on the other.

- Hodgson is not able to offer a theoretically reliable demarcation between the Islamic and the Islamicate beyond authoritative folk usage, nor is he able to reconcile Islam's absence of a "unity of life" with the presence of its "decisive continuity" in history.

- Shahab Ahmed's *What Is Islam?* relies on several profound misunderstandings about the nature of paradox and contradiction, rendering his conceptualization unusable, since one can call anything Islamic for any reason or for no reason at all.

- Talal Asad's notion of Islam as a "discursive tradition" is circular since "tradition" is defined as "a set of discourses," a conception that he applies to Islam unjustifiably by relying on Foucault's ideas about the nature of knowledge and power.

- Asad's notion of "discursive tradition" and Ahmed's notion of "inherent contradiction" both turn out to be different versions of the "Islam is whatever Muslims do" fallacy, despite the fact that both authors wish to reject that notion.

- Both varieties of "Islam is whatever Muslims do" evacuate Islam of stable moral or intellectual principles, either because Islam is open to any and all contradictions (Ahmed), or because such principles are really the interplay of power and resistance (Asad).

- Kevin Reinhart's approach in *Lived Islam* is a thoroughgoing anti-essentialism that treats Islam as an object with "no ontology." Islam is that which Muslims *believe* unites them, i.e., Muslims do not believe the same thing but only believe that they do.

- Anti-essentialism, like relativism and skepticism, is never a real practice but is a form of performative self-contradiction whose very rejection of essences presupposes the very thing it claims to deny.

- The anti-essentialist claim with respect to Islam is also empirically self-undermining, since scholars must and in practice do presuppose and even describe a certain "core" that abides in various manifestations of Islam.

- Ethnography has difficulty with Islam's intellectual tradition, which does not present itself as an easy anthropological object. Rather than incorporate this dimension of Islam, Reinhart's "Lived Islam" arbitrarily excludes the "Islam of texts."

Conclusion

The Sighted Men and the Elephant

Asking whether Islam is an institution is akin to asking whether a human being is a body. In one sense the answer is yes, but in another, clearly no. It is not *merely* so, and the answer depends entirely on what one has in mind as the meaning of "body" and upon one's ultimate assumptions. If one starts from the presuppositions about the reality of shared thinking as outlined in this book, then indeed Islam is a community, a practice, a legacy; it is stable, dynamic, and purposive; it is constituted by accounts, heuristics, and norms, but that conceptualization must also take into account its own metaphysical implications. The preceding chapters discussed a certain meaningful minimum of metaphysics—essentially a rejection of antidualism and the affirmation of the soul—but that is hardly enough to fully account for a reality such as Islam. To speak of a community practicing its legacy does not explain how human beings come to be, how their faculties work, how their souls are nourished and sustained, and what the cosmos is such that they are able to exist as conscious beings within it. We know that our shared thinking is stable, dynamic, and purposive, but this book did not delve into the deeper metaphysics and arguments behind that collection of attributes. Accounts, heuristics, and norms can be either right or wrong in the various ways someone can call something "right," but clearly this book did not attempt to address the many questions of history and experience that would lead human beings toward the right ones as opposed to the wrong ones. In earlier chapters we considered the image of human beings journeying together on a terrain navigating toward a destination, and one should remember that the terrain of life is not an abstract featureless space.

247

As with earthly terrain, there are realities one can either see or miss, one can choose good and bad routes, and one can direct oneself to good or bad destinations. In other words, one can be right or wrong about what is real, right or wrong about what is possible, and right or wrong about what is good. Understanding the invariant conditions of our journeys together as a conceptual matter—which has been the scope of this book—is very different from the actual task of traveling. One journey might lead you through brambles and off a cliff, while another might take you along a shaded path to an oasis. The general conditions of both journeys are the same, but the terrain, route, and destination are different. Understanding what makes any journey a journey—or any metaphysical institution a metaphysical institution—can be helpful along the way.

One lesson of this work is that there is no standpointless place from which to theorize the concept of "institution" and certainly not ultimate institutions such as Islam. It is not as though previous conceptualizations of our tetrad were agnostic to metaphysical questions and one could simply explore them *historically* while the current book is conceptualizing them *Islamically*. When the liberal theorist John Rawls, for example, argued that his conception of fairness was "political, not metaphysical," he cited a range of metaphysical positions that he thought were equally relevant or irrelevant. Although he deserves credit for addressing an issue that many serious thinkers simply ignore (which is why he is being mentioned here), his argument is surprisingly anemic. He first says, "There is no accepted understanding of what a metaphysical doctrine is," as if that matters. Would the statement "There is no accepted understanding of what politics is" be an argument against the notion that everyone has a politics? Certainly not. Later, Rawls articulates precisely the argument against himself only to dismiss it diffidently:

> One might say . . . that to develop a political conception of justice without presupposing, or explicitly using, a metaphysical doctrine, for example, some particular metaphysical conception of the person, *is already to presuppose a metaphysical thesis*: namely, that no particular metaphysical doctrine is required for this purpose. One might also say that our everyday conception of persons as the basic units of deliberation and responsibility *presupposes, or in some way involves, certain metaphysical theses* about the nature of persons as moral or political agents. Following the method of *avoidance*, I should not want to deny these claims. What should be said is the following. If we look at the presentation of justice

as fairness and note how it is set up, and note the ideas and conceptions it uses, no particular metaphysical doctrine about the nature of persons, distinctive and opposed to other metaphysical doctrines, appears among its premises, *or seems required* by its argument. If metaphysical presuppositions are involved, *perhaps* they are so general that they would not distinguish between the distinctive metaphysical views—Cartesian, Leibnizian, or Kantian; realist, idealist, or materialist—with which philosophy traditionally has been concerned. In this case, they *would not appear* to be relevant for the structure and content of a political conception of justice one way or the other.[1]

There is an equivocation here between metaphysics as a set of expressed *doctrines* and metaphysics as one's always already always active presuppositions about the nature of things. Why does Rawls avoid an ironclad logical argument about the nature of presuppositions, which he articulates with clarity, in favor of what *seems* or *appears* to be? Setting aside his relatively provincial sense of metaphysics (essentially European), the entire point Rawls seems unwilling to fully accept is that one's politics can exist only within the possibilities created by one's metaphysics and one simply has no choice in the matter. One does not think politically and *then* adjust that politics according to one's metaphysics. One's metaphysics constitutes the very conditions for conceiving of anything real, possible, or good in the first place.[2] What kind of being is free to care about fairness at all? Durkheim also failed to see this same truth when he said: "Firstly [sociology] is independent of all philosophy. . . . Sociology does not need to choose between the great hypotheses which divide metaphysicians. It needs to embrace free will no more than determinism. All that it asks is that the principle of causality be applied to social phenomena."[3] What could be more metaphysical (or indeed, philosophical) than the nature of causality? Unlike such a metaphysics-less posture, this book's concept of institutions ought to be understood exactly as one should understand as any such exploration one will encounter from any scholar: as a heuristic (or set of heuristics, see below) that presupposes certain accounts as its inputs and is oriented toward outputs determined by certain norms, and which is communicated by a member of a community who is practicing a legacy, fulfilling a certain purpose by creatively elaborating upon certain ideas that have remained constant over time. That is what Rawls was doing with respect to fairness, for example, whether he would say so or not.

One might object that the present work's emphasis on presuppositions is itself a form of relativism or anti-essentialism, or that it sets one on a path toward such pitfalls. Indeed, many relativistic philosophies rely on some version of saying that human beings can see things only from where they are and are "always already" in some set of conditions. That inference toward relativism, however, relies upon and presupposes a certain metaphysics as opposed to another. The insight that we are "always already" part of a *we*, which is one way of characterizing a major premise of the argument of this book, does lead some people to a kind of determinism and to a belief in an invisible boundary beyond which exist forces that control us in ways that we cannot ever actually know, where we are produced by a structure from which there is no escape, no getting on the outside of. But this inference from the "always already" to a cultural determinism or relativism relies upon hidden but necessary premises, namely a certain vision of what a human being is and what the world is. The fact of "always already" is not enough to conclude that cultural determinism or relativism is true. One requires also an understanding of *what* is already always there, and also *who* is plunged into that always already. If there is always already a "structure," then what is that structure and what is it made of?

Some have criticized Alasdair MacIntyre on such grounds, arguing that his emphasis on the "tradition-dependence" of rationality commits him to a form of relativism. MacIntyre himself notes:

> What I have to do, then, is to provide an account of the rationality presupposed by and implicit in the practice of those enquiry-bearing traditions with whose history I have been concerned which will be adequate to meet the challenges posed by relativism and perspectivism. In the absence of such an account the question of how the rival claims made by different traditions regarding practical rationality and justice are to be evaluated would go unanswered, and in default of an answer from the standpoint of those traditions themselves, relativism and/or prospectivism might well appear to prevail. Notice that the grounds for an answer to relativism and perspectivism are to be found, not in any theory of rationality as yet explicitly articulated and advanced within one or more of the traditions with which we have been concerned, but rather with a theory embodied in and presupposed by their practices of enquiry, yet never fully spelled out.[4]

Such a "theory" of rationality is not yet spelled out because it *cannot* be spelled out, because one is dealing not only with a theoretical or conceptual question but with the very being that asks the questions and produces the theory. That which is "presupposed" is not an articulation or an expression but rather the very human reality that enables meaning and understanding to exist in the world. What is humanly universal is not some form or expression—no form as such can be universal—but the faculties and powers that mean and understand. Rationality is not that which is expressed any more than sight is that which is seen or hearing that which is heard. It would seem that MacIntyre expects to find some universal form or expression over the horizon, but that is to leave unanswered the question of what human beings are such that they are capable of generating such ideas. An implication of the argument of this book is that with the right understanding of what human beings are one would never expect to find a universal procedure or theory of rationality, but rather one should aim to realize and awaken the reality of rationality that is already presupposed in such an expectation.[5] What makes rationality within a tradition possible is not some metatradition or metarationality in the form of a system of expressions, just as what makes communication in language possible is not the possibility or potential of a metalanguage. One must always beware of the structure-behind-structure fallacy, and repudiate it when it appears.[6]

To make this point more clear, let us use the analogy of bodily space: one always begins from somewhere in three-dimensional space, remains in it, and always ends up somewhere else in three-dimensional space, but this physical "always already" cannot, on its own, tell us how or why that movement happens. In other words, the very fact of always already being in a particular spot in three spatial dimensions is an incomplete account of one's conditions with relation to explaining change in location. The three dimensions are there from beginning to end, but that does not tell us how to interpret movement.

Suppose one wanted to reach a metal ball that was buried a few inches deep in sand. According to a purely mechanistic physical theory of bodies and movement, one would have to *first* move some of the sand touching that ball *before* one could move the ball, because the only way to move the ball is to touch the ball or to touch things that are in contact with it—like the sand. But according to another theory that includes non-mechanical electromagnetism, the ball can be moved without moving any sand and in fact rather than the sand acting on the ball the ball would act on the sand. (In the latter theory, *both* ways of moving the metal ball can work—it can be moved mechanically through touch contact, or it can be moved magnetically without touch contact.)

If, as in the mechanical philosophy of the early moderns, one supposes that everything happens by contact causation, then the only way that an object can move from one point in space to another is by being pushed around by other objects in its direct vicinity. But if mechanistic metaphysics is wrong and there are nonmechanical forces, then the explanation for how objects move in those three dimensions is different. In both explanations— movement by contact causation or by invisible forces—the very same three dimensions are always present and the ball is always starting from somewhere and ending somewhere. The fact that there is a ball and sand and both of them are always already located in a particular place in three dimensions of space cannot tell us which theory of movement is right. If one sees the metal ball move, and one is constrained by the mechanical philosophy, one could only say, "The sand moved it (or something moved the sand to move the ball)." But if one is not constrained and understands other causes, one could also say, "The ball moved through the sand itself toward a magnet not visible in the system."

By analogy, the arguments of this book—that there can be no *I* that does not grow and flourish in a *we*, that no human being can explore metaphysics without being within a metaphysical institution, that all conceptualizations are necessarily by someone for someone for some reason at a particular place and time—do not lead to relativism when they are understood against the background of the right metaphysics.

Yes, human beings have all sorts of conscious and even unconscious beliefs about what is real, what is rational, and what is right. We begin as children in a state of deference, imitation, and immaturity and grow into adults. But what brings about that growth, maturation, and change? What is the nature of refinement, development, and edification? How do institutions come to be, and how to human beings grow and flourish within them? There is as little agreement on the growth and development of institutions as there is on their definition. What one can say is that they clearly grow and deteriorate over time in multifarious ways, but how and why these changes take place will be understood differently depending on one's view of certain ultimate questions and one's view of history. To recall the journey metaphor once again, we may indeed always start out and end up somewhere on the terrain, but what accounts for how we can move from place to place? Sometimes human beings are moved by the sand, but sometimes we move the sand and move ourselves through it. The scope of this work does not allow a full discussion of the metaphysics of how consciousness comes to be and grows, but let us register at least that the soul is not like a sand dune changing shape and size over time. It is a different kind of thing. Being awake is not just another configuration of being asleep.

It is important to emphasize that one must think metaphysically and not only historically about these matters. As vital and illuminating as historical explorations of the terms discussed in this book can be, there will always remain certain philosophical problems that they can never solve. What are human beings and what is the world such that these concepts mean what they do? What do "we" assume to be real about human beings, believe to be possible from them, and deem to be good for them such that these terms are used in just the way they are? No amount of chronicling will answer those questions fully, and yet the answers are hugely consequential. I cannot know what a scholar means by "cultural" or "religious" until I grasp a meaningful minimum of what he means by "human being."

Tradition and Traditional

Let us return to the difference between thing and attribute (discussed in chapter 6). It is only at the level of ultimate questions that one can truly understand the difference and overlap between *a* civilization and *civilization,* or between *a* culture and *culture,* at least as those words are typically used by most modern people, namely, as a thing and as an attribute. Despite the fact that the notion of *civilization* is not used in the singular as it once was, it being now common to recognize that there is more than one of them, it nevertheless is the case and must be the case that civilization is not simply a fact or subdivision but also a process or "destination,"[7] as are culture, religion, and tradition depending on who is judging the matter. Any particular civilization must possess the attributes necessary to count as such a thing, and that attribute is also called *civilization* (or alternatively, *being civilized*). For a culture to count as *a* culture, it must have *culture.* One is the thing, the other is the attribute, and inevitably they are used equivocally in language for this reason (not unlike the case of English as a language and English at the attribute of being correct in a particular language). How human beings living together reach and maintain that special attribute is understood against the background of the general metaphysical and historical picture by which this change or realization is imagined to occur.

Reaching that "destination" state of civilization or culture is commonly conceived of as a historical evolutionary process governed by the constraints of antidualism, where the actualization of potential is a variation of "matter in motion," although in modern intellectual culture of the past few centuries there have been nonmaterialistic conceptions of how this evolution takes place, such as certain interpretations of Hegel's world spirit. In the evolutionary framework, the state of civilization (for example) would be the culmination of a process that starts from the low and ends at the high, a movement from primitive to advanced, from backward to forward, a stage of development from underdevelopment, a level of organization from disorganization, and so forth.

This is one decisive way in which tradition, or Tradition as elaborated by the who have made the concept of tradition once again central in its *normative* sense, differs from those conceptions that emphasize culture or civilization as evolutionary outcomes of essentially antidualist processes. For Tradition, the fullest actualization of potential and the realization of a true together-journey is not a question merely of a historical cascade of material or social factors but also and ultimately of the presence of the sacred and transcendent in the world that awakens and makes possible certain human possibilities. It is the magnet that pulls us through the sand. Even at the more mundane level, the civilization and culture of nontraditional and even antitraditional societies can exist only because human beings are what they are and have the capabilities that they do, which they would not possess if antidualism were true.

Thus, many scholars today employ "tradition" and "traditional" the way scholars of other philosophical perspectives might speak of "culture" and "cultural," namely, as terms meant to designate the *right* way to have and to be within a metaphysical institution—the destination or state that human beings reach and *ought* to reach. "Traditional" in this sense is used to characterize human beings, their practice, and their legacy when they are as they should be in light of what human beings are and what the world is (a state of things that Edward Shils called "traditionality"). The attribute of Tradition or the fact of being traditional, understood this way, means that one has the right accounts, the right heuristics, the right norms—truth, rationality, and goodness. It is the ideal form by which shared thinking is realized in the world, by which true community is kept from deteriorating into identity, by which practice is protected from becoming mere routine, by which legacy is saved from becoming a disregarded relic. It does not force false choices between imitation and creativity, or between deference and freedom, between change and stability, or between dogmatic acceptance and personal realization. It does not carve reality into separate spheres of ultimate concern—with questions about what is real here, questions of what is possible over there, and questions of what is good somewhere else. Its accounts are not mere assertions, its heuristics not mere reflexes, its norms not mere demands. Tradition understands the difference between "I know" and "we know" and that one cannot have one without the other. To be traditional, or to be of tradition, does not place one in the predicament of trying to hide one's reliance upon authority in the name of a chimerical autonomy or to make one's own metaphysical institution into a metareality that does not conform to the features of social reality. Tradition does not hide from dogma, imitation, deference, and trust any more than it hides from creativity, experience, discovery, or heroism. To deny dogma is simply to be confused about one's own dogma. To deny imitation and trust is to be oblivious to one's own inevitable reliance upon others.

This sense of "tradition" and "traditional" is not used by everyone, but in that respect "traditional" is no different from our other terms, since using "traditional" in this fashion requires the presupposition of a certain metaphysics, just as the use of "cultured" or "civilized" as something better than being "religious" or "traditional" presupposes another. When one omits to mention the metaphysical implications of one's use of our tetrad of terms, it is not because such implications do not exist but because they are being overlooked or masked. One cannot evade these implications and presuppositions, but one can be explicit about them when it is appropriate to do so.

René Guénon said, "There is nothing and can be nothing truly traditional that does not contain some element of a superhuman order."[8] In the words of Seyyed Hossein Nasr,

> Tradition implies both the Sacred as revealed to humanity through revelation and the unfolding and development of that sacred message in the history of the particular human community for which it was destined; it implies both horizontal continuity with the Origin and a vertical connection that relates each moment in the development of the life of any single tradition to the metahistorical Transcendent Reality . . .
>
> Tradition, therefore, is like a tree, the roots of which are sunk through revelation in the Divine Nature and the trunk and branches of which have grown over the ages. At the heart of the tree of tradition resides religion, and the sap of this tree consists of that grace, or barakah, that, originating with the revelation, makes possible the continuity of the life of the tree. Tradition implies the sacred, the eternal, the immutable Truth;

the perennial wisdom as well as the continuous application of its immutable principles to various conditions of space and time.[9]

Where to Go from Here?

It would be vain for anyone to attempt to revolutionize the meaning of religion, culture, civilization, and tradition or their corresponding adjectives. They are too rich in their history and far too prevalent in everyday language as well as in scholarly discourse for anyone to overturn their current patterns of use. If a scholar of the stature of Wilfred Cantwell Smith could not bring about any real change in the use of the word "religion" then it is doubtful that anyone can. Karl Popper theorized about a "rationalist tradition" of science, but this approach has not been adopted by anyone either. A good deal of Edward Shils's book on tradition demonstrates that science (and much modern intellectual culture) operates exactly like a tradition even though it claims to be "inimical to tradition,"[10] and yet the way moderns talk about science and tradition remains largely unchanged since that book's publication. The words "culture," "civilization," "religion," and "tradition" are going to continue to be used to communicate certain ultimate intuitions about what is real, what is possible, and what is good. No doubt some of their already existing senses can be emphasized or rehabilitated (as in the case of tradition), but in large part we must take them as they are. People will use them in different but overlapping ways, and they will never have consensus definitions or "useful concepts."

It is possible, however, to improve the situation by using the conceptualizations offered in this book. The usage of our tetrad of terms (and related and derivative ones) can be disciplined so as to avoid unnecessary sloppiness—for example, when exploring a question such as "What is Islam?" Being able to use folk concepts against a background of theoretical rigor is better than using those folk concepts uncritically. One can continue using these terms as rich idioms or figures of speech (see chapter 5) while still being able to analyze them according to our model of institutions, the way one can continue using old-fashioned street directions while also being able to consult a detailed map or use GPS on one's phone. One does not need GPS to get around one's town (at least that is how it once was), but GPS can have its uses especially in cases of interminable confusion and disagreement.

Moreover, it is good to avoid those cases where intellectuals reach for some way of recharacterizing certain complex realities and repurpose these terms in ways that are not idiomatic. It is quite common, for example, to call a disfavored ideology "religious" or even "theological" when one means really that one's opponents are being irrational and dogmatic in some way that one has not been able to find a concept for. Nationalism, secularism, and other isms are often called "religions" or "theological" by their critics, a label that depends on certain inherited associations (usually negative). In such cases, the parameters offered by this book's conceptualization of institutions can be a helpful option rather than extending an existing term such as "religion" or "tradition." In that spirit, this book did not attempt to use an unwelcome label such as "the Modern Religion" or "the Modern Tradition" and preferred to borrow the preexisting and uncontroversial "Modern Project," as "project" is nevertheless nearly synonymous with "institution" in the relevant aspects.

One possible strategy, in the case of Islam at least, is to simply stop using these words and revert to using untranslated traditional terms such as *din*, *ummah*, *sunnah*, *nihlah*, or *millah* regardless of the language one is using, with the hope that doing so would eliminate or set aside the impact of the logical problems (not to mention historical associations) discussed in this book. For better or worse, however, we live in a global intellectual culture dominated or heavily influenced by the Modern Project, and as a consequence these Islamic terms are almost always used together with and are compared to religion, culture, civilization, and tradition (and related concepts such as science, philosophy, art, and secularism) in many sometimes bewildering ways—even, or especially, in contemporary Muslim-majority languages such as Arabic, Turkish, and Persian.[11] Therefore, any coherent or sophisticated discourse about *din* (typically translated as religion), *ummah* (nation, people), *sunnah* (way, culture), *nihlah* (creed, sect), or *millah* (community, creed) at this moment in history will always have to contend with the logical and definitional problems around our original tetrad of terms and related ideas, and that means having the right conceptual tools to overcome the ambiguities endemic to discourse around Islam.

Muslims did indeed have a very sophisticated discourse about ideas such as *millah*, *ummah*, *nihlah*, *din*, and *sunnah* but, unlike the case for our tetrad of terms, they did not leverage them as analytical categories in order to evoke a ranking between the good and bad acts, true and false ideas, advanced and primitive societies. These words did not represent the boundary between maturity and immaturity, primitive versus advanced, evolved versus unevolved. Premodern Muslims theorizing different *adyān, milal, niḥal, umam,* and *sunan* knew that they themselves were also one of these things in the relevant discussion. They did not use these terms to decide which one (e.g., Islam or Hinduism) had more truth, more rationality, more goodness, more maturity, or more wisdom. Whatever they understood the term *niḥlah* to mean, the Muslims constituted one and the other group constituted another one. Muslims are an *ummah,* and they too are one. It never became necessary to repurpose such terms to decide more particular questions. There was no case where, for example, one evolved, grew, or improved from being an *ummah* to being a *millah,* or from being a *sunnah* to becoming a *dīn.* There are true and false *adyān* (pl. of *dīn*), good and bad *milal* (pl. of *millah*), *sunan* (pl. of *sunnah*) that were saved and those that were destroyed by God, but there is no sense that by having the right beliefs, right practices, and right ideals that some people are thereby promoted from one category to the other—the way a collectivity might *become* a civilization or *mature* from religion to culture. Like religion, culture, civilization, and tradition, the Arabic terms *dīn, millah, sunnah, niḥlah,* and *ummah* are rich folk terms, but unlike their modern counterparts they were used in Islamic intellectual life without unjustified theoretical pretensions. No argument stands or falls on the fact that people are not able to agree on just what is meant by a *sunnah* or a *millah* in relation to each other. They are ambiguous in an appropriate way, meaning that they are not too ambiguous for the purposes they are called upon to fulfill. Sometimes they referred to a community of people, sometimes to a practice, sometimes to certain ideas, but they do not lull anyone into a false sense of rigor or insight. Everyone knows that the Quran speaks of God's Sunnah, that it calls previous civilizations *sunan,* and that the Islamic tradition came to make the Prophet's *sunnah* the primary denotation of that word (not to mention the label of *sunnah* as denoting a recommended but not obligatory action in the *sharīʿah*), but such equivocations did not lead to statements like "Scholars have yet to agree on what makes a *sunnah* a *sunnah.*" The parameters and the nature of ambiguity of such terms was always ready at hand, unlike the case for our tetrad of terms. There is no judgment associated with assigning the label *millah* to one group and *dīn* to another and *niḥlah* to another. Everyone has one, and there is no question of calling this a "*millah* practice" and that a "*dīn* practice." There are of course distinctions such as *dīnī* and *dunyawī* (roughly "religious" and "secular," or hereafter versus "worldly," etc.), but that is a different kind of demarcation that is not the subject of this book.[12]

Indeed, in all major civilizations there have always been names for such realities that have here been analyzed within the rubric of "metaphysical institutions," but they were not called upon to act like clarifying concepts bundling together multiple irreducible judgments about the nature of the real, the possible, and the good, resulting in generations-long efforts at demarcating them from each other with no success. The Modern Project, which is a major metaphysical institution despite its self-image, is unable to or unwilling to acknowledge itself as one among many such analogous realities, and there will never be reliable concepts of religion, culture, civilization, and tradition within the framework of modern intellectual life because it is logically impossible to take an irreducibly complex bundle of judgments about good and bad and make it into a neutral analytical procedure by which to sort phenomena into various categories.

Three Heuristics

To conclude this book, let us recall the old parable of the blind men and their first encounter with an elephant, in which each man mistakes a part of the elephant for something else (a tree, a snake, a wall, a spear). We can invert that parable and make it instead about sighted men with a lifetime of experience of elephants. The model of metaphysical institutions in this book provides three problem-solving rules of thumb akin to three questions that these men might pose when encountering elephants: (1) Ask: Where is the rest of the elephant?, (2) Ask: What part of the elephant do you mean?, and (3) Ask: What is an elephant at all?

For scholars in many different fields, it is inevitable that in exploring religion, culture, civilization, or tradition one will be approaching it from some particular aspect first—a belief, a practice, an artifact, a law, a custom—and thence one's attention may open up to other dimensions of the reality in question. In most real-life cases scholars are not dealing with the totality of a civilization or a religion but are interested in some specific part of it. The conceptualization of institutions in this book, despite being totalizing and general in scope, can be very helpful in such instances. One cannot use this conceptualization to somehow bring to mind spontaneously, all at once, the nature of a community, and its way, and its legacy, and within each of those the aspects of memory, mastery, moral authority, communication, creativity, correctness, availability, intelligibility, and importance, and within each of those categories differentiating between accounts, heuristics, and norms. These things have to be dealt with at a normal human-scale reasonable pace and in cognitively manageable bites. Moreover, as stated in chapter 5, it is literally impossible to conceive of these things simultaneously even if one tried.

What this conceptualization can do, however, is to allow a scholar to recognize that one is in fact exploring an aspect of a metaphysical institution (for example, Islam) and, having recognized that, proceed more deliberately and rigorously. If a sighted person who knows what elephants are subsequently sees a trunk, or a tusk, or a giant flappy ear, or a treelike leg, he knows that if he expands his view he will see a whole elephant. In this sense, the conceptualization of institutions in this book can serve as a *heuristic for defragmentation*, whereby one knows that trunks, tusks, treelike legs, and big flappy ears do not just appear by themselves but always show up together. Within one triad of our conceptual ennead, one element implies the other two. But it is also the case that each triad implies the other triads, and that each of the twenty-seven elements in the fully elaborated model imply all the others. When it comes to an institution, one may encounter an account such as a certain doctrine about the creation of the world, but one can then recall that such accounts imply heuristics and norms, and also implies that it is a legacy that is a product of a community's practice, and so forth.

The elephant parable can work in another way. Imagine hearing someone call a thing "elephantine" without it being specified which attribute of elephants is meant: does the thing in question have a good memory, tremendous size, or is it loud like a trumpet, or does it have tusk-like appendages? If one knows what an elephant is, one can ask the appropriate questions. Analogously, when one encounters a descriptor like "religious" or even "Islamic," using this book's conceptualization one can have a way of grasping it as a figure of speech and a starting point for discerning some aspect of what that term encompasses as opposed to others that might not be meant in that particular instance. The conceptualization thus also offers a *heuristic for disambiguation*.

Finally, the conceptualization also serves as a *heuristic for metaphysics*, since the nature of the conceptualization implies the question "What are human beings?" and by implication "What is possible and good for human beings?" Our new elephant parable does not work unless we all know what an elephant really is, and that it is not a bicycle. The right conceptualization of shared thinking helps one to displace in one's mind the all-too-common metaphors of "structure" as well as the misapplied physical science metaphors, allowing one to recall that institutions are not mere mechanical systems but are constituted by thinking beings thinking together in a whole world in which such beings are capable of existing.

If some sectors of scholarship now insist on reducing communities to identities and identities to bodies, then perhaps it is high time to reemphasize that human beings are souls wayfaring together through life, whether everyone realizes this truth or not. It was not so long ago that in everyday English one spoke of human beings traveling together as "souls" (airline pilots still speak of how many souls are on board, not how many bodies), and it would be good to think of meaningful collectivities of human beings using the image of souls on a journey, rather than as moist machines bumping and jostling in a sprawling structure. It would have the benefit of actually supporting a coherent idea of how human beings share consciousness.

Synopsis

- Asking whether Islam is an institution is akin to asking whether a human being is a body. In one sense the answer is yes, but in another, clearly no. It depends on one's ultimate assumptions about what human beings are and what the world is.

- For human beings to be already always situated in a metaphysical institution only leads to relativism when understood through a certain metaphysics. One's metaphysics constitutes the very conditions for conceiving of anything real, possible, or good.

- How human beings living together reach the "destination" or state of civilization, culture, tradition, or religion is understood against the background of the metaphysical and historical picture in which this change or realization is believed to occur.

- Tradition and traditionalism differ from most contemporary interpretations in its view of metaphysics and history, which is based in the presence of the absolute and a notion of human fulfillment that is meaningful only in light of the presence of the sacred.

- Resorting to untranslated Islamic terms such as *millah, ummah, niḥlah, dīn,* and *sunnah* will not overcome the conceptual problems with our tetrad of terms, owing to the interconnected nature of global intellectual culture dominated by the Modern Project.

- The conceptualization in this book offers a *heuristic for defragmentation*, whereby one can see particular objects of study as aspects of larger institutional realities.

- It also offers a *heuristic for disambiguation*, whereby modifiers such as "religious" and "cultural" are recognized as idioms that encompass many irreducibly complex realities.

- Finally, it offers a *heuristic for metaphysics*, whereby it reminds us of the role of ultimate assumptions as well as helping to displace misleading images such as "structure" and other misapplied metaphors from physical science.

Notes

Introduction

1. This is a subject that is touched upon briefly in chapter 7 but that the author will take up more fully in a future work, *insha Allah*.

2. One has in mind, as respective examples, Ibn Khaldūn (d. 1406), Ibn Sīnā (d. 1037), al-Ghazālī (d. 1111), Ibn Taymiyyah (d. 1328), ʿUmar Khayyām (d. 1131), and Jalāl al-Dīn Rūmī (d. 1273).

Chapter 1

1. Wilfred Cantwell Smith, *The Meaning and End of Religion* (Minneapolis: Fortress Press, 1991), 17.

2. Brent Nongbri, *Before Religion: A History of a Modern Concept* (New Haven, CT: Yale University Press, 2015), 7.

3. Daniel L. Pals, *Eight Theories of Religion*, 2nd ed. (New York: Oxford University Press, 2006), 293.

4. A. L. Kroeber and Clyde Kluckhohn, *Culture: A Critical Review of Concepts and Definitions* (New York: Vintage Books, 1985), 357.

5. H. Spencer-Oatey, "What is Culture? A Compilation of Quotations," 2012, available at GlobalPAD Open House, https://warwick.ac.uk/fac/soc/al/globalpad-rip/openhouse/interculturalskills_old/core_concept_compilations/global_pad_-_what_is_culture.pdf 1.

6. For a helpful survey of the history of the term, see Brett Bowden, "Civilization and Its Consequences," in *Oxford Handbook Topics in Politics*, ed. Oxford Handbooks Editorial Board, 1st ed. (Oxford: Oxford University Press, 2016), available at https://doi.org/10.1093/oxfordhb/9780199935307.013.30.https://doi.org/10.1093/oxfordhb/9780199935307.013.30.

7. Fernand Braudel and Richard Mayne, *A History of Civilizations* (New York: Penguin Books, 1995), 5.

8. Abbey Perumpanani, "Civilization Defined," *Comparative Civilizations Review* 68, no. 68 (2013): article 3, available at https://scholarsarchive.byu.edu/ccr/vol68/iss68/3 10.

9. Samuel P. Huntington, *The Clash of Civilizations and the Remaking of World Order* (New York: Simon & Schuster, 1996), 325–26n5.

10. Huntington, *Clash of Civilizations,* 43.

11. Huntington, *Clash of Civilizations,* 42.

12. Huntington, *Clash of Civilizations,* 41.

13. Huntington, *Clash of Civilizations,* 42.

14. Huntington, *Clash of Civilizations,* 47.

15. Huntington, *Clash of Civilizations,* 43 (emphasis added).

16. Huntington, *Clash of Civilizations,* 43.

17. An annotated bibliography about the concept of tradition by James Adam Redfield, "The Concept of Tradition: 30 Key Works," can be found online at https://www.academia.edu/30716343/The_Concept_of_Tradition_30_key_works.

18. James Alexander, "A Systematic Theory of Tradition," *Journal of the Philosophy of History* 10 (2016): 6.

19. The situation has not changed that much with regard to "tradition" and "traditional" since 1919, when T. S. Eliot wrote,

> In English writing we seldom speak of tradition, though we occasionally apply its name in deploring its absence. We cannot refer to "the tradition" or to "a tradition"; at most, we employ the adjective in saying that the poetry of So-and-so is "traditional" or even "too traditional." Seldom, perhaps, does the word appear except in a phrase of censure. If otherwise, it is vaguely approbative, with the implication, as to the work approved, of some pleasing archaeological reconstruction. You can hardly make the word agreeable to English ears without this comfortable reference to the reassuring science of archaeology. (T. S. Eliot, "Tradition and the Individual Talent," in *The Sacred Wood: Essays on Poetry and Criticism* [Mansfield Centre, CT: Martino Fine Books, 2015], 42)

In "The Concept of Tradition" (1958), Josef Pieper pointed out, "Whoever happens to look into one of the philosophical dictionaries to orient himself in this subject will at once discover that the key word 'Tradition' and 'Uberlieferung' usually are absent." Josef Pieper, "The Concept of Tradition," *Review of Politics* 20, no. 4 (October, 1958): 469, stable URL: https://www.jstor.org/stable/1404856. Meike Bal notes that tradition is "a word we tend to take for granted as expressing a cultural value to be endorsed or rejected" (*Travelling Concepts in the Humanities: A Rough Guide* [Toronto, Canada: University of Toronto Press, 2002], 251).

20. The mercurial and evocative sense of "tradition" can be found in passages such as this from J. Pelikan: "Tradition without history has homogenized all the stages of development into one statically defined truth; history without tradition has produced a historicism that relativized the development of Christian doctrine in such a way as to make the distinction between authentic growth and cancerous aberration seem completely arbitrary. In this history we are attempting to avoid the pitfalls of both these methods. The history of Christian doctrine is the most effective means available of exposing the artificial theories of continuity that have often assumed normative status in the churches, and at the same time it is an avenue into the authentic continuity of Christian believing, teaching, and confessing. Tradition is the living faith of the dead; traditionalism is the dead faith of the living." Jaroslav Pelikan, *The Emergence of the Catholic Tradition: A History of the Development of Doctrine*, vol. 1, *The Emergence of the Catholic Tradition, 100–600 A.D.* (Chicago, IL: University of Chicago Press, 1971), 9.

21. Popper defended the idea of a "rationalist tradition." See his "Towards a Rational Theory of Tradition" in *Conjectures and Refutations: The Growth of Scientific Knowledge*, Routledge Classics (London: Routledge, 2002).

22. Pelikan did not spend much time defining tradition but simply took it as understood well enough to be dealt with both as a Christian concept and also more generally: "We shall have occasion in this volume to examine the concept of tradition as it was formulated over and against ancient heresy, and repeatedly in later volumes we shall be referring to the formal issue of tradition, particularly when it became a matter of doctrinal controversy or a factor in doctrinal development, but we shall be dealing *not so much with the formal as the material issue of tradition*." Pelikan, *Emergence of the Catholic Tradition*, 7 (emphasis added).

23. See, for example, his *Truth and Method*, 2nd ed., trans. Joel Weinsheimer and Donald G. Marshall (NY: Crossroad, 1992). Gadamer has quite a lot to say about tradition but does not do much to elevate the folk understanding of it. He is concerned with the excesses of certain stances toward tradition, and of course he is interested in all aspects of hermeneutics, but what is tradition for him? It is rather sensed or at best felt.

24. Edward Shils, *Tradition* (Chicago, IL: University of Chicago Press, 1981), 8.

25. Shils, *Tradition*, 10.

26. See above article on tradition and James Alexander, "Three Rival Views of Tradition (Arendt, Oakeshott and MacIntyre)," *Journal of the Philosophy of History* 6 (2012): 20–43.

27. René Guénon, *The Reign of Quantity and the Signs of the Times*, 4th rev. ed., Collected Works of René Guénon (Ghent, NY: Sophia Perennis, 2001), 169n4 and 210.

28. The friends of the slave revolt leader Spartacus (as portrayed in the 1960 movie of the same name) stand up one after another and shout, "I'm Spartacus!" making it impossible for the Romans to identify him from among his men, or for

Spartacus to give himself up. One could call this the Spartacus Problem: a proliferation of definitions each claiming to be the right one, but with no theoretical
framework for deciding between them. Each definition of religion, culture, and
civilization is shouting to the researcher, "I'm Spartacus!"

29. Nongbri notes, "What interests me is the impulse to which Lincoln refers
at the outset—those 'things one intuitively wants to call "religion."' There are certain
'things' that people in the modern world are conditioned to regard as 'religion,'
and attempts at definition are always subject to that impulse to be consistent with
everyday speech. . . . It is the desire to be consistent with this everyday usage [of
modern languages] that drives the continued production of definition upon definition
of the term" (*Before Religion*, 17–18).

This "impulse to be consistent with everyday speech" is, I would argue, the
same for the theorization of the terms "culture" and "civilization," and, to a certain
degree, "tradition."

30. Commenting on the "What is Islam?" question, Mairaj Syed notes,
"It is better to regard the role of definitions as functioning to facilitate communication between scholars. A scholar stipulates a definition of a term just in case
she uses it in a way that departs from the meaning assumed by her audience and
because it facilitates communication." "The Problem with 'What Is . . . ?' Questions, the Literalism of Islamic Law, and the Importance of Being Islamic," *Journal
of Law and Society* 43, no. 4 (2016): 668, http://www.jstor.org/stable/451799
63.

31. Donald Davidson, "The Folly of Trying to Define Truth," ed. John Smy-
lie, *Journal of Philosophy* 93, no. 6 (1996): 264, https://doi.org/10.2307/2941075.

32. In this connection Nongbri says, "In this book, I have interrogated the word
'religion,' and in doing so, I have been somewhat cavalier in my use of other words
such as 'culture,' 'society,' and 'ethnicity,' to name just three. All these terms could
(and should) be subjected to the kind of scrutiny that I have applied to 'religion.'
But all these terms also form important parts of the vocabulary that historians use
all the time. To simply jettison them wholesale is impractical"; *Before Religion*, 157.
Indeed, such jettisoning is neither desirable nor practical, but something "wholesale"
should be done, which is the intent of the work at hand.

33. For a helpful survey of various definitions and formulations specifically
regarding the term "social institution," see Seumas Miller, "Social Institutions,"
Stanford Encyclopedia of Philosophy (Summer 2019 edition), ed. Edward N. Zalta,
https://plato.stanford.edu/archives/sum2019/entries/social-institutions/.

34. Francesco Guala, *Understanding Institutions: The Science and Philosophy of
Living Together* (Princeton, NJ: Princeton University Press, 2016), xvii–xviii.

35. John R. Searle, "What Is an Institution?" *Journal of Institutional Economics* 1, no. 1 (June 2005): 1–22, *DOI.org (Crossref)*, https://doi.org/10.1017/
S1744137405000020. Searle concludes the article by saying, "I see the theory of

institutions as still in its childhood. (Maybe not in its infancy any more, but still its childhood.)"

36. Wolfgang Streeck and Kathleen Ann Thelen, *Beyond Continuity: Institutional Change in Advanced Political Economies* (Oxford: Oxford University Press, 2005), 9–10.

37. Thomas R. Voss, "Institutions," in *International Encyclopedia of the Social & Behavioral Sciences*, ed. James David Wright, 2nd edition (Amsterdam: Elsevier, 2015), 190, http://dx.doi.org/10.1016/B978-0-08-097086-8.32076-1.

38. "Institution," Oxford Reference, last accessed July 11, 2023, https://www.oxfordreference.com/view/10.1093/oi/authority.20110803100005339.

39. Anthony Giddens, *Introduction to Sociology*, 11th ed. (New York: W. W. Norton, 2018).

40. Thomas B. Lawrence and Masoud Shadnam, "Institutional Theory," in *The International Encyclopedia of Communication*, ed. Wolfgang Donsbach (Oxford: Blackwell, 2008), 2289 (emphasis added).

41. The survey by Voss of conceptions of institutions is particularly helpful in showing the variety of ways that scholars speak of the notion of the institution and its conceptual near neighbors such as organizations.

42. Popper, "Towards a Rational Theory," 133.

43. Arnold J. Toynbee, *A Study of History*, 12 vols. (London: Oxford University Press, 1934–61), 1:455n1.

44. See H. A. R. Gibb, "An Interpretation of Islamic History" in *Studies on the Civilization of Islam*, ed. Stanford J. Shaw (Princeton, NJ: Princeton University Press, 1982), 3–33. (Thanks to Esra Köşeli for the reference.)

45. The term "Modern Project" is chosen instead of simply "modernity" or "modernism" to highlight the existence of a veritable institutional reality with all its features as defined in this book, and not merely a historical period or tendency. Moreover, it is perhaps the only acceptable such term that moderns append to themselves. Habermas, to use just one of numerous examples, speaks of the project of modernity in his article "Modernity—an Incomplete Project," but few self-identified modern persons would refer to a modern *tradition* or modern *religion*. (For Habermas's essay and a group of responses to it see, Maurizio Passerin d'Entrèves and Seyla Benhabib, *Habermas and the Unfinished Project of Modernity: Critical Essays on "The Philosophical Discourse of Modernity,"* [Cambridge, MA: MIT Press, 1997].) When terms such as "modern civilization," "modern society," or "modern culture" are used, they denote certain features or aspects of being modern, not the entirety of the institution in question; it is the difference between "a culture" and "culture" (see conclusion). It is important to the overall argument of this book that the Modern Project be seen in its particularity (see chapter 7). For a critical approach that uses this term, see Rémi Brague, *The Kingdom of Man: Genesis and Failure of the Modern Project* (Notre Dame, IN: University of Notre Dame Press, 2018).

46. The misleading morphology of this term often leads people to wrongly imagine metaphysics as the realm of "beyond the physical" or "supernatural" but it originates in the naming convention whereby certain works of Aristotle were called those that came "after the [books of] physics." The relevant boundary is not between what we today would call physical versus nonphysical but between changing and unchanging, necessary and contingent, or always and sometimes. One cannot say "I have no metaphysics" any more than one can say "I have no politics." To deny metaphysics simply is one's metaphysics. For a survey of the term, see Peter van Inwagen, Meghan Sullivan, and Sara Bernstein, "Metaphysics," in *The Stanford Encyclopedia of Philosophy* (Summer 2023 edition), ed. Edward N. Zalta and Uri Nodelman, https://plato.stanford.edu/archives/sum2023/entries/metaphysics/.

47. Kroeber and Kluckhohn enumerate dozens of such brief conceptions in *Culture*, 81ff.

48. Quoted in Nongbri, *Before Religion*, 17.

49. Kroeber and Kluckohn provide many such examples throughout their book *Culture*.

50. *The Constitution of Society: Outline of the Theory of Structuration* (Berkeley: University of California Press, 1984), 24. Cited in Miller, "Social Institutions."

51. Anthony Giddens, *Central Problems in Social Theory: Action, Structure, and Contradiction in Social Analysis* (Basingstoke, UK: Macmillan, 2000), 65.

52. Giddens, *Central Problems in Social Theory,* 64.

Chapter 2

1. The connection between these two aspects of things is much more important than it may first appear. The relationship between a spatiotemporal essence (*ṣūrah*) and nonspatiotemporal essences (*maʿnā*) is a very important aspect of Islamic epistemology, and while there was a highly developed understanding of the difference between them and the faculties of the soul corresponding to them, these different kinds of essences did not belong to separate domains of subject and object as came to be commonplace in the wake of Kant, for whom space and time themselves are provided by the subject and not the object. Islamic thinkers took it for granted that when one saw shapes and colors in the world that one was actually seeing them; geometry and arithmetic (shapes and numbers) were part of the same objective world and perceived by the same subject. The case of the philosophy of mathematics shows just how totally Kant's conception of the spatiotemporal has dominated modern thought: mathematical theorists such as Richard Dedekind (d. 1916) and Gottlob Frege (d. 1925) were adamant to frame mathematics in terms of "pure number" and insisted "that one should have no recourse at all to geometric intuitions or first principles when founding the theory of the real numbers." In a

clear Kantian statement Dedekind said, "I consider the number-concept entirely independent of the notions or intuitions of space and time." (cited in Neil Tennant, "Logicism and Neologicism," *The Stanford Encyclopedia of Philosophy* (Winter 2017 Edition), ed. Edward N. Zalta, https://plato.stanford.edu/archives/win2017/entries/logicism/). Their assumption was that number (not geometric intuitions or principles) somehow allowed us to connect with the real world and not only with appearances. (One can think here of how a materialist philosopher like Quine somehow found himself assuming, strangely, the *objective* existence of numbers even though they were not material.) Considering how totally the sense of meaning as a "computation" arithmetically understood—not geometrically—or as resulting from the physical structure of the brain came to dominate later philosophy ("meaning" will be taken up in chapter 4), it is highly significant to maintain the relationship between the "geometric" and "arithmetical" aspect of things and not deem them to be completely separate epistemological domains. This will be taken up further in a future work *insha Allah*.

2. The word "identity" is used in various contexts, such as logic (e.g., the law of identity whereby each thing is identical with itself), philosophy of mind (e.g., the identity of the brain and the mind), and psychology (e.g., personal traits that are said to make one unique). The present discussion pertains to the notion of identity as found in the social sciences, being roughly equivalent to belonging in some way to a population group of some kind, e.g., national or ethnic identity.

Chapter 3

1. Ronald Desmet and Andrew David Irvine, "Alfred North Whitehead," in *The Stanford Encyclopedia of Philosophy* (Fall 2018 edition), ed. Edward N. Zalta, https://plato.stanford.edu/archives/fall2018/entries/whitehead/.

2. For a discussion of this term and related ones such as "antimentalism," especially as regards the field of psychology, see Jose E. Burgos, "Antidualism and Antimentalism in Radical Behaviorism," *Behavior and Philosophy* 43 (2015): 1, which states, "Antidualism is the rejection of ontological dualism, the partition of reality into physical and nonphysical."

3. Bas C. van Fraassen, *The Empirical Stance* (New Haven, CT: Yale University Press, 2002), 59.

4. John R. Searle, *The Construction of Social Reality*, Penguin Books Philosophy (London: Penguin, 1996), xi–xii.

5. For background on the acceptance and rejection of different forms of "transcendental" reasoning in modern philosophy (that is not of one kind and that can be motivated by very different presuppositions), see "The Fate of Transcendental Reasoning," in James Chase and Jack Reynolds, *Analytic Versus Continental: Argu-*

ments on the Methods and Value of Philosophy (Montreal, Canada: McGill-Queen's University Press, 2010). http://www.jstor.org/stable/j.ctt130hczx.15.

6. Karl-Otto Apel and Benjamin Gregg, "Can an Ultimate Foundation of Knowledge Be Non-Metaphysical?" *Journal of Speculative Philosophy* 7, no. 3 (1993): 181, http://www.jstor.org/stable/25670073.

7. Charles Taylor, "The Validity of Transcendental Arguments," *Proceedings of the Aristotelian Society* 79, no. 1 (June 1979): 165, *DOI.org (Crossref)*, https://doi.org/10.1093/aristotelian/79.1.151.

8. It hardly seems fair for modern scientists and philosophers to invoke contentless ideas such as "dark energy" and "dark matter" instead of saying "We do not know what most of the universe is made of" and then to demand that one's interlocutors provide an explanation of everything.

9. In C. P. Ragland and Sarah Heidt, eds., *What Is Philosophy?* (New Haven, CT: Yale University Press, 2001), 172–73.

10. Thomas Nagel, a rare exception who critiques those philosophers who wish to limit the scope of philosophy in this way, says, "If we find it undeniable, as we should, that our clearest moral and logical reasonings are objectively valid, we are on the first rung of this ladder. It does not commit us to any particular interpretation of the normative, but I believe it demands something more. We cannot maintain the kind of resistance to any further explanation that is sometimes called quietism. The confidence we feel within our own point of view demands completion by a more comprehensive view of our containment in the world." *Mind and Cosmos: Why the Materialist Neo-Darwinian Conception of Nature Is Almost Certainly False* (Oxford: Oxford University Press, 2012), 31.

11. Hilary Putnam, *Renewing Philosophy* (Cambridge, MA: Harvard University Press, 1998), 60.

12. "I'm a theist, I believe in God, which is regarded as really very primitive on the part of many of my friends." Video: "The Depths and Shallows of Experience—Hilary Putnam, Hubert Schwyzer and Bruno Latour," YouTube, posted August 20, 2012, https://youtu.be/DPQZfsAHgSg?t=4505.

13. Hilary Putnam, "Sense, Nonsense, and the Senses: An Inquiry into the Powers of the Human Mind," *Journal of Philosophy* 91, no. 9 (September 1994): 447, *DOI.org (Crossref)*, https://doi.org/10.2307/2940978.

14. One prominent writer in this area even goes so far as to question the understanding of causality in order to rescue antidualism: "It is not obvious that mere natural supervenience must imply epiphenomenalism in the strongest sense. It is clear that the picture it produces looks *something like* epiphenomenalism. Nevertheless, the very nature of causation itself is quite mysterious, and it is possible that when causation is better understood we will be in a position to understand a subtle way in which conscious experience may be causally relevant." David John Chalmers, *The Conscious Mind: In Search of a Fundamental Theory*, Philosophy of Mind Series (New York: Oxford University Press, 1996), 150.

Chapter 4

1. There are many other terms as well. For a survey of these views, see Dwayne Moore, *The Causal Exclusion Problem* (New York: Peter Lang, 2014); and an article by the same author, "Mind and the Causal Exclusion Problem," in *The Internet Encyclopedia of Philosophy*, ed. James Feiser and Bradley Dowden, https:// iep.utm.edu/mind-and-the-causal-exclusion-problem/. For a discussion of these issues in sociology, see Nigel Pleasants, "Free Will, Determinism and the 'Problem' of Structure and Agency in the Social Sciences," *Philosophy of the Social Sciences* 49, no. 1 (January 2019): 3–30, https://doi.org/10.1177/0048393118814952. The author states, "The metaphysical problem of free will and determinism arises from the difficulty of reconciling two seemingly unavoidable, but mutually contradictory, core beliefs about ourselves as human beings and the wider world of which we are a part. The first is that it is *free will* that distinguishes human beings from all others; the second is that human beings are wholly *natural* creatures, embedded in the ongoing causal order of the universe" (6). It is not, in fact, unavoidable to believe that human beings are "wholly natural" creatures, especially since there is no conception of what "natural" is beyond a certain trust that scientists know what is real.

2. Anthony Giddens, for example, says, "[Talcott] Parsons understands action in relation to what he calls 'voluntarism,' and has sought to reconcile the latter with a recognition of the 'emergent properties' of social systems. The reconciliation is achieved through the influence of normative values on two levels: as elements of personality and as core components of society. As 'internalised' in personality, values provide the motives or need-dispositions which impel the conduct of the actor; while on the level of the social system, as institutionalised norms, values form a moral consensus that serves to integrate the totality. 'Voluntarism' here thus becomes largely reduced to making space in social theory for an account of motivation, connected via norms to the characteristics of social systems." Giddens, *Central Problems in Social Theory: Action, Structure, and Contradiction in Social Analysis*, Contemporary Social Theory (Basingstoke, UK: Macmillan, 2000), 51–52.

3. For a survey of some of these issues as relates to anthropology, see for example, Sherry B. Ortner, "Theory in Anthropology since the Sixties," *Comparative Studies in Society and History* 26, no. 1 (January 1984): 126–166, https://doi.org/10.1017/S0010417500010811.

4. Paul Grice, "Method in Philosophical Psychology (from the Banal to the Bizarre)," *Proceedings and Addresses of the American Philosophical Association* 48 (1974): 23, https://doi.org/10.2307/3129859, 30–31.

5. This relationship between theoretical formalisms and the nontheoretical concrete models that communicate them and are used to make them cohere is far more complicated (and much less well understood) than might commonly be assumed. On these issues, see Roman Frigg and Stephan Hartmann, "Models in Science," in

The Stanford Encyclopedia of Philosophy (Spring 2020 edition), ed. Edward N. Zalta, https://plato.stanford.edu/archives/spr2020/entries/models-science/.

6. On the proliferation of approaches, see Ken Turner, ed., *The Semantics/Pragmatics Interface from Different Points of View*, 1st ed. (Oxford, UK: Elsevier, 1999); and also Ilse Depraetere, *Semantics and Pragmatics: Drawing a Line* (New York: Springer Berlin Heidelberg, 2016). Zoltán Gendler Szabó notes that "the theory of utterance interpretation is still an ambitious enterprise we have no clear idea how to pursue," which shows just how little is settled in this area. "The Distinction between Semantics and Pragmatics," in *The Oxford Handbook of Philosophy of Language*, ed. Ernest Lepore and Barry C. Smith, Oxford Handbooks in Philosophy (Oxford: Oxford University Press, 2008), 378.

7. Scott Soames's critique of Quine exposes a prominent (perhaps preeminent) example of this self-undermining feature of certain physicalist arguments about meaning: "What [Quine] asserted, believed, and argued for has the character that the very act of asserting, believing, or arguing for it is itself sufficient to falsify it. Can Quine avoid this kind of self-undermining? Well, it is tempting to think that he may do so by claiming that he didn't state, assert, believe, or argue for his theses. But even this won't help, since if he claims that he didn't state, believe, or argue for anything, then he still will have claimed something, and that is enough to falsify his theses." Scott Soames, "The Indeterminacy of Translation and the Inscrutability of Reference," *Canadian Journal of Philosophy* 29, no. 3 (1999): 357, https://www.jstor.org/stable/40232060.

8. There is no term "thinker" in the classical technical vocabulary of Islamic thought that corresponds precisely with the boundaries of what is being discussed here, although there are many terms that overlap with it. Within Islamic spirituality (*taṣawwuf*), theology (*kalām*), and philosophy (*falsafah/ḥikmah*) there have been multiple ways that the inner reality of human beings has been characterized and classified, a vast topic that cannot be elaborated here. A good starting point for these issues is Muhammad U. Faruque, *Sculpting the Self: Islam, Selfhood, and Human Flourishing* (Ann Arbor: University of Michigan Press, 2021).

Chapter 5

1. For example, acupuncture requires one to visualize channels of qi that are, as it were, the lower bounds of the soul and the upper bounds of the body, but even the cosmology behind acupuncture does not allow one to literally imagine the whole soul. This topic cannot be explored here but is worth at least mentioning.

2. See the author's "Language Is Not Mechanical, and Neither Are You," *Renovatio: The Journal of Zaytuna College* 2, no. 2 (Fall 2018): 107–20, https://renovatio.zaytuna.edu/article/language-is-not-mechanical-and-neither-are-you.

3. It is important to recall that this was *not* the conception of the early moderns. Descartes, Newton, and Galileo did not reduce consciousness to the workings of the body. Even for Descartes, to call something (such as language) "mental" was to recognize that it did not obey the laws of mechanical entities.

4. Cited in Christoph Durt, "The Embodied Self and the Paradox of Subjectivity," *Husserl Studies* 36, no. 1 (April 2020): 70, https://doi.org/10.1007/s10743-019-09256-4.

5. Cited in Durt, "Embodied Self," 70.

6. This will be a major theme of an upcoming book by the author about metaphysics, *insha Allah*.

7. See note 1 in chapter 2.

8. Edwin A. Abbott, *Flatland: A Romance in Many Dimensions* (1884), unabridged (New York: Dover Thrift Edition, 1992).

9. In sociology, for example, one began with what came to be called functionalism and later structural functionalism. Figures such as Comte, Durkheim, Spencer, and Parsons were luminaries at a time when the prevailing metaphors used to describe society were mechanical and organic (e.g., Durkeim's division into mechanical and organic solidarity), but since organisms were already at that time conceived of as being a kind of machine that worked through the function of parts (hence the metaphor of structure), one was really dealing with different modes of mechanism. The main criticisms of structural functionalism were not interested in changing the basic view of what constituted a society (parts in a structure) but shifted focus to different forms of conflict. Even those qualifications that tried to point out that people are not trapped in their structures and that the individual agent is important (e.g., Giddens's "Structuration") provide no account of the agent that enables this to make any sense. For example, what explains that an agent can move outside the structure?

10. For an illuminating discussion of the use of quantitative empirical methods over qualitative theorizing in the field of international relations, see John J. Mearsheimer and Stephen M. Walt, "Leaving Theory Behind: Why Simplistic Hypothesis Testing Is Bad for International Relations," *European Journal of International Relations* 19, no. 3 (September 2013): 427–57, https://doi.org/10.1177/1354066113494320. They quote C. H. Achen, who says, "Empirical work, the way too many political scientists do it, is indeed relatively easy. Gather the data, run the regression/MLE with the usual linear list of control variables, report the significance tests, and announce that one's pet variable 'passed.' This dreary hypothesis-testing framework is sometimes seized upon by beginners. Being purely mechanical, it saves a great deal of thinking and anxiety, and cannot help being popular. But obviously, it has to go. Our best empirical generalizations do not derive from that kind of work" (452).

11. "For Newton it was 'absurd' to regard gravity as acting between bodies at a distance, without the mediation of material bodies, and he persistently tried

to find a modus operandi for how gravitational attraction was conveyed through a medium. Yet even without that physical theory, gravitational attraction was *not* to be regarded as unintelligible: its intelligibility resided in the lawful account of its action. The law of gravitation could be used for explanatory ends even if no mechanical cause could be specified." Steven Shapin, *The Scientific Revolution* (Chicago, IL: University of Chicago Press, 1996), 64.

12. Alan Lightman, "Science: Magic on the Mind Physicists' Use of Metaphor," *American Scholar* 58, no. 1 (1989): 101, http://www.jstor.org/stable/41211647.

13. Isaac Asimov structured his best-selling *Foundation* novels around the notion of "psychohistory," a new science wherein a sufficiently sophisticated algorithm can predict the course of human society. It remains science fiction.

Chapter 6

1. In recent years language identification has usually been done through software, but software does not program itself and crucially depends on the trial and error of its users for input, and works through brute force, not understanding.

2. There's also another point here: an English speaker might go his or her whole life never hearing or speaking the words "cerulean" or "crimson" or indeed most of the words that count as English. One may simply not have any meaningful ideas or concern about a certain level of detail about color. That is, *not* using "cerulean" does not imply that one *therefore* uses "ultramarine." One can use neither one and still be an English speaker, but a different level of English speaker compared with someone who, all else being equal, knows how to use "cobalt," "cerulean," "navy," and "indigo." The difference between two such speakers is not correctness but rather level of mastery or expertise, two parameters that are different but related. So, in Islam the difference between one form of practice and another might not be between correct and incorrect, or between Islam and not-Islam, but a depth of use. Is *wahdat al-wujūd* incorrect, or is it not-Islam, or is it simply a different mode of metaphysical language? In other words, it could be conceived of as simply another form of correctness.

3. As Sajjad Rizvi notes in connection with Shahab Ahmed's work, "How does that question [Is *x* Islamic?] relate to other questions such as: 'is it right,' 'is it proper,' 'is it ethical,' or 'is it culturally authentic'?" "Reconceptualization, Pre-Text, and Con-text," *LA Marginalia Review of Books Forum*, http://marginalia. lareviewofbooks.org/reconceptualization-pre-text-con-text-sajjad-rizvi/.

4. To use just this specific example of a technical term from Islamic law, Umar F. Abd-Allah notes, "The appearance and development of theories and terminologies must not be confused with the radically different process of intuiting conceptual processes and forming working guidelines for them. Searching out terms for analogy in primary sources is not a viable methodology for discovering if the concept

existed in the early period, although it is useful toward other ends. . . . I found no instance of Mālik himself using the word 'analogy' (*qiyās*), but he employs a variety of alternative expressions for it." *Mālik and Medina: Islamic Legal Reasoning in the Formative Period*, Islamic History and Civilization 101 (Leiden: Brill, 2013), 146–47.

5. This and related questions are dealt with by Sherman Jackson in his article "The Islamic Secular," in which he theorizes the *sharī'ah*'s scope and boundaries in Islam, and corrects the impulse to "burden Sharia with the responsibility for speaking effectively to all and sundry matters." "The Islamic Secular," *American Journal of Islam and Society* 34, no. 2 (April 1, 2018): 21, https://doi.org/10.35632/ajiss.v34i2.184. (The article has been expanded to a book not yet released at the time of this writing.) I would argue that Jackson's concept of "the non-*shar'ī* realm [of the Islamic]" as implied and presupposed by its "*shar'ī* realm" is the decisive demarcation in his work, and his new concept "Islamic secular" is entirely derivative of it. Any effort to delineate an Islamic (in this context, religious) "secular" will always run up against the practical indefinability of "religion." Jackson himself notes, "As for the charge that I do not define religion, I plead guilty" ("Islamic Secular," 40). Indeed, the religious/secular conceptual divide he describes is conceptually downstream of all the other substantive categories he lays out (drawn from the Islamic legal tradition). It thus serves to translate the substantive Islamic theoretical framework into a modern idiom, yet remains fully intelligible and illuminating without reference to the notion of the "secular" at all.

6. See Mas'ūd ibn 'Umar al-Taftāzānī, *A Commentary on the Creed of Islam: Sa'd al-Dīn al-Taftāzānī on the Creed of Najm al-Dīn al-Nasafī*, trans. E. E. Elder (New York: Columbia University Press, 1950), 6–7.

7. For what still remains an excellent survey, see Annemarie Schimmel, *Mystical Dimensions of Islam* (Chapel Hill: University of North Carolina Press, 1981).

8. Mohamed Zakariya, an American calligrapher who is a living representative of this tradition, notes, "In the flow of calligraphic history, certain masters at certain times have been associated with revolutionary flashes of creativity and invention." He distills certain features of a "critical theory of calligraphy" drawn from Mahmud Yazır (d. 1952), a rubric consisting of schools (*mekteb*) of calligraphy and their branches (*kol*), which evince certain methods (*üslub*), styles (*tarz*), and manners (*tavır*), and also a calligrapher's accent (*şive*) and state (*hal*), which latter pertain to the individual artist's contribution and "unique look." The correct understanding of this discipline thus includes both long-standing tradition and individual creativity. "An Ottoman Murakkaa and the Birth of the International Style," in *God Is Beautiful and Loves Beauty: The Object in Islamic Art and Culture*, ed. Sheila Blair, Jonathan Bloom, and Museum of Islamic Art (Dawḥah, Qatar) (New Haven, CT: Yale University Press, 2013), 18.

9. Among the several *ḥadīths* on this topic one can cite "Whoever does not recite the Quran beautifully is not one of us" (*Ṣaḥīḥ al-Bukhārī* K. al-tawḥīd #7621, *laysa minnā man lam yataghanna bi'l-Qur'ān*).

10. Ṣaḥīḥ Muslim, *K. al-ṣayd wa'l-dhabā'iḥ* #5167 (*inna'Llāha kataba'l-iḥsāna 'alā kulli shay'*).

11. To state it in Jackson's technical language, "Non-*shar'ī* culturally informed charm and winsomeness can clearly be seen as serving the *shar'ī* interest of marital harmony" ("Islamic Secular," 16).

12. Sunan al-Tirmidhī, *K. al-birr wa'l-silah* #2043 (*laysa minnā man lam yarḥam ṣaghīranā wa yuwaqqir kabīranā*).

Chapter 7

1. On these topics, see the author's *Ibn Al-'Arabī and Islamic Intellectual Culture: From Mysticism to Philosophy*, Routledge Sufi Series 18 (London: Routledge / New York: Taylor & Francis Group, 2019).

2. For more on this metaphysical trifurcation, see the author's "Wisdom in Pieces," *Renovatio: The Journal of Zaytuna College* vol. 1 no. 2 (Dec. 8, 2017): 5–16. https://renovatio.zaytuna.edu/article/wisdom-in-pieces

3. "Philosophy and Literature with Iris Murdoch and Bryan Magee" (interview), Manufacturing Intellect, YouTube, last accessed July 11, 2023, https://www.youtube.com/watch?v=pBG10XnxQaI.

4. Theodor Adorno and E. B. Ashton, *Negative Dialectics* (London: Routledge, 2010), 15.

5. Adorno and Ashton, *Negative Dialectics*, 69.

6. Adorno and Ashton, *Negative Dialectics*, 63.

7. Adorno and Ashton, *Negative Dialectics*, 15.

8. Adorno and Ashton, *Negative Dialectics*, 109.

9. C. P. Ragland and Sarah Heidt, eds., *What Is Philosophy?* (New Haven, CT: Yale University Press, 2001), 76.

10. Shahab Ahmed, *What Is Islam? The Importance of Being Islamic* (Princeton, NJ: Princeton University Press, 2015), 108.

11. Ahmed, *What Is Islam?*, 108 (underline added; italics in original).

12. Ahmed, *What Is Islam?*, 108.

13. Ahmed, *What Is Islam?*, 82 (underline added; italics in original).

14. Ahmed, *What Is Islam?*, 129 (emphasis in original).

15. Ahmed, *What Is Islam?*, 107.

16. Ahmed, *What Is Islam?*, 303.

17. Much has been written on the subject of "Orientalism" and the ways that scholarship about Islam has served the interest of Western domination over the Islamic world and continues to do so, and of course many examples of such intellectual activity can be found in history and today. But there is also a way in which domination and power serve the interests of a certain kind of understanding of the world and of the self. Yes, human beings rationalize their greed and lust for

power through false narratives and unfair representations of the other, but they also act on their beliefs about themselves that they have formed for all kinds of reasons. It is the nature of these beliefs, at the deepest level, that is the focus of the present argument, without denying other highly significant economic and political factors. On this topic readers are strongly encouraged to consult Wael Hallaq's *Restating Orientalism: A Critique of Modern Knowledge* (New York: Columbia University Press, 2018) and in particular his chapter on "the subversive author."

18. Ahmed, *What Is Islam?*, 107.

19. In Kuhn's language, the paradigm is in the state of adding ad hoc hypothesis created to deal with recalcitrant data.

20. It is important to mention, lest there be any misunderstanding, that of course many of the scholars who study Islam actually love their subject matter, are personally enriched by it, and have rich and illuminating historical knowledge. They admire the figures and works they study, and would gladly speak of how Islam and the Islamic have nourished them intellectually and even morally and spiritually. They would rank the figures of the Islamic tradition as not any less than the luminaries of the Modern Project in terms of their intrinsic qualities of rationality, morality, imagination, and value of their contribution. I would categorize them as good neighbors and welcome guests in the land of Islam. They come as interested travelers, not would-be tutors. These remarks are not really directed at such scholars, who tend not to busy themselves with trying to "conceptualize" Islam or to redefine the religion on behalf of the people who cannot seem to define it themselves. They are, rather, interested in interesting things and want to participate in good faith inquiry into the world.

21. Ovamir Anjum, for example, discusses what he takes to be the "fact" that "Muslims are at least as aware of the diversity of interpretation and practice of Islam as are Western anthropologists," but there is little evidence that the conceptualizers of Islam from the Modern Project generally accept this fact. "Islam as a Discursive Tradition: Talal Asad and His Interlocutors," *Comparative Studies of South Asia, Africa and the Middle East* 27, no. 3 (2007): 656–72, muse.jhu.edu/article/224569, 657.

22. "A natural language has no metalanguage that is not dependent in turn on an interpretation in that (or another) natural language." Jürgen Habermas, *On the Pragmatics of Social Interaction: Preliminary Studies in the Theory of Communicative Action*, trans. Barbara Fultner (Cambridge, MA: The MIT Press, 2001), 73.

23. If a person speaks more than one language fluently, that person nevertheless speaks two languages, not a metalanguage, and moreover can speak only one language at a time and cannot mix grammars or syntax. The analogy is meant to foreground the impossibility of a metalanguage, which is not changed by the existence of bilingual people. As for the possibility that a person could be "bilingual" in one's metaphysical institution, one could ask: are there people who carry the kind of moral authority (as set out in the book's model) both in the Modern Project and in Islam to determine what counts as modern and also what counts as Islamic? I am not aware of such a person.

24. No doubt in many settings it makes perfect sense to speak without qualifiers and caveats. One does not, in a graduate seminar about Wittgenstein's *Tractatus*, say, "Let us analyze this keeping in mind that by analysis I mean . . ." One knows what "analysis" means in that room, and one follows along. But if the circumstances required distinguishing that particular procedure of analysis form others, then the Wittgensteinian ought to be able to situate it on the spectrum of different forms of analysis—when asked to speak about the global history of philosophy, for example. A Muslim knows that *taḥqīq* (verification, realization) will for the Sufis mean one thing (a transformation of the soul) and that in a commentary on a book of later *kalām* it will probably mean another (a mode of analytical demonstration), and one does not need to belabor the distinctions every time it appears. But books devoted to definitions of such technical terms exist in Islamic civilization precisely because such polyvalence exists and no one gets to monopolize *taḥqīq* in the way that some humanities and social science scholars usurp "theory" or "critique."

25. It is thought that Edward Said, through his hugely influential *Orientalism* (1978), had overcome a certain essentializing, imperial, and ethnocentric approach to scholarship about the Islamic world, but, as Wael Hallaq notes, the field today is "nothing but a more sophisticated version of its former self, largely due to Said's influence" (*Restating Orientalism*, 174). In Hallaq's terminology, Said was a *dissenter* (one who "does not question the mainstays of the system, or the epistemological structures or forms of knowledge that define the worldview through the prism in which problems in the field are solved" and for whom "these foundations and epistemic edifices are left in place, accepted and intact [172]). He was not truly *subversive*, and, "through his powerfully dissenting voice, Said reinforced modern academia and the foundations on which it stands" (174).

Chapter 8

1. Marshall G. S. Hodgson, *The Venture of Islam*, vol. 1, *The Classical Age of Islam*, paperback ed. (Chicago, IL: University of Chicago Press, 1974).

2. Shahab Ahmed, *What Is Islam? The Importance of Being Islamic* (Princeton, NJ: Princeton University Press, 2016).

3. A. Kevin Reinhart, *Lived Islam: Colloquial Religion in a Cosmopolitan Tradition*, 1st ed. (New York: Cambridge University Press, 2019).

4. Talal Asad, "The Idea of an Anthropology of Islam," *Qui Parle* 17, no. 2 (2009): 1–30, http://www.jstor.org/stable/20685738.

5. Hodgson, *Venture of Islam*, 1:59 (emphasis added).

6. Hodgson, *Venture of Islam*, 1:57 (emphasis added).

7. Hodgson, *Venture of Islam*, 1:58 (underline added, italics in original).

8. Hodgson, *Venture of Islam*, 1:87.

9. Hodgson, *Venture of Islam*, 1:80–81.

10. Hodgson, *Venture of Islam*, 1:81.

11. Hodgson, *Venture of Islam*, 1:80–81.

12. Hodgson, *Venture of Islam*, 1:81.

13. Hodgson, *Venture of Islam*, 1:82.

14. Hodgson, *Venture of Islam*, 1:27.

15. Hodgson, *Venture of Islam*, 1:27.

16. Hodgson, *Venture of Islam*, 1:88–89.

17. Hodgson, *Venture of Islam*, 1:88n6 (emphasis in original).

18. Hodgson, *Venture of Islam*, 1:30; see also his discussion of other historians of civilization such as Toynbee, Spengler, and Turner on 120n11.

19. Hodgson, *Venture of Islam*, 1:31.

20. For example, Hodgson says, "The civilization that united the lands from Nile to Oxus [Hodgson's term for the broader Middle East] in the Islamic period could be regarded, for some purposes, as no independent cultural body but simply the latest phase in a long-term Irano-Semitic civilization continuous from the time of the ancient Sumerians." *Venture of Islam*, 1:91.

21. One can observe that Samuel Huntington would have benefitted greatly from Hodgson's more sophisticated and astute remarks about the nature of civilization, but it does not appear that he was familiar with them, a surprising omission considering Huntington's focus on Islam's borders and Hodgson's prominence as a historian of Islamic civilization.

22. Hodgson, *Venture of Islam*, 1:85 (emphasis added).

23. Hodgson, *Venture of Islam*, 1:86 (emphasis added).

24. Hodgson, *Venture of Islam*, 1:94.

25. Ahmed, *What Is Islam?*, 366 (emphasis in original).

26. "Ahmed gives his readers no single example of something or someone that would not qualify for the rubric of hermeneutical engagement—even when touching upon the difficult issue of violence committed in the name of Islam. . . . Anything can be potentially Islamic and nothing is explicitly named as not Islamic." Raissa von Doetinchem de Rande, "Ahmed, Shahab: *What Is Islam: The Importance of Being Islamic*. 2016," *Orientalistische Literaturzeitung* 113, no. 1 (2018): 68, https://doi.org/10.1515/olzg-2018-0019.

27. Ahmed, *What Is Islam?*, 363.

28. Ahmed, *What Is Islam?*, 373.

29. In his review Alireza Doostdar notes, "Indeed, to the extent that Ahmed uses the word 'contradiction' to indicate 'difference' or 'disagreement' (and he often does exactly this), it is not clear why Islam should be conceptualized any differently than other traditions of 'hermeneutic engagement'—like Christianity, feminism, or particle physics—that similarly accommodate divergent viewpoints." *Shi'i Studies Review* 1, no. 1–2 (2017): 279.

30. Ahmed, *What Is Islam?*, 404.

31. Ahmed, *What Is Islam?*, 404.

32. Ahmed, *What Is Islam?*, 98.

33. Ahmed, *What Is Islam?*, 397n197.

34. Ahmed, *What Is Islam?* 397–98n197.

35. Ahmed, *What Is Islam?*, 398.

36. See, for example, the author's "Metaphor, Symbol, and Parable in the Quran," in *Routledge Companion to the Qur'an*, ed. George Archer, Maria Massi Dakake, and Daniel A. Madigan, 1st ed. 1st ed. Routledge Religion Companions (New York: Routledge, 2021), 191–99.

37. Different versions of this old story exist both in Islamic sources and in European adaptations. In one version, the Angel of Death visits Solomon and gives a strange look to a certain man. That man, fearing death, beseeches Solomon to use the wind to send him to India. Solomon then asks Death why he gave the man a strange look, whereupon Death responds that he was surprised to see the man because he was meant to collect his soul in India that day.

38. Ahmed, *What Is Islam?*, 405 (emphasis in original).

39. Ahmed, *What Is Islam?*, 136.

40. Ahmed, *What Is Islam?*, 104.

41. These analytical problems are all the more astounding since Ahmed's critiques of other logically incoherent conceptions of Islam in *What Is Islam?* are often excellent and invaluable, but he seems to have a blind spot for his own constructions. It is as though *What Is Islam?* were two books: one a catalog of devastating and erudite critiques of previous conceptualizations of Islam, and the other his own theorization of Islam that seems to violate some of the very principles he uses—often with great subtlety and skill—to critique others. It is frustrating for such valuable observations—of which there are many isolated examples in *What Is Islam?*—to be marred by analytical blunders such as "coherent dynamic of internal contradiction," and one is saddened to see so much erudition and illuminating critique of existing scholarship put to the service of what turns out to be a logically untenable argument.

42. For an interesting discussion of the impact of Asad's ideas in this area on other scholars, see Samuli Schielke, *Second Thoughts about the Anthropology of Islam, or How to Make Sense of Grand Schemes in Everyday Life*, vol. 2, ZMO Working Papers (Berlin: Zentrum Moderner Orient, 2010).

43. Asad, "Idea of an Anthropology," 20 (emphasis in original).

44. Mohammed Sulaiman, "Between Text and Discourse: Re-Theorizing Islamic Orthodoxy," *ReOrient* 3, no. 2 (April 1, 2018): 140–62, 10.13169/reorient.3.2.0140.

45. Alasdair C. MacIntyre, *Three Rival Versions of Moral Enquiry: Encyclopaedia, Genealogy, and Tradition: Being Gifford Lectures Delivered in the University of Edinburgh in 1988* (Notre Dame, IN: University of Notre Dame Press, 1990), 45.

46. Although there is some uncertainty regarding Foucault's position on the metaphysics of these questions, as will be discussed in the conclusion.

47. Asad, "Idea of an Anthropology," 23.

48. Ovamir Anjum, "Islam as a Discursive Tradition: Talal Asad and His Interlocutors," *Comparative Studies of South Asia, Africa and the Middle East* 27, no. 3 (2007): 656–72, muse.jhu.edu/article/224569, 670.

49. Even Ahmed's conceptualization, perhaps the most ambitious to date, excludes quite a large part of the Islamic world outside of the "Balkans-to-Bengal" complex.

50. Reinhart, *Lived Islam*, 8.

51. Reinhart, *Lived Islam*, 12.

52. Reinhart, *Lived Islam*, 10.

53. Reinhart, *Lived Islam*, 32.

54. Reinhart, *Lived Islam*, 44–45 (emphasis in original).

55. Reinhart, *Lived Islam*, 68.

56. One can peruse at random the commentary of *The Study Quran* to see this range of opinions. Seyyed Hossein Nasr, Caner K. Dagli, Maria Massi Dakake, Joseph E. B. Lumbard, and Mohammed Rustom, *The Study Quran: A New Translation and Commentary* (New York: HarperOne, An Imprint of HarperCollins Publishers, 2015).

57. Reinhart, *Lived Islam*, 42.

58. Reinhart, *Lived Islam*, 40.

59. Reinhart, *Lived Islam*, 50.

60. Reinhart, *Lived Islam*, 129.

61. Reinhart, *Lived Islam*, 139.

62. In the important book *A Culture of Ambiguity: An Alternative History of Islam*, ed. Thomas Bauer, Thomas Hinrich Biesterfeldt, and Tricia Tunstall (New York: Columbia University Press, 2021), Bauer occasionally veers outside his illuminating chronicle of the important ways Muslims have cultivated a sophisticated sense of polyvalence and unnecessarily includes statements such as, "A further calamitous fallacy of Western interpreters of Islam sets in: *the* Islam, as a religion, was nowhere to be found. Religious elements, however, were to be found in quite diverse areas of society" (135). Would the Muslims whose works he studies see it this way? He elsewhere attributes to Islamic culture "a suspension of truth throughout centuries in the interest of a theory of probabilities presupposes a high tolerance of ambiguity" (103). Again, would his objects of study accept that a suspension of truth is the price that must be paid for the tolerance of ambiguity? None of the authors Bauer rightly praises would ever claim that they were "suspending truth." Would al-Jazarī (the fourteenth- to fifteenth-century scholar of Quranic recitations to whom Bauer devotes many pages) say the Quran was an "open text" (88) without qualification, as Bauer seems to imply, so much so that he ponders whether his approach could be characterized as "postmodern" (72)? Talk of suspending truth, postmodernism, and "open texts" is superfluous and counterproductive to Bauer's otherwise worthy and impressive discussion of the Islamic "culture of ambiguity" and how modernists and fundamentalists have both succumbed to "Cartesian modernity" with its "insistence on a single meaning for each Quranic passage, solely correct at all times" (77).

63. Reinhart, *Lived Islam*, 32.
64. Reinhart, *Lived Islam*, 33.
65. Reinhart, *Lived Islam*, 33.
66. Reinhart, *Lived Islam*, 10.
67. Reinhart, *Lived Islam*, 10.
68. Reinhart, *Lived Islam*, 10.
69. Reinhart, *Lived Islam*, 92.
70. Reinhart, *Lived Islam*, 119.

Conclusion

1. "Justice as Fairness: Political Not Metaphysical," *Philosophy & Public Affairs* 14, no. 3 (1985): 223–51, http://www.jstor.org/stable/2265349, 240 (emphasis added).

2. Without referencing metaphysics explicitly, Seamus Miller makes a similar point: "Philosophers, such as John Rawls, have developed elaborate normative theories concerning the principles of justice that ought to govern social institutions. Yet they have done so in the absence of a developed theory of the nature and point of the very entities (social institutions) to which the principles of justice in question are supposed to apply. Surely the adequacy of one's normative account of the justice or otherwise of any given social institution, or system of social institutions, will depend at least in part on the nature and point of that social institution or system." "Social Institutions," in *The Stanford Encyclopedia of Philosophy* (Summer 2019 edition), ed. Edward N. Zalta, https://plato.stanford.edu/archives/sum2019/entries/social-institutions/.

3. Emile Durkheim and Steven Lukes, *The Rules of Sociological Method*, 1st American ed. (New York: Free Press, 1982), 159. Cited in Nigel Pleasants, "Free Will, Determinism and the 'Problem' of Structure and Agency in the Social Sciences," *Philosophy of the Social Sciences* 49, no. 1 (January 2019): 3–30, https://doi.org/10.1177/0048393118814952.

4. Alasdair C. MacIntyre, *Whose Justice? Which Rationality?* (Notre Dame, IN: University of Notre Dame Press, 1988), 359. For an extremely subtle discussion of the "transcendental" move MacIntyre seems to be making in this passage, as well as a discussion of how some critics see an inevitable contradiction in MacIntyre's claim that one can reason only within a tradition in light of his own practice of seeming to move between traditions, see Jennifer Herdt, "Alasdair MacIntyre's 'Rationality of Traditions' and Tradition-Transcendental Standards of Justification," *Journal of Religion* 78, no. 4 (1998): 524–46, http://www.jstor.org/stable/1206573.

5. I confess that in reading MacIntyre I am unable to pinpoint his position on metaphysics in a way that I find fully satisfying. For example, even after reading his *First Principles, Final Ends, and Contemporary Philosophical Issues* (The Aquinas Lecture 1990, [Milwaukee, WI: Marquette University Press, 1990]), which is entirely

about metaphysics, it is very hard to say for sure where he has settled down. Even good faith efforts to explain his position are hard to sort out: "A few years after the publication of *After Virtue*, MacIntyre became a Thomist and accepted that the teleology of human action flowed from a metaphysical foundation in the nature of the human person. . . . Nonetheless, MacIntyre has the main points of his ethics and politics of human action have remained the same. MacIntyre continues to argue toward an Aristotelian account of practical reasoning through the investigation of practice. Even though he has accepted Thomistic metaphysics, he seldom argues from metaphysical premises, and when pressed to explain the metaphysical foundations of his ethics, he has demurred. MacIntyre continues to argue from the experience of practical reasoning to the demands of moral education. MacIntyre's work in *Whose Justice, Which Rationality, Dependent Rational Animals, The Tasks of Philosophy, Ethics and Politics*, and *God, Philosophy, University* continue to exemplify the phenomenological approach to moral education that MacIntyre took in *After Virtue*." Christopher Stephen Lutz, "Alasdair Chalmers MacIntyre (1929–)." in *Internet Encyclopedia of Philosophy*, ed. James Feiser and Bradley Dowden, https://iep.utm.edu/mac-over/.

6. To put it in Islamic terms, the *fiṭrah* is not a theory.

7. See Brett Bowden, "Civilization and Its Consequences," in *Oxford Handbook Topics in Politics*, edited by Oxford Handbooks Editorial Board, 1st ed. (Oxford: Oxford University Press, 2016), https://doi.org/10.1093/oxfordhb/9780199935307.013.30.

8. René Guénon, *The Reign of Quantity and the Signs of the Times*, 4th rev. ed. Collected Works of René Guénon (Ghent, NY: Sophia Perennis, 2001), 211.

9. Seyyed Hossein Nasr, *Islam in the Modern World: Challenged by the West, Threatened by Fundamentalism, Keeping Faith with Tradition* (New York: HarperOne, 2012), 4.

10. Nasr, *Tradition*, 102.

11. For example, terms related to "tradition," such as *turāth* and *taqlīd* in Arabic, "gelenek" in Turkish, or *sunnatī* in Persian, are all of recent coinage or recent change of use (that is, they either did not exist until recently, or if they did, they were until recently used quite differently) and cannot be understood outside of the intellectual culture of the modern world, especially since the nineteenth century, a period that was also a key turning point for many related terms in Western languages. For another example—the use of the term *ḥaḍaruḥ* and similar terms in Arabic for "civilization"—see Badrane Benlahcene, "The Term 'Civilization' in the Muslim Intellectual Traditions: Changing Vocabulary and Varied Conceptions," *International Journal for Innovation Education and Research* 5, no. 4 (April 30, 2017): 44–49, https://doi.org/10.31686/ijier.vol5.iss4.653.

12. S. H. Nasr discusses this topic in his "The Meaning of 'Religion' in the Islamic Tradition," in *Religion: Eine europäisch-christliche Erfindung? Beiträge eines Symposiums am Haus der Kulturen der Welt in Berlin*, ed. Hans-Michael Haussig and Bernd Michael Scherer (Berlin: Philo, 2003), 111–21. For more on these topics and

a bibliography for further reading, see also Rushain Abbasi, "Islam and the Invention of Religion: A Study of Medieval Muslim Discourses on Dīn," *Studia Islamica* 116, no. 1 (May 11, 2021): 1–106, https://doi.org/10.1163/19585705-12341437h.

Works Cited

Abbasi, Rushain. "Islam and the Invention of Religion: A Study of Medieval Muslim Discourses on Dīn." *Studia Islamica* 116, no. 1 (May 11, 2021): 1–106. https://doi.org/10.1163/19585705-12341437.

Abbott, Edwin A. 1884. *Flatland: A Romance in Many Dimensions.* Unabridged. New York: Dover Thrift Edition (1992).

Abd-Allah, Umar F. *Mālik and Medina: Islamic Legal Reasoning in the Formative Period.* Islamic History and Civilization 101. Leiden: Brill, 2013.

Adorno, Theodor, and E. B. Ashton. *Negative Dialectics.* London: Routledge, 2010.

Ahmed, Shahab. *What Is Islam? The Importance of Being Islamic.* Princeton, NJ: Princeton University Press, 2015.

Alexander, James. "A Systematic Theory of Tradition." *Journal of the Philosophy of History* 10 (2016): 1–28, doi: https://doi.org/10.1163/18722636-12341313.

———. "Three Rival Views of Tradition (Arendt, Oakeshott and MacIntyre)." *Journal of the Philosophy of History* 6 (2012): 20–43.

Anjum, Ovamir. "Islam as a Discursive Tradition: Talal Asad and His Interlocutors." *Comparative Studies of South Asia, Africa and the Middle East* 27, no. 3 (2007): 656–72. muse.jhu.edu/article/224569.

Apel, Karl-Otto, and Benjamin Gregg. "Can an Ultimate Foundation of Knowledge Be Non Metaphysical?" *Journal of Speculative Philosophy* 7, no. 3 (1993): 171–90. http://www.jstor.org/stable/25670073.

Asad, Talal. "The Idea of an Anthropology of Islam." *Qui Parle* 17, no. 2 (2009): 1–30. http://www.jstor.org/stable/20685738.

Bal, Mieke. *Travelling Concepts in the Humanities: A Rough Guide.* Toronto, Canada: University of Toronto Press, 2002.

Bauer, Thomas, Hinrich Biesterfeldt, and Tricia Tunstall. *A Culture of Ambiguity: An Alternative History of Islam.* New York: Columbia University Press, 2021.

Benlahcene, Badrane. "The Term 'Civilization' in the Muslim Intellectual Traditions: Changing Vocabulary and Varied Conceptions." *International Journal for Innovation Education and Research* 5, no. 4 (April 30, 2017): 44–49. https://doi.org/10.31686/ijier.vol5.iss4.653.

Bowden, Brett. "Civilization and Its Consequences." In *Oxford Handbook Topics in Politics*, edited by Oxford Handbooks Editorial Board. 1st ed. Oxford: Oxford University Press, 2016. https://doi.org/10.1093/oxfordhb/9780199935307.013.30.

Brague, Rémi. *The Kingdom of Man: Genesis and Failure of the Modern Project*. Notre Dame, IN: University of Notre Dame Press, 2018.

Braudel, Fernand, and Richard Mayne. *A History of Civilizations*. New York: Penguin Books, 1995.

Burgos, Jose E. "Antidualism and Antimentalism in Radical Behaviorism." *Behavior and Philosophy* 43 (2015): 1–37.

Chalmers, David John. *The Conscious Mind: In Search of a Fundamental Theory*. Philosophy of Mind Series. New York: Oxford University Press, 1996.

Chase, James, and Jack Reynolds. "The Fate of Transcendental Reasoning." In *Analytic versus Continental: Arguments on the Methods and Value of Philosophy*, 89–114. Montreal, Canada: McGill-Queen's University Press, 2010. http://www.jstor.org/stable/j.ctt130hczx.15.

Dagli, Caner K. *Ibn al-ʿArabī and Islamic Intellectual Culture: From Mysticism to Philosophy*. Routledge Sufi Series 18. London: Routledge / New York: Taylor & Francis, 2019.

———. "Language Is not Mechanical, and Neither Are You." *Renovatio: The Journal of Zaytuna College* 2, no. 2 (Fall 2018): 107–20. https://renovatio.zaytuna.edu/article/language-is-not-mechanical-and-neither-are-you.

———. "Wisdom in Pieces." *Renovatio: The Journal of Zaytuna College* 1, no. 2 (Dec. 8, 2017): 5–16. https://renovatio.zaytuna.edu/article/wisdom-in-pieces.

———. "Metaphor, Symbol, and Parable in the Quran." In *Routledge Companion to the Qur'an*, edited by George Archer, Maria Massi Dakake, and Daniel A. Madigan, 191–99. 1st ed. Routledge Religion Companions. New York: Routledge, 2021.

Davidson, Donald. "The Folly of Trying to Define Truth." *Journal of Philosophy* 93, no. 6 (1996): 263–78. https://doi.org/10.2307/2941075.

de Rande, Raissa von Doetinchem. "Ahmed, Shahab: *What Is Islam: The Importance of Being Islamic*. 2016." *Orientalistische Literaturzeitung* 113, no. 1 (2018): 65–69. https://doi.org/10.1515/olzg-2018-0019.

Depraetere, Ilse. *Semantics and Pragmatics: Drawing a Line*. New York: Springer Berlin Heidelberg, 2016.

Desmet, Ronald, and Andrew David Irvine. "Alfred North Whitehead." In *The Stanford Encyclopedia of Philosophy* (Fall 2018 edition), edited by Edward N. Zalta. https://plato.stanford.edu/archives/fall2018/entries/whitehead/.

Doostdar, Alireza. Review of *What Is Islam? The Importance of Being Islamic* (Shahab Ahmed). *Shi'i Studies Review* 1, no. 1–2 (2017): 277–82.

Durkheim, Emile, and Steven Lukes. *The Rules of Sociological Method*. 1st American ed. New York: Free Press, 1982.

Durt, Christoph. "The Embodied Self and the Paradox of Subjectivity." *Husserl Studies* 36, no. 1 (April 2020): 69–85. https://doi.org/10.1007/s10743-019-09256-4.

Eliot, T. S. "Tradition and the Individual Talent." In *The Sacred Wood: Essays on Poetry and Criticism*. Mansfield Centre, CT: Martino Fine Books, 2015.

Faruque, Muhammad U. *Sculpting the Self: Islam, Selfhood, and Human Flourishing*. Ann Arbor: University of Michigan Press, 2021.

Frigg, Roman, and Stephan Hartmann. "Models in Science." In *The Stanford Encyclopedia of Philosophy* (Spring 2020 edition), edited by Edward N. Zalta. https://plato.stanford.edu/archives/spr2020/entries/models-science/.

Gadamer, Hans-Georg. *Truth and Method*. 2nd ed. Translated by Joel Weinsheimer and Donald G. Marshall. New York: Crossroad, 1992.

Gibb, Hamilton A. R. "An Interpretation of Islamic History." In *Studies on the Civilization of Islam*. Edited by Stanford J. Shaw. Princeton, NJ: Princeton University Press, 1982.

Giddens, Anthony. *Central Problems in Social Theory: Action, Structure, and Contradiction in Social Analysis*. Contemporary Social Theory. Basingstoke, UK: Macmillan, 2000.

———. *The Constitution of Society: Outline of the Theory of Structuration*. Berkeley: University of California Press, 1984.

———. *Introduction to Sociology*. 11th ed. New York: W. W. Norton, 2018.

Grice, Paul. "Method in Philosophical Psychology (from the Banal to the Bizarre)." *Proceedings and Addresses of the American Philosophical Association* 48 (1974): 23. https://doi.org/10.2307/3129859.

Guala, Francesco. *Understanding Institutions: The Science and Philosophy of Living Together*. Princeton, NJ: Princeton University Press, 2016.

Guénon, René. *The Reign of Quantity and the Signs of the Times*. 4th rev. ed. Collected Works of René Guénon. Ghent, NY: Sophia Perennis, 2001.

Habermas, Jürgen. *On the Pragmatics of Social Interaction: Preliminary Studies in the Theory of Communicative Action*. Translated by Barbara Fultner. Cambridge, MA: The MIT Press, 2001.

Hallaq, Wael B. *Restating Orientalism: A Critique of Modern Knowledge*. New York: Columbia University Press, 2018.

Herdt, Jennifer A. "Alasdair MacIntyre's 'Rationality of Traditions' and Tradition-Transcendental Standards of Justification." *Journal of Religion* 78, no. 4 (1998): 524–46. http://www.jstor.org/stable/1206573.

Hodgson, Marshall G. S. *The Venture of Islam*. Vol. 1, *The Classical Age of Islam*. Paperback ed., Chicago, IL: University of Chicago Press, 1974.

The Clash of Civilizations and the Remaking of World Order. New York: Simon & Schuster, 1996.

Jackson, Sherman A. "The Islamic Secular." *American Journal of Islam and Society* 34, no. 2 (April 1, 2018): 1–38. https://doi.org/10.35632/ajiss.v34i2.184.

Jensen, Klaus Bruhn, Robert T. Craig, Jefferson Pooley, and Eric W. Rothenbuhler, eds. *The International Encyclopedia of Communication Theory and Philosophy.* Chichester, UK: John Wiley & Sons, 2016.

Kroeber, Alfred L., and Clyde Kluckhohn. *Culture: A Critical Review of Concepts and Definitions.* New York: Vintage Books, 1985.

Lawrence, Thomas B., and Masoud Shadnam. "Institutional Theory." In *The International Encyclopedia of Communication*, ed. Wolfgang Donsbach, 2288–93. Oxford: Blackwell, 2008.

Lightman, Alan P. "Science: Magic on the Mind Physicists' Use of Metaphor." *American Scholar* 58, no. 1 (1989): 97–101. http://www.jstor.org/stable/41211647.

Lutz, Christopher Stephen. "Alasdair Chalmers MacIntyre (1929–)." In *The Internet Encyclopedia of Philosophy*, ed. James Feiser and Bradley Dowden. https://iep.utm.edu/mac-over/.

MacIntyre, Alasdair C. *First Principles, Final Ends, and Contemporary Philosophical Issues.* The Aquinas Lecture 1990. Milwaukee, WI: Marquette University Press, 1990.

———. *Three Rival Versions of Moral Enquiry: Encyclopaedia, Genealogy, and Tradition: Being Gifford Lectures Delivered in the University of Edinburgh in 1988.* Notre Dame, IN: University of Notre Dame Press, 1990.

———. *Whose Justice? Which Rationality?* Notre Dame, IN: University of Notre Dame Press, 1988.

Mearsheimer, John J., and Stephen M. Walt. "Leaving Theory Behind: Why Simplistic Hypothesis Testing Is Bad for International Relations." *European Journal of International Relations* 19, no. 3 (September 2013): 427–57. https://doi.org/10.1177/1354066113494320.

Miller, Seumas. "Social Institutions." In *The Stanford Encyclopedia of Philosophy* (Summer 2019 edition), edited by Edward N. Zalta. https://plato.stanford.edu/archives/sum2019/entries/social-institutions/.

Moore, Dwayne. *The Causal Exclusion Problem.* New York: Peter Lang, 2014.

———. "Mind and the Causal Exclusion Problem." In *The Internet Encyclopedia of Philosophy*, ed. James Feiser and Bradley Dowden. https://iep.utm.edu/mind-and-the-causal-exclusion-problem/.

Nagel, Thomas. *Mind and Cosmos: Why the Materialist Neo-Darwinian Conception of Nature Is Almost Certainly False.* Oxford: Oxford University Press, 2012.

Nasr, Seyyed Hossein. *Islam in the Modern World: Challenged by the West, Threatened by Fundamentalism, Keeping Faith with Tradition.* 1st HarperCollins paperback ed. New York: HarperOne, 2012.

———. "The Meaning of 'Religion' in the Islamic Tradition." In *Religion: Eine europäisch-christliche Erfindung? Beiträge eines Symposiums am Haus der Kulturen der Welt in Berlin*, ed. Hans-Michael Haussig and Bernd Michael Scherer, 111–21. Berlin: Philo, 2003.

Nasr, Seyyed Hossein, Caner K. Dagli, Maria Massi Dakake, Joseph E. B. Lumbard, and Mohammed Rustom. *The Study Quran: A New Translation and Commentary.* New York: HarperOne, 2015.

Nelson, Richard R. "Physics Envy: Get Over It." *Issues in Science and Technology* 31, no. 3 (2015): 71–78. http://www.jstor.org/stable/43314857.

Neumann, Birgit, and Ansgar Nünning, eds. *Travelling Concepts for the Study of Culture.* Concepts for the Study of Culture 2. Boston, MA: De Gruyter, 2012.

Nongbri, Brent. *Before Religion: A History of a Modern Concept.* New Haven, CT: Yale University Press, 2015.

Ortner, Sherry B. "Theory in Anthropology since the Sixties." *Comparative Studies in Society and History* 26, no. 1 (January 1984): 126–126. https://doi.org/10.1017/S0010417500010811.

Pals, Daniel L. *Eight Theories of Religion.* 2nd ed. New York: Oxford University Press, 2006.

Passerin d'Entrèves, Maurizio, and Seyla Benhabib. *Habermas and the Unfinished Project of Modernity: Critical Essays on "The Philosophical Discourse of Modernity."* Cambridge, MA: MIT Press, 1997.

Pelikan, Jaroslav. *The Emergence of the Catholic Tradition: A History of the Development of Doctrine.* Vol. 1, *The Emergence of the Catholic Tradition, 100–600 A.D.* Chicago, IL: University of Chicago Press 1971.

Perumpanani, Abbey. "Civilization Defined." *Comparative Civilizations Review* 68, no. 68 (2013): article 3. Available at https://scholarsarchive.byu.edu/ccr/vol68/iss68/3 10.

Pieper, Josef. "The Concept of Tradition." *Review of Politics* 20, no. 4 (1958): 465–91. http://www.jstor.org/stable/1404856.

Pleasants, Nigel. "Free Will, Determinism and the 'Problem' of Structure and Agency in the Social Sciences." *Philosophy of the Social Sciences* 49, no. 1 (January 2019): 3–30. https://doi.org/10.1177/0048393118814952.

Popper, Karl R. "Towards a Rational Theory of Tradition." In *Conjectures and Refutations: The Growth of Scientific Knowledge,* 161–82. Routledge Classics. London: Routledge, 2002.

Putnam, Hilary. *Renewing Philosophy.* Cambridge, MA: Harvard University Press, 1998.

———. "Sense, Nonsense, and the Senses: An Inquiry into the Powers of the Human Mind." *Journal of Philosophy,* vol. 91, no. 9 (September 1994): 445. *DOI.org (Crossref).* https://doi.org/10.2307/2940978.

Ragland, C. P., and Sarah Heidt, eds. *What Is Philosophy?* New Haven, CT: Yale University Press, 2001.

Rawls, John. "Justice as Fairness: Political Not Metaphysical." *Philosophy & Public Affairs* 14, no. 3 (1985): 223–51. http://www.jstor.org/stable/2265349.

Redfield, James Adam. "The Concept of Tradition: 30 Key Works." Academia.edu. https://www.academia.edu/30716343/The_Concept_of_Tradition_30_key_works.

Reinhart, A. Kevin. *Lived Islam: Colloquial Religion in a Cosmopolitan Tradition.* 1st ed. New York: Cambridge University Press, 2019.

Rizvi, Sajjad. "Reconceptualization, Pre-Text, and Con-text." *LA Marginalia Review of Books Forum.* http://marginalia.lareviewofbooks.org/reconceptualization-pre-text-con-text-sajjad-rizvi/.

Schielke, Samuli. *Second Thoughts about the Anthropology of Islam, or How to Make Sense of Grand Schemes in Everyday Life.* Vol. 2. ZMO Working Papers. Berlin: Zentrum Moderner Orient, 2010.

Schimmel, Annemarie. *Mystical Dimensions of Islam.* Chapel Hill: University of North Carolina Press, 1981.

Searle, John R. *The Construction of Social Reality.* Penguin Books Philosophy. London: Penguin, 1996.

———. "What Is an Institution?" *Journal of Institutional Economics* 1, no. 1 (June 2005): 1–22. *DOI.org (Crossref).* https://doi.org/10.1017/S1744137405000020.

Shapin, Steven. *The Scientific Revolution.* Chicago, IL: University of Chicago Press, 1996.

Shils, Edward. *Tradition.* Chicago, IL: University of Chicago Press, 1981.

Smith, Wilfred Cantwell. *The Meaning and End of Religion.* Minneapolis, MN: Fortress Press, 1991.

Soames, Scott. "The Indeterminacy of Translation and the Inscrutability of Reference." *Canadian Journal of Philosophy* 29, no. 3 (1999): 321–70. https://www.jstor.org/stable/40232060.

Spencer-Oatey, H. (2012) "What Is Culture? A Compilation of Quotations." Available at GlobalPAD Open House. https://warwick.ac.uk/fac/soc/al/globalpad-rip/openhouse/interculturalskills_old/core_concept_compilations/global_pad_-_what_is_culture.pdf.

Streeck, Wolfgang, and Kathleen Ann Thelen. *Beyond Continuity: Institutional Change in Advanced Political Economies.* Oxford: Oxford University Press, 2005.

Sulaiman, Mohammed. "Between Text and Discourse: Re-Theorizing Islamic Orthodoxy." *ReOrient* 3, no. 2 (April 1, 2018): 140–62. https://doi.org/10.13169/reorient.3.2.0140.

Syed, Mairaj. "The Problem with 'What Is . . . ?' Questions, the Literalism of Islamic Law, and the Importance of Being Islamic." *Journal of Law and Society* 43, no. 4 (2016): 661–71. http://www.jstor.org/stable/45179963.

Szabó, Zoltán Gendler. "The Distinction between Semantics and Pragmatics." In *The Oxford Handbook of Philosophy of Language,* ed. Lepore, Ernest, and Barry C. Smith. Oxford Handbooks in Philosophy. Oxford: Oxford University Press, 2008, 361–392.

al-Taftāzānī, Masʿūd ibn ʿUmar. *A Commentary on the Creed of Islam: Saʿd al-Dīn al-Taftāzānī on the Creed of Najm al-Dīn al-Nasafī.* Translated by E. E. Elder. New York: Columbia University Press, 1950.

Taylor, Charles. "The Validity of Transcendental Arguments." *Proceedings of the Aristotelian Society* 79, no. 1 (June 1979): 151–66. *DOI.org (Crossref)*. https://doi.org/10.1093/aristotelian/79.1.151.

Toynbee, Arnold J. *A Study of History.* 12 vols. London: Oxford University Press, 1934–61.

Turner, Ken, ed. *The Semantics/Pragmatics Interface from Different Points of View.* 1st ed. Oxford, UK: Elsevier, 1999.

Van Fraassen, Bas C. *The Empirical Stance.* New Haven, CT: Yale University Press, 2002.

van Inwagen, Peter, Meghan Sullivan, and Sara Bernstein. "Metaphysics." In *The Stanford Encyclopedia of Philosophy*, Summer 2023 edition), ed. Edward N. Zalta and Uri Nodelman. https://plato.stanford.edu/archives/sum2023/entries/metaphysics/.

Voss, Thomas R., "Institutions." In *International Encyclopedia of the Social & Behavioral Sciences*, edited by James David Wright, 190–95. 2nd ed. Amsterdam: Elsevier, 2015. https://doi.org/10.1016/B978-0-08-097086-8.32076-1.

Zakariya, Mohamed. "An Ottoman Murakkaa and the Birth of the International Style." In *God Is Beautiful and Loves Beauty: The Object in Islamic Art and Culture*, ed. Sheila Blair, Jonathan Bloom, and Museum of Islamic Art (Dawḥah, Qatar), 273–300. New Haven, CT: Yale University Press, in association with the Qatar Foundation, Virginia Commonwealth University, and Virginia Commonwealth University School of the Arts in Qatar, 2013.

Index

academia, 185, 186, 187, 193–194, 206, 207, 237–238
accounts: defined, 49–50, 67; logical relationship with heuristics and norms, 51; as part of twenty-seven parameters of an institution, 54–56; empirical variation of, 60, 61; between reason and imagination, 100–104, 106; in language, 139–140. *See also* assertions
Adorno, Theodor, 182
aesthetics, 163
agency, 89
Ahmed, Shahab, 185–186, 189, 211, 219–227, 232–234, 237
allegory. *See* metaphor
always-already, 250, 251
ambiguity, 2, 13, 16–18, 21, 23, 28, 29, 30–31, 33, 37, 46, 75, 100, 101, 105, 106, 122, 123, 125, 126, 212–213, 224, 225, 227, 257, 258, 260
anthropology, 10, 13, 18, 132, 217, 228, 230, 231, 233, 243, 271n3, 277n27
antidualism, 83–93, 95–100, 107, 110, 111, 113, 116, 117, 131, 247, 253, 254, 269n2, 270n14
Apel, Karl-Otto, 90, 92
Aristotelianism, 113, 283n5

art, 163–164, 211; as apex metaphysical community, 181–184; and universality, 188, 189; and Islamic world, 190–191
artifacts, 58, 112–113
Asad, Talal, 211, 228–232, 232–234, 237, 238, 239, 241
Ash'arī, al-, 154
Ash'arite school, 161
assertions, 67, 72, 198, 255. *See also* accounts
authority. *See* moral-authority
availability (as feature of institutions), 48, 62, 63, 64
Avicenna (Ibn Sīnā), 195, 197

beauty, 113, 163–164
Black Americans, 68–69
blind men and the elephant allegory, 259–261
body, 110–112, 116, 127, 131, 247, 251–252, 261, 272n1, 273n3. *See also* consciousness
brain, 86, 116–117, 131, 269n1
Brandom, Robert, 182
Braudel, Fernand, 10, 19

calligraphy, 58, 162, 163, 275n8
civilization: definition of, 10–12, 16–17, 22–23, 26, 41; as normative